PRAYING
WITH
POWER

Lloyd John Ogilvie

Guideposts®

CARMEL • NEW YORK 10512

This Guideposts edition is published by
special arrangement with Regal Books.

The translation of all Regal books is under the direction of GLINT. GLINT provides technical help for the adaptation, translation and publishing of books for millions of people worldwide. For information regarding translation contact: GLINT, P.O. Box 6688, Ventura, California 93006.

Published by Regal Books
A Division of GL Publications
Ventura, California 93006
Printed in U.S.A.

Library of Congress Cataloging in Publication Data

Ogilvie, Lloyd John.
  Praying with power.

  Includes bibliographical references.
  1. Prayer. I. Title.
BV215.037 1983   248.3'2   83-17742

TABLE OF CONTENTS

INTRODUCTION

Every week I receive hundreds of letters containing questions and expressions of urgent need from my congregation and my church's national television ministry. The deepest need expressed in dozens of ways is to learn how to pray with power.

I have kept a record of what people ask about prayer. These provided me the basis of a prolonged study of the Scriptures on the theme of prayer. The result was not only an opportunity to respond personally from the Bible to each letter, but to do a series of messages on the television program in direct response to the questions people raised. The fresh insight the Lord revealed to me about the power of prayer is the thrust of this book.

What breathing is to our physical life, prayer is to our spiritual life. It is the very essence of the abundant life. Why then do we find so much difficulty in praying? Why do we have so many questions about how to pray effectively?

I am convinced that it is because of a profound misunderstanding of prayer, who initiates it, and what should happen to us when we pray. The purpose of this book is to expose what God meant prayer to be and what He has said about the secret of dynamic conversation with Him when we pray.

Prayer is more than saying our prayers. It is communion with the Lord who wants to give us His mind, guidance, and power. Most of all, He wants to give us the gift of Himself. He calls us into prayer to impart that awesome gift.

There is a central theme that runs all through this book. It is that prayer starts with God. He is the initiator, instigator, and inspiration of prayer. I try to weave that exciting conviction through all the chapters which deal with the deepest needs and urgent questions which people constantly ask about prayer. With the essential secret of prayer as God's idea, I deal with how to talk with Him, how to make all of life a prayer, how prayer transforms us, how to pray for people, and what to do when our prayers seem to be unanswered. Then I press on to deal with how prayer enables healing, why we pray in Jesus' name, and how God can guide our decisions. The final chapter offers the much needed gift of endurance when life brings us to the end of our resources and we're tempted to give up.

The whole book is meant to be a dialogue between friends who long to discover how to pray with power. Everywhere I go, I talk to people who are struggling to find power to live life more fully—to discover how to realize their full potential. Here's my formula worked out over the years of studying the Scriptures and the great prayer warriors of the ages.

I am thankful for the fact that these chapters have been written in conversation with a congregation seeking to discover all that the Lord offers through prayer. Each chapter was preached and then revised in the light of insights and comments by my friends in my congregation and the television audience. These front line troops of the Lord were the focus of my efforts to explore the deeper mysteries of prayer power. The result is a book that has been tested and tried by real people who echo Jesus' disciples' plea, "Lord, teach us to pray!" That was also my urgent quest as I wrote this book—to put into your hands as my readers, the practical and applicable insights the Lord gave me and deepened in conversation with real people like you who seek to pray with power.

My special thanks to Jeri Gonzalez, my administrative assistant, for her typing of the manuscript and for her enthusiasm for this project.

Now I want to open my heart and mind to you and pour out the exciting, fresh vision the Lord has given me for you about adventuresome prayer.

Lloyd John Ogilvie

Chapter One

PRAYER STARTS WITH GOD

I want to share a revolutionary thought. It has changed my life. My whole perception of prayer has been transformed by it. As a result, my prayers and praying have become more exciting than ever.

I've been a Christian for thirty-five years. Far too many of those years were spent with a totally incorrect conception of prayer. I labored with the misapprehension that prayer was my idea, that conversation with God was initiated by me. That idea took on the heavy baggage of believing that I had to get God's attention and that He would listen and respond if I said the right words and led a life worthy of His condescension. Prayer became burdensome, laborious. Often I was reluctant to pray when I needed to the most because of things I'd done or said which made me feel ashamed or embarrassed by a less than perfect life. The conception that prayer was initiated by me left it up to my moods and spiritual readiness.

Then one day a few years ago, I happened on a combination of Scriptures from the Old and New Testaments which exploded the tight, constricted, and limited view of prayer I had held. They all thundered forth a truth which I desperately needed to learn and live.

Stated simply it is this: prayer starts with God. It is His idea. The desire to pray is the result of God's greater desire to talk with us. He has something to say when we feel the urge to pray. He is the initiator. The keen desire to begin and end the day with prolonged prayer is His gift. The sense of need to pray for challenges or opportunities throughout the day is because He has wisdom and insight He wants to impart. When we face crises and suddenly feel the urge to pray for strength, that feeling is a response to the Lord's invasion of our minds which triggers the thought of needing help which is congealed into the desire to pray. He, not us, was the author of the longing for His help.

I want to share these Scriptures with you which have caused this renaissance in my prayers. The message they convey tells us something magnificent about God and the wondrous way He has created us for communion and conversation with Him. He is the instigator, implementor, and inspiration of prayer.

The Answer Is Prepared Before We Pray

The first is Isaiah 65:24. Listen to what the Lord Himself tells us about prayer. "It shall come to pass that before they call, I will answer; and while they are still speaking, I will hear." That tells us that the answer to our prayers is prepared before we pray. The desire to talk to the Lord about our needs comes from Him. Prayer begins in the mind of God, invades our minds, is formulated into a clarification of what He wants to do or give, and then is articulated in our words. He is more ready to hear than we are to pray!

This propitious promise of the Lord was made in response to an excruciating question asked by Israel, recorded in Isaiah 64:12. The people had sinned and felt the judgment of God. They were distant from Him; He had never left His people. Their sorrow had reached its height when they cried out, "Wilt thou keep silent . . . ?" *(RSV)*. The response of grace was mediated through the prophet. There will come a time when not only will the Lord answer, but His answer will precede the petition, and prayer will be the response of God's call rather than just His response to our call. This prophetic revelation of the nature of prayer is in anticipation of the messianic age when God Himself would come to reconcile and redeem His people. The people to whom Isaiah wrote never fully appreciated the wondrous offer God made in this statement. It was only after the incarnation and Pentecost that a new creation was prepared to appropriate it. It was not until the liberation of the bondage of the will took place on Calvary and the new creatures in Christ were filled with His Spirit at Pentecost that a new Israel, the Church, was born and could accept and utilize the awesome promise the Lord had made so long before.

Thomas Carlyle once said, "Prayer is and remains a native and deep impulse of the soul of man." That sounds lovely, but I don't believe it. No one naturally desires to pray. Our volitional capacity is debilitated until we are loved, liberated, and regenerated by Christ. It is after we have been transformed by the cross and filled with the Spirit that we can experience the enlivening of the "native and deep impulse" to pray. And even after we've been born again, it is the Lord who motivates us to pray. It is part of His prevenient, beforehand grace. Not even the longing for God is our accomplishment. It is birthed in our souls by the Lord who created us for communion with Him.

Commenting on this promise in Isaiah, Luther said, "Our prayer pleases God because He has commanded it, made promises, and given form to our prayer. For that reason, He is pleased with our prayer, He requires it and delights in it, because He promises, commands, and shapes it . . . . Then He says, 'I will hear.' It is not only guaranteed, but it is actually already obtained."[1]

He Is the Implementor of Prayer

At the same time I was pondering the implications of the Lord's offer in Isaiah, He led me to rediscover another passage which deepened my understanding of that promise. I read 1 John 5:12-15 with new eyes in my heart. The Lord comes to us as the implementor of prayer. The Apostle John asserted the secret of dynamic praying in the context of our life in Christ. "He who has the Son has life; he who does not have the Son of God does not have life" (v. 12). The apostle wanted his readers in the early Church to be sure of their relationship, now and forever, in Christ. He went on to state the reason why he had written was: "that you may know that you have eternal life, and that you may continue to believe in the name of the Son of God" (v. 13). For John, the Son was *Immanuel*, God with us, and continuing with us to guide us. His Christian life was not an anxious searching for the Lord but moment by moment response to His impinging, invading imminence. Then in verses 14 and 15, John sounds the same joyous note we heard in the Isaiah promise. "Now this is the confidence that we have in Him, that if we ask anything according to His will, He hears us. And if we know that He hears us, whatever we ask, we know that we have the petitions that we have asked of Him."

I quickly checked the Greek text to review words I had studied so often before. Now they came alive in new vitality and freshness. The words for "confidence" and "in Him" leaped off the page. Confidence is *perresia* in the

Greek. The word means boldness. It is a compound word made up of *pan*—all, and *ressia*—to tell, meaning freedom to speak boldly. Prayer is freedom to speak freely and boldly to the Lord who has instigated our prayer. But then I discovered again that the English translation of the next words do not catch the exciting implication of the original Greek. The confidence we have in prayer is what "we have in Him." *Pros auton* really means "toward Him" or "face-to-face" with Him. *Pros* is from *prosōpton*, "face." Prayer, for John, was face-to-face communication with Christ as a part of the eternal quality of life we have in Him which gives us boldness. Face to face, first we listen to Him intently and then we can speak with intrepidity.

And who starts the face-to-face conversation? The Lord! John makes that clear in 4:19, "We love Him because He first loved us." He is the prime mover in salvation, the gift of faith, and the initiation of prayer. In prayer, He makes known to us what is His will so that we can ask for what He longs to give. He calls us into His presence because He has the answer to our needs and questions. "If we ask anything according to His will, He hears us." Our assurance that He hears us is that He is the one who asked for the conversation. He would not call us to prayer and then refuse to listen or be inattentive to our prayer. That's the confidence, boldness, we have: prayer is our response to His call. In the time of face-to-face communion He makes clear what it is that we are to ask for in the needs He has come to us to help us solve.

So when we do ask, it is with the confidence that we are asking for what He is prepared to release for us. "And if we know that He hears us, whatever we ask, we know that we have the petitions that we have asked of Him." We know before we ask, because the content of our asking has been guided by Him. The same assurance had been stated by John earlier in his epistle. "And by this we know that we are of the truth, and shall assure our hearts before Him. For if our heart condemns us, God is greater than our heart, and knows all things. Beloved, if our heart does not condemn us, we have confidence toward God. And whatever we ask we receive from Him, because we keep His commandments and do those things that are pleasing in His sight. And this is His commandment: that we should believe on the name of His Son Jesus Christ and love one another, as He gave us commandment" (1 John 3:19-23). The basics of prayer have been given already in the commandment. The Lord reminds us of this as He calls us into prayer and then as the instigative agent of prayer, spells out the specific details of the commandment to believe and love in particular situations.

Allow me to illustrate. Recently one of my friends was in trouble. He needed my help, and yet was not sure I had time to help. So I asked one of my sons to talk to the man and offer my help. My son said to him, "My dad really wants to help and he's willing to do the following things." He enumerated the personal and practical assistance I wanted to give. The intervention of someone as close to me as my son convinced the man of my real heart in the matter. When the man came to me with the request he did not have to wonder about my readiness to help. He came with the confidence of inside information of what I was willing to do. When he asked me to do exactly what I'd offered through my son, I did it immediately.

Or consider the world of negotiation in business. A man in my congregation confided that settling a difficult matter is so much easier when he knows what the other person is willing to do. If he can get someone to intercede for him to find out what the other party's terms are, he can make an offer which he knows will be accepted. On the other hand, when he wants someone to bid at a price he is willing to accept, he gets an emissary to go to the person to disclose his willingness to sell and the price he's open to accept. When the offer comes, he responds because it complies with his terms.

Some years ago, I needed a grant from a large foundation for a strategic program in my church. A trusted friend interceded for me. He talked to the head of the foundation and arranged for an interview for me. The man liked the idea and suggested how I should draft the proposal to be sure it was met with enthusiasm and approval by the board of directors in charge of the foundation. When I followed his suggestions, the proposal was accepted by the foundation and the grant was made. All the guesswork was taken out of my application. The board was responsible for distribution of funds provided by a great benefactor in America. It had to distribute the funds; all I had to do was prepare something which was within the qualifications of the policies of the board. I could not have known that without the help of the head of the board who helped me ask in a way I could be confident would be accepted.

These illustrations touch only the fringes of the central truth John is seeking to communicate. Christ is the heart of God with us. He guides us in what and how to ask. When we ask in keeping with what He has revealed to us, we ask with the boldness that the answer is on the way. "We know that we have the petitions that we have asked of Him." The word "know," *oidamen,* is used twice: If we know that He hears us, then we know that we have what He has guided us to ask. A.T. Robertson says that the Greek implies "the confidence of possession by anticipation."[2] The Lord gives us boldness to say what He has told us to pray!

Inspiration Comes from Him

The third passage of Scripture which confirmed for me this truth that prayer starts with God is Romans 8:26-30. This particular passage affirms that the inspiration for praying comes from Him. Again the Spirit of the Lord, the present Christ, is the initiator of the desire, content, and assurance of prayer. Note how Paul developed the same sublime theme. "Likewise the Spirit also helps in our weaknesses. For we do not know what we should pray for as we ought, but the Spirit Himself makes intercession for us with groanings which cannot be uttered. Now He who searches the hearts knows what the mind of the Spirit is, because He makes intercession for the saints according to the will of God. And we know that all things work together for good to those who love God, to those who are the called according to His purpose. For whom He foreknew, He also predestined to be conformed to the image of His Son, that He might be the firstborn among many brethren. Moreover whom He predestined, these He also called; whom He called, these He also justified; and whom He justified, these He also glorified."

The full impact of this is realized by starting at the end. We are called and appointed to belong to the Lord. That election and call was according to His predestined plan. We did not choose; we were chosen. That's where it all began. The Lord singled us out to belong to Him. As His children, He wants us to accept His love lavishly given on the cross and offered in His own presence in His Spirit. He wants to make us like Himself. That requires the quality of face-to-face communion which is prayer. His desire is for all things in our lives to work together to accomplish the plan He has for each of us. That plan is His will for us. The word *the-lēma* is used in Greek for "will" in this passage. It means desire. The Lord has a desire for all of us, a purpose for us to accomplish. But He does not leave us, after we are born again, with no training or help in accomplishing this purpose of being conformed into His own image. He invades our subconscious with preconscious longings and urgings which are manifested in the conscious desire to pray, seeking His desires for us. The Father, the Son, and the Holy Spirit are one. The Spirit is the reigning glorified Christ with us. This is what Paul made undeniably clear to the Galatians. "And because you are sons, God has sent forth the Spirit of His Son into your hearts, crying out, 'Abba, Father!' " (Gal. 4:6). The Spirit of the Son comes to us in our weaknesses. He calls us to prayer and then gives us the "groanings which cannot be uttered." What does this mean? My understanding is that the groanings are the preconscious longings which He eventually articulates through us in helping us to put into words what He wants us to pray. It is not that the intercession is done for us, for that would deny the cooperation with the Lord for which we were created. At first the invasion of the Spirit produces the longing to pray. Then when we feel the need to pray, but still don't know how or what to pray, He provides that also. Because He knows our hearts and is the heart of the Lord, He brings them into congruity. His purpose is to bring our desires into alignment with His desires so we can ask for that which will be part of all things working together for good.

Recently I had a misunderstanding with a cherished friend which resulted in a broken relationship. The startling thing was that for a time I didn't want to find a reconciliation. I chalked it up to irreconcilable differences which precluded the possibility of forgiveness and a new beginning. I was hurt and angry. My plan was to forget the whole mess. Some weeks later, an uneasiness began to grow in me. I couldn't shake the man out of my mind. That was followed by a mysterious desire to pray about him. When I responded to the inner urgings to pray, I noticed a difference in my attitude. As I prayed, I was given new empathy for what might have caused the man's behavior. I was given a completely different picture of the needs inside him; and then I asked for a way to communicate acceptance and forgiveness. As I lingered in prayer, a strategy was unfolded for what I needed to do and say. I had the deep conviction that the plan came from the Lord. Therefore when I asked for His help to accomplish His will in the matter, I could ask with boldness. The inner disquiet, like an inaudible wordless groaning, turned into clarity and was articulated in a request for strength to do what the Lord had promised He would do through me if I were willing. A new, ready will worked with my imagination to form the picture of how it would be accomplished. And that's exactly the way it turned out. The Lord was initiator and inspiration from start to finish.

The same process occurred in a tough decision I had to make recently. I thought I knew what the Lord wanted and did not pray a lot about it. When the decision was made, I had no peace. There was a jangling static in my spirit. It lasted for days. When sleep was interrupted by the disturbance, I knew something was very wrong. I asked the Lord to be very clear. I asked Him how to pray. A specific request was given me to make. If the disturbance was from Him I asked that it continue and grow. If the decision I had made was right and the disquiet was simply my own fear of implementing it, I was led to ask that the disturbance be taken away. You guessed it: the static grew to unbearably high decibles. That led me to confess, "Lord, now I know I'm on the wrong track. Show me what you want me to do." After hours of quiet listening, I reversed the hastily made decision. As I prayed, a new direction formed in my mind, pictured by my imagination. When I decided to follow the new direction, the jangling static inside subsided. An inner calm and confidence grew in its place. Then with holy boldness, I asked for what the Spirit had formed in my mind. When I asked I knew that I was assured of the answer. Subsequently, the decision was worked out by the Spirit's power exactly as He detailed it in prayer. Again, He had been the source of the disturbance, the desire to review the previous decision, the architect of the new plan, the communicator of the different direction, and the instigator of a boldness to ask for what He had imparted.

All these passages I have shared with you are the basis of everything else I want to say about prayer. Hold that basic thought. It will be woven through all that we will discuss together. *Prayer starts with God.* Our desire to pray is the result of His call to prayer. He has something to say. Our responsibility is to listen to what He wants to give us for our problems and potentials. He will make it clear. Then we can say with boldness:

> I sought the Lord, and afterward I knew
>> He moved my soul to seek Him, seeking me;
> It was not I that found, O Savior true,
>> No, I was found of Thee. [3]

Notes

1. Hilton Oswald, *Luther's Works, Isaiah* (Saint Louis: Concordia Publishing House, 1975), vol. 17, p. 393.
2. A. T. Robertson, *Word Pictures in the New Testament* (Nashville: Broadman Press, 1930), vol 6, p. 243.
3. Author unknown.

EIGHT STEPS TO EFFECTIVE PRAYER

Successful prayer is not measured by how much we get from God, but how much of Him gets into us and our daily circumstances and relationships. Prayer is not a "gimme game" but a grace gift. It is not being able to convince God of what we ought to have, but allowing Him to convince us of what we need and He is ready to give.

That's the magnificent truth Jesus taught His disciples when they came to Him with the request, "Lord, teach us to pray" (Luke 11:1). His response was to give them an example of prayer in what we have called the Lord's Prayer. In it we discover the steps of effective prayer. And then to drive home the context in which these steps were to be realized, the Lord gave several parables which stressed God's availability, His readiness to hear and respond, and His desire to give us Himself.

He startles us with the parable of the importune friend who goes to a neighbor seeking bread at midnight and is refused at first and then, because of his persistence, is granted his request. No such importunity is necessary with God. Jesus says, "And I say to you, ask, and it will be given you; seek, and you will find; knock, and it will be opened to you. For every one who asks receives, and he

who seeks finds, and to him who knocks it will be opened"
(Luke 11:9-10). The gracious generosity of God is established as the ambience in which we pray.

If that startles us, the second parable shocks us. "If a
son asks for bread from any father among you, will he give
him a stone? Or if he asks for a fish, will he give him a ser-
pent instead of a fish? Or if he asks for an egg, will he offer
him a scorpion?" (vv. 11-12). We feel a tug on our filial
hearts. What parent would do that? Jesus has our attention, indeed! We are ready to hear His "how much more"
comparison of God to earthly parents. "If you then, being
evil, know how to give good gifts to your children, how
much more will your heavenly Father give the Holy Spirit
to those who ask Him!" (v. 13). What Jesus is saying to us
is that the purpose, power and progression of prayer is a
gift of the Holy Spirit. When we ask how to pray, God
gives Himself. He gives us the motive and power to pray.
He instructs us in the progression of our conversation with
Him. In a vivid way Jesus is predicting His own return in
the presence of the Holy Spirit to guide us in our prayers.
He creates the longing to pray, helps us to know what to
say, and then guides us each step of the way. Prayer is to
expand our hearts until they are capable not just of saying
our prayers, but of receiving the Lord Himself.

In the power of the Spirit, the Lord comes to us and
says, "Behold, I stand at the door and knock. If anyone
hears My voice and opens the door, I will come in to him
and dine with him, and he with Me" (Rev. 3:20). As the
honored guest of our hearts He shows us how to pray. He
created us and knows how crucial it is that our capacity of
desire be directed creatively. Emerson said, "Prayer is the
soul's sincere desire." Desire marshals our energies and
prioritizes what we think is important. That's why the
Lord wants to shape our desires as He guides our prayers.

We are desiring all the time and, therefore, are really praying all the time. We need prolonged times with the Lord so that we can experience the reorientation of our desires around His desires for us.

Robert Murry M'Cheyne said something which has radically changed my conception of how this works. He said, "If I could hear Christ praying for me in the next room, I would not fear a million enemies. Yet distance makes no difference. He is praying for me." Profound prayer is listening in on our Lord's prayers for us and then praying after Him what He has modeled for us to pray. Prayer is not getting the Lord's attention, but allowing Him to lead us in praying for what He is more ready to give than we may be to ask.

The essence of this quality of prayer was expressed by a son who tenderly said to his dad, "I really appreciate all you've done for me, but my deepest desire is just to be with you . . . . I want to become like you, Dad." That's the dominant desire the Lord creates within us for our prayers. And then we are ready to hear from Him how to pray. In my experience, He leads us through the following eight steps of effective conversation.

Adoration

All great praying begins with adoration. God does not need our praise as much as we need to give it. Praise is like a thermostat that opens the heart to flow in communion with God. Hallowing God's name is enumerating His attributes. When we think magnificently about God's nature we become open to experience afresh His glory in our lives. I once took a course in creative conversation. The key thing I rediscovered was that there can be no deep exchange with another person until we have established the value of that person to us. Just as profound con-

versation with another person results from our communicating that person's worth to us, so too, we become
receptive to what God wants to do in our lives when we
have taken time to tell Him what He means to us. Don't
hurry through adoration. Everything else depends on it.
Tell God what He means to you, pour out your heart in
unhurried moments of exultation. Allow Him to remind
you of aspects of His nature you need to claim in the subsequent steps of prayer. Don't forget He is the leader of
the conversation. The more we praise the Lord, the more
we will be able to think His thoughts after Him throughout
our prayer. He loosens the tissues of our brains to become
channels of His Spirit.

Praise is the ultimate level of relinquishment. When
we praise God for not only all He is but what He is doing in
our lives, we reach a liberating stage of surrender. Often
when we begin our prayers, we don't feel like adoration.
Sometimes we wonder what God is doing with us in the
difficulties and trials of life. Praising Him reestablishes the
fact in our minds that He knows what He is doing and
makes us receptive to His guidance in those very needs.

I've experienced that repeatedly. When I'm inundated
with problems, my temptation is to rush past adoration to
tell the Lord the particular thing I think He ought to do to
help me. It never works. When I take time to reflect on
the greatness of God in spite of my circumstances, I am
much more ready to receive fresh wisdom when I pray
about specifics.

A good way to recapture the power of praise is to read
the Psalms. I find a creative two-week adoration assurance is to read Psalms 95 through 108, one each day as a
prelude to my own praise. They reestablish my trust in
God's power, providence, and all-knowing love. My heart
begins to sing again and then soar in communion with the

Lord. The point is that God wants us to enjoy Him! He delights to bless us when we let go of our worries and fears in unfettered praise.

There are times when I've found it helpful to begin my prayers by saying, "I love you, Lord. Let me tell you why." Then I rehearse in my mind all that He's been for me. Soon He takes over and leads me in remembering His goodness and grace. In times of difficulty, dark moods are lifted, troubled spirits are transformed, and an unwilling heart is made receptive. Or in bright times of success and smooth sailing, my happiness is maximized into pure joy. But whatever the circumstances of life, adoration creates the sublime delight of being in the presence of the Lord. Worship in the ancient English means "worth-shape," or establishing the worth, the wonder, and the glory of God in our minds and hearts. Adoration is the beginning of powerful praying. God created us to receive and return His love.

Contrition

The heights of our adoration prepares us for the depths of our confession. *The second step of prayer is contrition.* Once we have beheld the holiness of God, we become aware of our need to talk to Him about anything we've done or said that has denied His plan and purpose for us. But here again, the secret of confession is to allow the Lord to guide us. We think of confession as our act of setting things right with God. Not so! In Hebrew, confession means to show, point out, or acknowledge. In Greek the word is *homologeō,* "to say the same after." Authentic confession is to allow the Lord to press to the deeper levels of our lives to point out what He wants us to confess. So often we rehearse the surface failures. He digs deeper into the motive of our rebellious hearts. Often things which we decided to hide or equivocate become the focus of His all-knowing eye. Confession is to say, "Lord, show me anything which you see that is standing between you and me or between me and any other human being which needs to be confessed, or said after you." Sin means to miss the mark. What we consider our sins may be far less serious than what the Lord wants to cleanse from us. It is an awesome experience to allow the Lord to show us ourselves. We cannot take the shock apart from His love which will not let us go.

> Search all my sense, and know my heart
>   Who only can make known
> And let the deep, the hidden part
>   To me be fully shown.[1]

We cannot pray like that anywhere but at the foot of the cross. We can confess what God tells us to say after Him when we are sure we are forgiven even before we acknowledge the deeper sin beneath our more obvious sins. What is involved in true confession is to surrender the management of our lives to the Lord. He wants to make us new creatures. He knows what needs to be changed, amended, or corrected.

I am constantly amazed at how this happens. Recently, I felt a twinge of jealousy because of an opportunity given to a friend of mine. The next day I spread out the whole situation to the Lord. Much to my astonishment, He dug down into the roots of the sin. The longer I lingered in the confession portion of my prayers that day, the more I realized that I had drifted into a lack of appreciation for the tremendous opportunities the Lord had lavished on me. That changed jealousy into praise for the unique, different ways the Lord had decided to use me and my friend. The feeling was gone and has not returned.

This personal illustration is duplicated in the lives of people with whom I counsel. So often they come to me with the need to confess some sin which is unsettling them. I've learned from experience to help people ask the Lord to show them the deeper cause and motivation. Then prayer therapy with them in which we are silent after asking the Lord to probe deeper, usually exposes the raw nerve which really needs His healing forgiveness. The Lord is up to a great thing in transforming us and He wants nothing in His way. "Would not God search this out? For He knows the secrets of the heart" (Ps. 44:21). It is a source of comfort that He knows all about us. Peace comes when we say after Him what He knows and experience unlimited grace in spite of anything we've done or been.

Thanksgiving

And how shall we respond to a love like that? We are ready for the *next step which flows naturally—thanksgiving*. Thanksgiving is not just listing our blessings, but acknowledging the greatest blessing of all—the unmerited grace of the cross. It is from this side of Calvary and the open tomb of Easter that we can repeat Psalm 106, verse 1. "Praise the Lord! Oh, give thanks to the Lord, for He is good! For His mercy endures forever." The cross revealed the forgiving heart of God; the resurrection was His vindication and validation of Christ's atonement for our sins. How can we ever thank Him enough?

Here again the Spirit of the Lord leads us just as He did in adoration and confession. He brings to our remembrance all that He has done for us. We are all tempted to take the Lord's blessings for granted. We forget to say thanks. He knows that the attitude of gratitude is the key to greatness. The more we thank God for who He is and what He does for us the more He is able to bless us further.

Commitment

I have discovered that thanksgiving prepares me to commit all my problems and needs to the Lord. A survey of the past goodness of the Lord leads me to a confidence of trusting my relationships and responsibilities to Him. *Commitment is the fourth step of effective prayer.* On the cross, Jesus repeated a prayer which every Hebrew child learned at his mother's knee. "Into Your hand I commit my spirit" (Ps. 31:5). It is a good motto for this stage of our conversation with the Lord. Another is Psalm 37:5, "Commit your way to the Lord, trust also in Him, and He shall bring it to pass." The same releasing quality is expressed in Proverbs 16:3, "Commit your works to the Lord, and your thoughts will be established." All these Scriptures offer a great promise. Commitment leads to openness. We can discover the Lord's guidance in these challenges which have been turned over completely to Him.

I can't stress too much the crucial importance of this step of prayer. Commitment is the missing ingredient of contemporary Christianity and the reason so many miss the power of prayer. Many of us believe in the Lord, but have never made a commitment of our lives to Him. We are running our own lives. Prayer becomes a kind of magic to get God to do what we think is best for our lives. We break the first commandment: we have another god before the Lord—ourselves. When a crisis strikes we run to the Lord for help. It's usually to get His assistance to do what we've planned.

Too severe an analysis? How do you feel about that from your own experience of prayer? Ever sought God's help to accomplish plans that were never committed to Him or the result of His guidance?

When I talk with people who are experiencing a lack of power in their prayers or seldom sense the presence of the Lord, so often the cause is traced back to the absence of complete commitment. I talked to a man recently who was facing difficulties with his daughter. Her life did not reflect his values or his beliefs. Tension and hostility sparked like electricity whenever they were together. The man prayed about his daughter's problems daily. There was no question in his mind what his daughter should do and be, and he told God repeatedly. When he came to see me about what he called his "impossible problem," I felt led to ask him how he was praying about it. His response clearly indicated the real problem. He had never surrendered the need to the Lord, asking what He wanted him to be as a father and a communicator of affirmation and encouragement to his daughter's efforts to find out who she was and where she was going. He had to become a friend to establish the right to be heard. Imperious commands only caused greater rebellion. When he stopped telling the Lord what to do, and committed the broken relationship between him and his daughter, he began to see the quality of father she needed. He asked the Lord to show him the person he needed to be with her. The result was that he began empathizing instead of criticizing. He not only was able to help her make some crucial decisions about her life, but discovered the secret of dynamic prayer. The only things which can ultimately hurt us and those we love are the things we refuse to commit to the Lord's wise and incisive guidance.

What are the problems and perplexities on your mind right now? In what areas are you clenching your fists and saying, "I've got to take care of this on my own"? Open those fists and put the needs into the trustworthy hands of our Lord. He is worthy of the trust. He's been handling people and problems for thousands of years. He is able. Let go! When you do, you are ready for the adventure of the next step of conversation with the Lord.

Meditation

Commitment is followed by meditation. This is creative listening. When we unfold all our needs before the Lord and listen attentively, He will speak through the Scriptures, our thoughts, and our inner feelings. When we honestly say, "Lord, what do you want me to do?" He answers. The psalmist had that assurance. "The meditation of my heart shall bring understanding" (Ps. 49:3).

Keep meditation at the center of prayer. It is the most decisive aspect of prayer. Everything leads up to it; everything flows from it. From it we learn what to ask in subsequent portions of prayer for others, ourselves, and specific situations. Our theme in this book is emphasized again. God delights to reveal to us what He wants us to pray. Then our prayers are in keeping with what He has prepared to give.

Often I sit or kneel for a long time waiting for guidance on how to pray about particular needs. I would be less than honest if I suggested that an answer on what to pray for comes in the first few times I ask for guidance on how to pray about a situation. Patience is not my character trait. I want action from myself, others, even God, when I want it. But I have learned to give the Lord what I call conditioning time. When I see a need for guidance forming on the horizon of my future, I try to commit it to Him, renew that commitment daily, and be open for His perfectly timed direction. As the time for action or a decision draws near, there is a confluence of Scripture, the development of my thinking, and circumstances. I know how to pray when the time is right. The Lord knew all along what He wanted me to pray—it was I who needed to be prepared to ask according to His will.

In the process of meditation, the most complicated problems yield to solutions. We are given wisdom and insight we could not have achieved by ourselves. The wonder of it all is that the Creator and Sustainer of the universe is able and willing to inspire our thoughts so we know how to pray for what He wills and wants to give.

Intercession and Supplication

I have stressed meditation at length because it transforms *the next two steps of prayer—intercession and supplication*. Without meditation, prayers for others and ourselves will be ineffective and lacking in power.

Prayers for people will be dealt with more completely in a subsequent chapter. At this point I want to stress our calling to be part of the priesthood of all believers. The mystery of the Lord's providential management of the lives of His people is that He often waits to bless the people around us until we pray. Prolonged meditation about the needs of people gives us the content of our prayers of intercession. As priests of the Lord we have authority to go to Him about people and bring His assurance and courage to them. "You are a chosen generation, a royal priesthood" (1 Pet. 2:9). Our calling to be priests armed with the power of intercessory prayer goes back to the strategy of God given to Moses at Mount Sinai. The Lord declared that He wanted all His people to cooperate with Him in accomplishing His purposes through prayer for others.

The secret of how to intercede for others comes from Christ. Hebrews 7:25 shows us the way. "Therefore He is also able to save to the uttermost those who come to God through Him, since He ever lives to make intercession for them." In our prayers for others, our task is to listen in on His intercession. What would He pray for the people on our hearts? He reveals that in our meditation. Then we can pray with both authority and confidence. To pray for another person in Christ's name means by His power, but also through His guidance of what to pray. He gives us that discernment for our priesthood as intercessors. The Lord wants to bind His people together in mutual love and concern through prayer for each other. And the awesome thing is that through our prayers His blessings, power, healing, and guidance are given the people for whom we pray!

Prayer for our own needs is done in the same assurance. It is as if the Lord Jesus comes to us, puts His arms of love around us and says, "Dear friend, you've told me about your concerns, committed them to me and have asked how to pray. Now this is what I want for you." The one who said, "I will never leave you or forsake you" will not leave us confused or without direction for our prayers of supplication. Our Lord is faithful. He has a maximum plan for all of us. He will make it plain. The Lord never contradicts the Ten Commandments, His own message as Jesus of Nazareth, or the implications of His love for each situation. He will not guide us to do anything which will frustrate our union with Him. His ultimate will is that we know, love, and serve Him. He shows us what love demands and guides us in specific steps to take. When we miss His best and confess it to Him, He graciously weaves that into the tapestry of His final goal. We belong to Him, and if we are willing He will make each step of our path clearly lighted by daily, moment-by-moment guidance. We have a wonderful Friend to help us pray with power.

Dedication

Finally, He leads us into the last step of effective praying. He says, "Will you dare to implement your part in what I have guided you to pray?" Our actions either confirm or contradict what He has led us to pray. *Dedication is the action step of powerful prayer.* So often our prayers clarify what love demands in specific action. Our capacity to receive further intimacy with Him in prayer is dependent on implementing anything He clarifies we must do in faithfulness and obedience to Him. So often each step of prayer we've talked about leads to the necessity of following orders. Jesus put a great emphasis on the balance between hearing and doing. He closed the Sermon on the Mount with the parable of the builders to underline the importance of action. Those who hear but do not act are like the man who built on the instability of sand. The ones who hear truth and act on it, build the structure of their lives on rock.

I am convinced that the reason prayer becomes shallow and eventually hollow is because we resist the follow-through required. Often we return with the same personality difficulties because we were shown things about our character which required change and we resisted. Or the costly order for reconciliation or restitution in our relationships was mandated by the Lord and we resisted meliorating it into our behavior. When we return to the Lord in prayer, reiterating the same needs, He says, "Act on what I told you to do before and I will give you fresh guidance for the next phase of my unfolding strategy for you."

This outline of prayer is a guide for daily prayer. It follows the essential outline of prayer given in the Lord's Prayer and is offered in response to the human plea, "How can I maximize my prayers?" Each week I receive hundreds of letters from our church's national television audience. Among them are always dozens who ask how to pray. The quest is worded in a variety of different ways. And beneath different expressions of need is the longing to know how to listen to the Lord and share our deepest concerns with Him. I suggest at least fifteen minutes each day for these eight steps of prayer. They have been the lifeline for my prayers. I long for nothing less for you. Utilize them when you're at your best, morning or evening. Combine them with daily reading of the Bible. Then brief prayers can be added all through the day in each situation, problem, or opportunity. A prolonged time, not less than fifteen minutes, does not substitute for praying all through the day. How to do that, making all of life a prayer, is the awesome privilege to which we turn our attention in the following chapter.

Note

1. Author unknown.

WHAT A WONDERFUL WAY
TO LIVE!

A man came to see me about how to handle the mounting pressure in his life. I knew he believed in God, so I
asked him to tell me about his prayer life. He told me that
he had decided years ago to spend a period each morning
in prayer and Bible study. "It just doesn't last through the
day!" he said. "And things are so harried at work that
there's no time to get away from it all to pray."

"Why not pray your way through the day right on the
job?" I responded. He said he didn't think that would be
possible with people around him all the time. Then I
described the secret of prayer without ceasing and how to
retreat into the living center of his own soul sanctuary.

"You think with people around, don't you?" I asked.

"I'd better," he laughed, "or I'd lose my job!"

"Then why not also pray?" I asked.

We talked about the power of brief arrows of prayer
for wisdom, guidance, and help. I suggested that he send
an arrow of prayer to God for the people, problems, and
perplexities which were causing him tension. When things
got tough, all he needed to do was claim that the Lord was
present with him, that He was as concerned about carry-

ing on a conversation with him there at work as He was in the quiet early morning hours when he had his devotions.

"Think of it this way," I suggested. "One hundred ten and a fourth hours make one weak. Spell week, w-e-a-k."

"What do you mean?" the man asked, his interest peaked.

"Well," I said, "you have one hundred and sixty eight hours at your disposal every week—seven times twenty-four, right?" He agreed to the obvious, with a smile. "You sleep about eight hours a night," I continued, "so subtract fifty-six from that and you have one hundred and twelve left. Now you tell me you spend about fifteen minutes in prayer every morning—that's an hour and three fourths each week. Subtract that and you have one hundred and ten and one-fourth hours left uninspired by communion with the Lord and unprotected by His guidance and care. No wonder you're living under pressure," I said urgently. "The hours at work where you're in the bind of impossible schedules and difficult people are unclaimed for the Lord."

I explained that Christ is the Lord of all life, that for Him there is no division between the sacred and the secular. In fact the word "secular" comes from the Latin root *saecularis,* meaning "of the now, belonging to this age." Every "now" moment is sacred to the Lord. His wisdom can be given for our thinking about problems and opportunities, and His guidance is available for our moment-by-moment decisions. Then we talked about how to pray for each person as we talk to them or deal with them. In each problem-solving challenge we can pray, "Lord, I live with the results of so many poor decisions and wrong choices. Help me right now to think clearly and see all the facts of this complication. Show me what to be, do, and say."

The man's face brightened. He got the picture of living in the flow of supernatural power all through the unclaimed hundred and ten and a fourth hours at work, at home, at church, and in the community that had not been filled with the power of prayer. His response expressed excitement and the desire to experiment with praying all through the day. So I continued about prayer at night.

"And here's a way to claim those fifty-six night hours. Go to sleep praying. Ask the Lord to work in your mind all through the night and He will. You'll awake refreshed and have ideas and solutions that the day hours will demand."

"What a wonderful way to live!" my friend exclaimed.

"The only way to live adventuresomely and abundantly," I rejoined.

Marcus Aurelius once said, "The soul is dyed with the color of its leisure thoughts." I'd say that the soul is dyed with the color of our momentary thoughts all through the day. The author of Proverbs was right, "As we think in our hearts, so are we" (see Prov. 23:7). We become what we think about all the time and if the Lord is given access to our thoughts in only a brief time of prayer each day, we will become less than the persons He intends us to be. J.M. Barrie said, "To have faith is to have wings." Wings of prayer lift us above the present pressures so we can get perspective and receive power to be maximum for the Lord.

Wherever I go, people tell me that their greatest problem is living out their faith in the daily round of activities and challenges. So often they express the desire to get away from it all to rediscover their relationship with the Lord. Now I'm a firm believer in retreats for spiritual renewal and times away alone for prayer and planning. But these times can only strengthen us to discover the resources of prayer for the daily demands of living. It's what happens to us in the battle which shapes our lives.

Morning quiet times are absolutely essential to go

through the steps of effective prayer we talked about in the previous chapter, but it's throughout the day that we need the Lord to unfold the specific implications of His will. And He's ever ready to help. "God is our refuge and strength, a very present help in trouble. Therefore we will not fear . . . The Lord of hosts is with us" (Ps. 46:1-2, 7). That is what Archbishop William Trench claimed when he said, "Prayer is not overcoming God's reluctance; it is laying hold on His highest willingness."

We all want what I like to call the three *E*s of abundant living: Energy, Efficiency, and Endurance. We long to receive the energy of the Holy Spirit for our needs; we want to use the energies efficiently for His glory and our growth as persons; and we want to endure when the going gets rough. The Apostle Paul gives us three admonitions which cover all these needs in our lives. They cover the whenever, wherever, and whatever of our experience of praying through all our hours. Here is a practical, biblical guide for making all of life a prayer:

Whenever: "Pray without ceasing" (1 Thess. 5:17).

Wherever: "Therefore, I desire that the men pray everywhere, lifting up holy hands, without wrath and doubting" (1 Tim. 2:8).

Whatever: "Rejoice in the Lord always. Again I will say, rejoice! Let your gentleness be known to all men. The Lord is at hand. Be anxious for nothing, but in everything by prayer and supplication, with thanksgiving, let your requests be made known to God; and the peace of God, which surpasses all understanding, will guard your hearts and minds through Christ Jesus" (Phil. 4:4-7).

I want to consider each of these with you, plumbing the depths of what they can mean in specific application.

Whenever of Prayer

First, the "whenever" of prayer. We are invited to talk to the Lord and listen to Him to draw on His energy, efficiency, and endurance all the time, in all places, and in all circumstances. Some penetrating questions are helpful. Is there any time when God is unavailable? Is there any place where He is not? Is there any circumstance we could handle better without Him? Experience has taught us to answer all these questions with an emphatic "no!" Prayer without ceasing is built on that strong conviction.

Commenting on Paul's admonition for continuous prayer, Alexander McLaren, that great Scottish expositor of another generation, said, "A very high ideal, but a very reasonable one, for unless we can find some place where God is not, and where the telegraph between heaven and earth are beyond reach, there is no place where we should not pray. And unless we can find a place where we do not want God, nor need Him, there is no place where we should not pray. Because, then, everywhere is equally near Him, and the straight road to His throne is all the same length from every hole and corner of the world; therefore wherever people are, they ought to be clinging to His skirts."[1]

The challenge to pray whenever, in all times, becomes not only a source of strength for every moment, but also a good basis of making our choices about life-style and associations. Must God be excluded? Then it's best not to do it! Have we planned our life so cautiously that we're not attempting soul-sized challenges which only His power could help us achieve? Then life has lost its gusto. Are we spending our hours in things in which we'd be embarrassed to include the Lord? Then we've lived with the illusion that we have the power to exclude Him. The psalmist put it pointedly. "I have set the Lord always before me; because He is at my right hand I shall not be moved" (Ps. 16:8).

Paul lived his own advice to pray without ceasing. He claimed the companionship of prayer in victory, defeat, uncertainty, sickness, and persecution. Each move in his missionary journeys was guided by the Lord. He battled for faith alone as the basis of righteousness with the leaders of Israel as well as the Church; he communicated the gospel with freshness in each unique situation and to different types of personalities; he ministered relentlessly with supernatural strength; he confronted the resistance of friends and enemies; he was relentless in his purpose in triumph and tragedy. And the secret was that he was in constant communion with the Lord. From his decisive encounter with the Lord on the road to Damascus to his imprisonment in Rome, the reason for his spectacular life was: "All I care for is to know Christ, to experience the power of his resurrection" (Phil. 3:10, *NEB*).

"Whenever" prayer opens every moment to the resources of the Lord. He offers us His gifts: grace, faith, wisdom, discernment, and insight. The fruit of the Spirit is provided. Love, joy, peace, longsuffering, kindness, goodness, faithfulness, gentleness, self-control (Gal. 5:22-23). We need never be lonely for we are never alone.

Wherever of Prayer
Now claim these resources in the "wherever" of prayer. Based on his own experiences of the omnipresence and omniscience of his ubiquitous, ever-present Lord, Paul challenged people to pray everywhere. That covers the whole range of life's experiences. Alone, with people, at home, on the job, making money or making love, on vacation or in the battles of life. Psalm 139 describes David's

experience of the "everywhereness" of the Lord. "Where can I go from Your Spirit? Or where can I flee from Your presence? If I ascend into heaven, You are there; if I make my bed in hell, behold, You are there. If I take the wings of the morning, and dwell in the uttermost parts of the sea, even there Your hand shall lead me, and Your right hand shall hold me. If I say, 'Surely the darkness shall fall on me,' even the night shall be light about me; indeed, the darkness shall not hide from You, but the night shines as the day; the darkness and the light are both alike to You" (Ps. 139:7-12). The Lord of all life is not only always available for prayer, but He is inescapable. And in each moment He is calling us into prayer so that His best can be given to us and the people around us.

I find it helpful to think of prayer everywhere like breathing. All through the day I try to remember to breathe out the prayer, "Lord, I need you!" and then breathe in with the prayer of receptive gratitude, "Lord, I receive You!" It works wonders while studying or writing, talking with people, in staff or official board meetings, as well as in trying times of difficulty. Our minds are amazingly capable of doing several things at the same time. In a conversation, for example, we do not deny another person our full attention when at the same time we are praying for him or her. The same is true for preaching. While I am speaking I try to remember to pray all through the message that what is said will reach people's minds and hearts. When people listen and pray for what God wants to tell them through the message, powerful things happen. And the glory goes to the Lord!

A further aspect of Paul's word to Timothy that we should pray everywhere is that we should lift "holy hands without wrath or doubting." The Hebrew practice of lifting hands when in prayer, mentioned in the Old Testament

(Neh. 8:6), is probably what Paul referred to. The practice is customary in some churches today. I've found it to be a helpful and tangibly physical way of claiming the Lord's presence and power in various situations in which I pray for help.

The other day I was on a long flight from coast to coast. The hours had to be spent in a very strategic study and writing assignment. The need for clarity and accuracy was demanding. Often through the hours I would put my pen down, lift my arms and pray silently, "Lord, help me!" Later during the mealtime a woman across the aisle leaned over and said, "Sir, are you alright? You seem to be stretching a lot."

I laughed as I told her, "Yes, I was stretching, but also praying." She seemed interested in this gesture of prayer so I explained that what I was writing needed the Lord's word-for-word guidance and inspiration. That led to a visit about prayer and the Lord's intervening power in our affairs.

Just as the plane landed, she looked me in the eye and said, "I need you to do some stretching for me. I've got some difficult decisions to make in the next few days. Pray for me. And after what I've learned about prayer in our talk, you can be sure I'll be praying for the Lord's help. People in my office will probably think I'm stretching a lot also!" We both laughed and she went off to meet her particular set of impossibilities in which I am confident she discovered that with the Lord's intervention, all things are possible.

A friend of mine is a famous surgeon. He's also a committed Christian who believes that his skill is a gift of the Lord. The spiritual gift of healing is coupled with immense capabilities as a surgeon. One day in the operating room, a relatively new assistant asked him a question. "Why is it that at the most strategic, life-and-death moment of the surgery you pause, put down your instruments and stretch?" He explained that in tedious operations like that he needed the Great Physician's help and he paused to pray that he would know the exact thing to do. This brilliant surgeon had learned that the Lord was with him and his powers were dependent on His guidance.

I have another friend who leans back in his chair and lifts his hands at crisis points in meetings in the board room of his company. He is praying for wisdom. His associates are aware that his most ingenious suggestions are made after one of those "stretching times."

We needn't press that gesture of supplication too far. The Lord is no more available if we lift our hands in claiming His help. What is important is developing a technique of praying in all circumstances, everywhere.

Whatever of Prayer

That leads us to Paul's *third admonition to pray in all things.* This is the "whatever" of continuous prayer. "Be anxious for nothing, but in everything, by prayer and supplication, with thanksgiving, let your requests be made known to God" (Phil. 4:6). This is what George Tyrell called "a life of friendship with God." In this friendship we can depend on the Lord to be with us in whatever happens. All we have to do to realize His intervention is to take the feeling of anxiety as the signal to pray. When we talk to the Lord in the midst of the opportunity or challenge, we are to relinquish the management of the problem or potential to Him and thank Him for it.

You're probably thinking, "Listen, Lloyd, there are lots of things for which I'd find it difficult to thank the Lord!" I know that it is not easy to thank the Lord for troublesome people and turbulent problems. And yet, if we believe that the Lord is in charge, we can be sure that He will use what happens to us for what He wants to happen to and through us. Thanking Him in advance of solutions sets us free to discover what He may want to teach us. So often we look back at tough times and realize that we grew the most in the midst of them. The five words for a motto of victorious living are "Thank the Lord in trouble." When we do, we are released from the tension of facing it alone. The peace Paul talks about flows into our hearts.

In all the whenever, wherever, and whatever dimensions of living life as a prayer, the purpose is not just to get out of difficulties or solve problems or deal with troublesome people. All that will happen, but the greater result will be that we will come to know and love our God more profoundly as a friend. Not just in formal prayer times, but in the flow of life. Albert Day expressed that assurance. "This is the meaning of prayer—not to get things but to realize God. This is the greatest answer to prayer—not bread nor healing nor guidance, but companionship, Divine—human companionship."

One of the reasons I appreciate the poetry of Annie Johnson Flint so much is that it was written in physical pain. And yet she knew the Lord with an intimacy we all desire. Here's the reason.

> I dare not pray for any gift
>   Upon my pilgrim path to heaven;
> I only ask one thing of Thee
>   Give Thou Thyself, and all is given.[2]

Pray that prayer wherever, whenever, and in whatever life brings each day, and those one hundred and ten and one-fourth hours we talked about will make you strong. Indeed, what a wonderful way to live!

Notes

1. Alexander McLaren, *Expositions of Holy Scriptures* (Grand Rapids: Baker Book House, 1975), vol. 15, p. 354.

2. Annie Johnson Flint, "My Prayer," *Flint's Best Loved Poems* (Grand Rapids: Zondervan Publishing House, n.d.), p. 86.

THE TRANSFORMING POWER
OF PRAYER

The other day, as I was driving along in my car, my attention was arrested by a billboard. In bold, black letters it said, "Prayer changes things!" I thought a lot about that as I drove along. Does prayer change things? Well, yes and no. Certainly, when we pray God does intervene and make a difference in circumstances. But at the center of most of the difficulties and problems we face are people. Usually the way God changes things is to change those people. And yet, one of the greatest miracles of prayer is how God changes us and then frees us to cooperate with Him in changing people. Wonderful things begin to happen when, through prayer, we allow Him to change our attitudes toward the people and problems we face.

I want to communicate an astounding promise in this chapter. *We don't have to remain as we are.* We have been programmed for progress. William James said, "The most exciting discovery of our generation is that we can alter our person by altering our attitudes." Prayer is how it happens. There is a transforming power in prayer. George Bernard Shaw said, "Those who cannot change their minds cannot change anything." Prayer can be a mighty force in changing our minds about the people for whom we are concerned or distressed.

Look at it this way. When we have problems which are hassling our peace of mind, as we have said, the Lord instigates in us a desire to pray. We tell Him all about the problem and ask for His guidance. Or we are troubled about some person: a loved one who is in need, a friend whose life-style disturbs us, a fellow worker who doesn't measure up, or a neighbor who upsets us by the way he or she lives. Again the Lord is the initiator of the desire to pray about these people. Often we think that because we pray we can dispatch the Lord to straighten out these people according to the detailed specifications we have outlined to Him. When the answer isn't immediate, we wonder if He's heard us. Then a wonderful thing begins to happen. Our attitude of worry, judgment, impatience, or defensiveness begins to change. We begin to feel differently about the people. We see them through the eyes of our Lord. We feel love, understanding, and compassion. Often it is our changed attitude which gives them the desire to change. And even if they remain the same, we are able to cope much more effectively because of the transformation of our attitudes. We can't change most situations or people, until the Lord changes us. Changed people change situations around them. Beginning with them.

How does this happen? Paul tells us the secret in his second letter to the Corinthians. Though the word *prayer* is not mentioned in the passage I have in mind, it is really a description of how the Lord changes us, our attitudes, and subsequently, our relationships with people. It is through prayer that we appropriate this promise. "Now the Lord is the Spirit; and where the Spirit of the Lord is, there is liberty. But we all, with unveiled face, beholding as in a mirror the glory of the Lord, are being transformed into the same image from glory to glory, just as by the Spirit of the

Lord" (2 Cor. 3:17-18). Paul has given us the *purpose* of prayer, the transforming *power* of prayer, and the *promise* of prayer.

The Purpose of Prayer

The purpose of prayer is communion with the Lord who is the Spirit. "Now the Lord is the Spirit." The unity of Christ and the Holy Spirit is affirmed. The same Christ who came from the heart of God in the incarnation, returns to us in the Spirit to take up residence in us. Prayer is intimate communication in what Thomas Kelly called the divine center in each of us. It is from within us that the Lord does His work of changing us.

The task of the indwelling Lord is to introduce us to the real person who lives inside us. We are so much more than the outward person others see. He wants to liberate the unique, distinctly different person each of us is. "Where the Spirit of the Lord is, there is freedom." How does He do it? He told us plainly during His ministry. "If you abide in My word, you are My disciples indeed. And you shall know the truth and the truth will make you free . . . . Therefore if the Son makes you free, you shall be free indeed" (John 8:31-32,36). Jesus is telling us about freedom from sin. But what is sin? Not just the bad things we do, but the bound-up person we are. Sin is to miss the mark of the reason for which each of us was born. It is also the refusal to be the unique miracle each of us is. Christ sets us free from whatever binds the special person inside us.

The Transforming Power of Prayer

But mere liberation would be ineffective if the Lord didn't do something to shape and direct the person who is released. Liberation must be coupled with transformation.

And so Paul goes on. "We all, with unveiled face, beholding as in a mirror the glory of the Lord, are being transformed into the same image from glory to glory" (2 Cor. 3:18). This is in contrast to Moses' experience which the apostle had explained earlier in the passage. It reveals the different quality of prayer made possible after the incarnation, resurrection, and Pentecost. Moses' prayers to the Lord on Mount Sinai produced a radiance on his face. But the radiance would fade, so he placed a veil over his face so that the people would not see the diminishing radiance. Paul shows the difference in us as a result of the transforming power of prayer. Our communion with the Lord is meant to be consistent and constant; therefore the glory manifested in our personalities and on our countenances does not fade.

We are transformed by beholding. Prayer is beholding. And what do we behold? Paul's words can be interpreted in two ways. Beholding in a mirror the glory of the Lord can mean that we gaze into the gospel and behold Christ, who is the image of God. It may also mean something else. The Greek word used here for "beholding in a mirror" is a compound participle. *Katoptrizomenoi* is the present middle participle of *katoptrizō*, a verb from the noun *katoptron*, meaning "a mirror to see with"—*Kata*, with; *optron*, see.

The question is what Paul meant. What is reflected in the mirror into which we look? One meaning is that we behold the glory of God reflected in the face of Jesus Christ. Beholding Him we grow in His likeness. Another possible interpretation is that we are allowed to see our own faces with the glory of the Lord manifested on them. This second idea holds more closely to the Greek word for mirror. I think Paul mixed his metaphors and implied both meanings. Surely the whole thrust of the passage is that we have been given the privilege of beholding God face to face in Christ the Mediator.

"Glory" in Hebrew is *kabod* meaning value, weight, substance. When applied to God who is a Spirit the word *glory* is synonymous with the splendor of His presence and power. In Greek the word means manifestation. *Doxa* means the Lord's revelation of His nature and attributes. That's why the Scriptures speak of Christ as the glory of God. This is what Paul means when, a few verses later in chapter 4, he says, "For it is the God who commanded light to shine out of darkness who has shown in our hearts to give the light of the knowledge of the glory of God in the face of Jesus Christ" (v. 6). God who brought the light of day out of darkness in creation has illuminated our hearts with the knowledge and experience of His glory in Christ.

In prayer we behold the glory of Christ as we commune with Him. His glory in our hearts transforms us from within. We are changed into His likeness. The Greek word for transformation is *metamorphoō*. It means that there is a change which brings about a congruity between the inner and outer dimensions of our personalities. What's inside is manifested in character, action, attitude, and personality characteristics. We do not experience transformation by beholding the person we were, but by beholding Christ. But the exciting implication of the mirror metaphor may be that the Lord gives us the encouragement of being able to see the change as we look into the mirror and realize that beholding Him has made us progressively more and more like Him. This is hinted at in the *Living Bible* paraphrase of 2 Corinthians 3:18. "But we Christians have no veil over our faces; we can be mirrors that brightly reflect the glory of the Lord. And as the Spirit of the Lord works within us, we become more and more like Him." Could it be that the Lord also allows us the delight of seeing the change He is manifesting in us? Does

He enjoy sharing the progress with us? I am convinced He does.

Dr. F. B. Meyer put it clearly. "We reflect. The beauty of His face glancing on ours will be mirrored, as a man's eye will contain a tiny miniature picture of what he is beholding. Then we will be changed. If you try to represent Jesus in your character and behavior, you will become transfigured into His likeness. Love makes like. Imitation produces assimilation."[1]

What does all this mean to you and me and our discovery of how to pray with power? Everything! The Lord creates in us the desire to pray because He wants to make us like Himself. As we take time to be with Him in prayer we feel loved and affirmed. The result is not pride or complacency; strangely, it produces a desire to grow in Christlikeness. It isn't that we work out an idea of the person we want to be and then get His help to fulfill our plans. Rather, as we come to know Him better, changes take place inadvertently. In the pure light of His presence, we see ourselves as we are. We could not endure that experience if it were not for the fact that honesty about ourselves is enabled by His unlimited love.

We all want to press on in becoming mature men and women in Christ. It's a serious thing. I've never met a person who is totally satisfied with the man or woman he or she is. Whatever accomplishments we achieve, there is an inherent longing to press on. We are like the artist who was asked, "What is your greatest painting?" He responded, "The next one!" We'd all echo that about any project, day, or phase of our lives. Complete satisfaction with ourselves seems to be a luxury the Lord has decided to deny us so that we might press on in becoming more of the person He created us to become.

The amazing thing is the way the Lord works with us.

He does not plunge us into inordinate dissatisfaction or force us to be protectively defensive about ourselves. He does not allow us to get down on ourselves or be proud of our progress. In the ambience of His love we are shown things which cripple our freedom to be creative communicators of His love to others. His way of dealing with us is radically different from the current self-realization therapies of our time. He has a much greater purpose: His desire is to make us people who can be channels of His affirmation, assurance, forgiveness, and new life to others. In keeping with that, the thrust of the New Testament about the need for character transformation is always in the context of our calling to be ambassadors of hope, agents of reconciliation, and stewards of the manifold grace of the Lord. Whatever gets in the way is what the Lord wants to change in us. To do that He communicates forgiveness for what we've been and a vivid picture of what we can become.

Just the opposite of the way Christ works in us was depicted in a cartoon I saw recently. I like cartoons. They make me laugh at myself and, sometimes, even think. Ed Frascino is one of my favorite cartoonists. He loves to poke fun at "that stagnant, bound together with another person thing" of some middle-aged couples. One of his cartoons depicting that caught my attention. A grim, hatchet-faced woman was seated next to her equally grim, overbearing, and overweight husband. As she glared critically, she said, "What's your biggest fault and what are you going to do about it?"

That question is often implied, if not asked, in lots of relationships—by young and old, single and married. The last thing most of us need is to contemplate our faults without an atmosphere of affirmation in which we are encouraged to grow as persons. When another person is over against us with negative criticism we become rigidly intractable.

How differently Christ deals with us! His question is not, "What is your greatest fault and what are you going to do about it?" but "What would you be like if you allowed me to form your character and personality like mine?" In prayer He activates our imagination to picture the person we long to be by His transforming power and then offers us the help we need. He does that by removing the barriers to Christlikeness. Most of us are haunted with fears. These shape our personalities into inverted, cautious distortions. He helps us look at these one by one. Then He deals with the memories which lurk within—the times we failed, were hurt by others, or stunted in our personality growth by the debilitating experiences during the early years of our lives. The Lord allows us to look honestly at what our parents and our families did to encourage or discourage our emergence as self-accepting, life-affirming people capable of receiving and giving love. As we probe deeper with His loving guidance in prayer, He helps us receive and give forgiveness. Memories are expunged of their poison.

Now the Lord is ready to deal with habit patterns in our attitudes. Why do we react the way we do? What causes us to respond to some people and reject others? What lack of security in His love makes us negatively critical, judgmental, or hostile?

Consistently in prayer with the Lord we can look back over the previous day and affirm progress and question the deeper causes of any lack of freedom. He gently, but persistently, touches the raw nerve of the deeper causes.

Throughout the lifelong process of creative personality prayer therapy, as we are ready, subconscious repressions will surface and can be dealt with in conversation with the Lord. We will become progressively more liberated. We will find that we enjoy the person who lives in our skin and befriend his or her struggle to be whole. The delightful, evolving result is that we will begin to love ourselves as we are loved by the Lord. As Dr. Karen Horney explains, "The feeling of being loved and even more of being loveable is perhaps one of the greatest values in life." And one of the primary purposes of prayer is to give us the gift of both with the added plus of wanting to communicate both to the people around us.

In explaining this process of the transformation of personality through prayer, I do not want to negate the function of the trained Christian psychologist or psychiatrist. Often we need help in understanding what has conditioned and shaped our personalities. But even when the Lord uses another person to help us, eventually we must deal with the discoveries and insights ourselves in our relationship with Him. We cannot see ourselves as we are or gain a true picture of what we can become without His love and the strength for behavior modification.

Another source of help are Christian friends who will listen to us as we grapple with our assets and liabilities. Often prayer groups reach the level of intimacy in which we can talk out what the Lord is showing us about ourselves. When the action step of change is mandated, we need the prayers of others to spur us on. I have never been without a group like that. Presently I am in a group of fellow adventurers in growth in Christ. The participants communicate, listen, and give me courage to dare to grow and change. I can trust them because I know they too are on a personality pilgrimage of being formed into the image of Christ.

The Promise of Prayer

All this that I tried to share about prayer and personality in this chapter comes down to some personal questions. Have you ever thought of prayer as the dynamic communion with the Lord in which He seeks to transform you into His likeness? If so, are you presently yielding who you are to His healing and reformation? Have you ever asked Him to show you your full potential as His person? Do you dare to yield to His molding Spirit the future development of your personality?

"Therefore, if anyone is in Christ, he is a new creation; old things have passed away; behold, all things have become new" (2 Cor. 5:17). And for what purpose? To love as we've been loved! Prayer doesn't just change things. It changes us.

> Lord, what a change within us one short hour
> Spent in Thy presence will prevail to make!
> What heavy burdens from our bosoms take,
> What parched grounds refresh as with a shower!
> We kneel, and all around us seems to lower;
> We rise, and all, the distant and the near,
> Stands forth in sunny outline brave and clear;
> We kneel, how weak! we rise, how full of power!
> Why, therefore, should we do ourselves this wrong,
> Or others, that we are not always strong,
> That we are ever overborne with care,
> That we should ever weak or heartless be,
> Anxious or troubled, when with us is prayer,
> And joy and strength and courage are with Thee![2]

Notes

1. F. B. Meyer, *Great Verses Through the Bible, A Devotional Commentary on Key Verses* (Grand Rapids: Zondervan Publishing House, 1972), p. 427.

2. Richard Chenevix Trench, "Prayer," James Dalton Morrison, ed., *Masterpieces of Religious Verse* (New York: Harper & Row Publishers, 1948), p. 403.

PRAYER AND OUR WORRIES OVER PEOPLE

Focus in your mind's eye the people about whom you are concerned. The people about whom you worry. Who are they to you? Perhaps you are married to him or her. Maybe you're worried about one of your children. Or it may be a friend who's in trouble, or someone for whom you work or who works for you.

What Is Worry?

I want to share a secret of how to stop worrying about those people and start living. Intercessory prayer can break the worry bind. Worry is thinking turned toxic, concern degenerated into inner conflict. The old English word for worry is *wyrgan* which means to twist or strangle. Worry does that to our love for people. It both twists it into debilitating anxiety and strangles our capacity to discover what to do to help and do it in a way that does not multiply the problem about which we are troubled in another person.

Worry is that anxiety which fills the interface between what is and what we imagine should be. It is the insecure, unstable fill we dump into the caverns excavated by our human expectations. It is the marshy substance that will support no bridge of safe passage; it is the aching memory of what should have been and what should be but seldom is. Worry is unproductive because it is not based on the vision of what God promises He can and will do.

Intercessory Prayer Combats Worry

Intercessory prayer is the antidote to worry over people. But many of us pray for people about whom we are concerned, and still worry. A woman said to me recently, "I pray for my son, but can't seem to stop worrying about him. I talk to God about him and tell Him what my boy needs. But I get up from my knees and soon I am worrying as if I had never prayed." Ever feel like that? How can we pray for people and know that God has heard us, understood, and that He will do something?

Last summer, just before I left for my study leave in Scotland, a friend shared a profound problem he was facing. We spent hours talking it through, then we prayed together, and I departed. I told him I would pray for him each day. The difficulty he was facing was so serious for him and his marriage that I found him coming back to my mind often each day. When I prayed about him it sounded as if I were calling the Lord's attention to a problem about which He had little or no information. Because I thought I knew what the man had to do to save his marriage, I petitioned God almost hourly during the weeks of study and writing. Then one day during a long walk, a reorienting, transforming thought hit me. I had believed that intercessory prayer was my placing my burdens on God's heart. Or at least, that's the way my prayers sounded. Then that day, a totally new conception formed in my mind. It was consistent with the theme the Lord was giving me for this book. It came first as a thought and then was articulated into words in my mind. It is the secret I must share with you. *Intercessory prayer is God putting His burdens on our hearts.*

Like all prayer, intercessory prayer originates with God, not us. He has wisely decreed that His work will be done in His people cooperatively through the prayers of those on whose hearts He places His burden. If we won't pray, often He won't act. Notice I didn't say that He can't act. He can do anything He wants to do. But the mystery of His providential care of people is that He calls us into the process of His blessing, and often waits to bless a person until we pray.

The word *intercede* in the Latin means "to go or pass between": *inter,* between; *cedere,* go on, pass. The exciting idea the Lord has been giving me is that He is the original, initiating interceder. He intercedes with us, that is, He invades our worry with specific guidance on how to pray for another person. Jesus did that for us in the incarnation and the atonement. And He continues to do that in our prayers. "He ever lives to make intercession for them" (Heb. 7:25), first between us and the heart of God and then into our hearts to give the wisdom of what and how to pray for the people about whom we are tempted to worry.

But so often we worry over a person, finally decide that prayer is our last resort, and then go into God's presence to brief Him on the need and what He should do. Because we feel that it's up to us to persist and that God will bless someone because of the length and repetition of our prayers, we do not get free of the worry. We wonder, Have we said enough? Have we prayed often enough? Is our own life sufficiently in order to deserve an answer to our prayer for a loved one? Now added to our original worry is the concern about the adequacy of our prayers.

We are back in the syndrome of self-justification and bartered love.

It is the Lord who calls us into prayer for people. The thought of a person's need is because He wants to act in that person's life. Part of His strategy is to involve us in His unfolding answer.

I've had some humorous experiences with people's message beepers going off during my preaching. Doctors, and now busy people of all kinds, wear them or carry them in purses. Often they forget to turn down the volume of the beep before coming into worship. Recently, while I was preaching I asked the rhetorical question, "Who in your life needs your love and affirmation?" At that very moment, a doctor's turned-up beeper attached to his belt sounded, invading the quiet of the sanctuary with its loud persistence until the doctor was able to turn it off and leave his pew to return an emergency call from the hospital. The congregation laughed at the timing of my question and the beep. I tried to utilize the unexpected parable and suggested that there was probably a call for help waiting for all of us if we could only hear the plea in people's expressions and the meaning beneath their words. But what if we thought of our concerns over people as a beep from God calling us into prayer? Consider it this way in response:

> All that I feel of pity Thou hast known
> Before I was; my best is all Thy own
> From Thy great heart of goodness mine but drew
> Wishes and prayers, but Thou, O Lord, wilt do
> In Thine own time, by ways I cannot see,
> All that I feel when I am nearest Thee![1]

The impact of this growing understanding of intercessory prayer, subsequent to the insight from the Lord that afternoon as I walked, has broken the worry bind I have experienced so often when people's needs have the potential of starting the cycle of anxiety. The conviction which has gripped me ever since is that it is the Almighty God of power who has called me to join Him in the accomplishment of His plans and purposes for a person.

Look at it this way. If you or I go to a person for help for someone in trouble, the responsibility is ours to convince him or her of the need. Explanation, examples, and appeals to the potential benefactor are made with the hope of touching his or her heart and getting the desired assistance. The burden of proof is ours. Our plea must be convincing enough to motivate action. Even after we've presented the need we are left with the uncertainty about whether we have said the right thing. But most of all, we wonder if the person has the resources to help even after we have marshalled his or her desire to help. That's the way many of us think about intercessory prayer.

Now turn that around totally. Think of being called by someone who wants to help a friend or loved one of ours. There is no need of convincing or impassioned appeals. We are asked to be the mediator and implementor of the help. Our only task is to learn what the person wants to do or give. Our responsibility is not asking, but claiming what is offered. And that's the way our Lord wants us to think about our prayers for others.

Jesus Gave a Model

Jesus' priestly prayer for His disciples on the night before the crucifixion is an excellent model for our intercessory prayers. It's found in the seventeenth chapter of John. Read it over carefully. Note how Jesus reaffirms His oneness with the Father as the basis of His confidence in prayer. His claim and confidence is based on what the Father had already done and declared. Then the Lord prays for the disciples as people given Him by His Father. "I have manifested Your name to the men whom You have given Me out of the world. They were Yours, You gave them to Me, and they have kept Your word. Now they have known that all things which You have given Me are from You" (vv. 6-7). The prayer is more like reporting in for duty and a fresh update of vision already revealed. Jesus goes on to claim all that the Father had promised for the disciples. Then the prayer proceeds to include those who will become believers through the disciples. "I do not pray for these alone, but also for those who will believe in Me through their word; that they all may be one, as You, Father, are in Me, and I in You; that they also may be one in Us, that the world may believe that You have sent Me. And the glory which You gave Me I have given them, that they may be one just as We are one" (vv. 20-22).

The Lord's intercessory prayer was in perfect consistency with what He knew was the heart of God. Our response may be, "Well, Jesus was the Son of God; of course He knew what to pray." And yet, this is the key to unlocking the power of intercessory prayer. Immanuel, God with us, is with us still. Through His Spirit He teaches us what to pray for others. He does that by energizing our imaginations. He gives us a picture of what He wants to do, and then the content of our prayer is to claim that picture. Intercessory prayer is the risen, present Christ continuing His ministry through His chosen and called people.

The exchange between Simon Peter and Jesus in the Upper Room (Luke 22:31-34) helps us to understand the Lord's plans for us as agents of enabling prayers for others. To the then unstable and unconverted disciples He said, "Simon, Simon! Indeed, Satan has asked for you, that he may sift you as wheat. But I have prayed for you, that your faith should not fail; and when you have turned to Me, strengthen your brethren" (Luke 22:31-32). At that point Peter was not converted, did not have the gift of faith, and was incapable of ministering to the needs of others. After the resurrection and the empowering of the indwelling Christ at Pentecost he was converted. "Return to Me" is a translation of the Greek word *hepistripho,* to turn, to be transformed, to go in an entirely new direction. After the effluence of the Spirit at Pentecost, Peter is given the gift of faith to accept the atonement of the cross, claim the power of the resurrection, and begin doing what Jesus did (see John 14:12-14). The interceding prayer ministry of the incarnate Lord now is carried out by Peter and the Church. After our conversion our major ministry is praying for others.

The oft-repeated quote of E.M. Bounds underlines the crucial calling we have been given. "Talking to men for God is a great thing, but talking to God for men is greater still." It is a sublime expression of love. But when we allow God to talk to us about people, what we have to say to Him about them in our intercessory prayers is infused with His love and His wisdom.

The priestly prayer of Jesus gives us further insight in how to pray when we are concerned for others. The ultimate prayer is that "they may be one." That oneness with God is the deepest need in everyone for whom we pray. Oneness means love, communion, intimacy, closeness. The essential "I" meets the eternal God. Whatever need in a person drives us to our knees is insignificant in comparison to this. And when we are led to pray about a specific problem, our supreme concern is that the Lord will use what is happening to a person for introduction to a deeper relationship with Him.

Why God Needs Our Prayers

Having said all this, a question still lingers. Why does God need our prayers? If He knows what is best for someone, why doesn't He just do it without involving us? That's the other dimension of the oneness Jesus prayed for. He came not only to make us one with God, but to call us into oneness with each other. The reconciliation He died and rose to provide, and returned to impart, is both vertical and horizontal: it is with God and between us and others. That's why intercessory prayer is so crucial. The Lord wants us to be to one another what He has been to us in love, forgiveness, and unlimited concern. The mystery of it all is that often He will not bless another until we pray. When we do pray, His love flows through us to the other person. The help the Lord has reserved until we prayed is given because we have become agents of His intervention. When He is ready to give reconciliation, salvation, healing, strength, guidance, or the resolution of a seemingly unsolvable problem, He enlists us into partnership for the accomplishment of His will.

That is both a source of awe and a reason for alarm. The fact that God has decided to bless through the prayers of His people is humbling. But it is also startling when we realize how little time and effort we expend in intercessory prayer. We wonder about who in our lives may be enduring less than God's maximum because we have not taken our calling seriously. Saint Francis de Sales put it this way: "God did not deprive thee of the operation of His love, but thou didst deprive Him of thy cooperation."

Added to that, many relationships remain on a mediocre level because we pray so little for others. Nothing engenders love and delight over the unique miracle which each person is more than prayer. William Law said, "Intercession is the best arbitration of differences, the best promoter of true friendship, the best cure and preservative agent against unkind tongues, all anger and haughty passion." Intercessory prayer frees us to love the persons for whom we pray. We feel the pulsebeat of the Lord's love. Concern for them prompts forgiveness and patience. Our hearts are knit to theirs as we claim what the Lord has given us—the discernment and boldness to ask for them. We are on their side—for them. People desperately need that. God knows—He created us so that we could not be complete without Him or each other. Intercession is the mother tongue of the new creation in Christ.

And yet we've all prayed for people who have resisted what seemed to be best for them. We all have free will and some of the people for whom we pray are in what Luther called the "bondage of the will." There are times when people resist receiving what the Lord has prompted us to ask. That's a signal for our prayers to plunge deeper. The will can dominate both thought and emotion. People can will not to accept the Lord's blessing. The will is released from bondage of the imperious self-control only by the invasion of the Spirit of the Lord. No one decides to want God until He creates the desire in him or her. When a person is resistant, pray for the liberation of the will and trust that the gift of faith will be given. When God puts that need on our hearts, it is because that's exactly what He desires and is preparing to do.

Worry Is a Substitute for Intercession

A concern for a person is a call to intercessory prayer. Worry is a substitute for intercession. And worrying after we've prayed is a sure sign that we think of prayer as our effort and that perhaps God has not heard. Added to that, it is a lack of trust. And that may tell us more about our need than the person for whom we are praying. Worry is a cycle of unproductive thought whirling around a center of hidden fear. We cannot receive the cure of our worry until we allow the Lord to show us what fear in us is causing it. Perhaps we fear losing control or want to direct another person's life. Claiming that God is in charge may be very frightening. Or we may have asked the Lord for something in our own lives and it has not come on our timing or to our specifications. We have little confidence that He will hear us in our concerns for others any more than we think He hears us about our own set of problems. Worry is the natural result of unbelief.

Worry Becomes a Habit

The problem is that worry becomes a habit. After a while, we need it to feel secure. We are like dope addicts needing a fix. We can actually create situations about which we can worry. What can we do? The cure of worry is not just the belief that things will work out for good under the providence of God. It comes from wrenching our egos from the throne of our hearts. Worry is a manifestation that we are still living with our wills in control and our desires as the focus of our prayers. The worry syndrome is seldom broken until we are willing to be called into prayer to receive God's orders for what is best rather than tenaciously grasping what we are determined to convince Him should be done. Helmut Thielicke said, "Care can be cured only by care. Care about many things can be cured only by care about the one thing needful. This is the homeopathy of divine healing." And the one thing needful? Jesus said it was to seek first God's kingdom and all else would be given. The creative fear of missing the reason we were born displaces all secondary fears. When we put

God first in our lives, people and their needs become a close second. The ministry of prayer is not an option for those so inclined by nature. Our new nature in Christ is manifested in the willingness to be called by Him into a ministry of listening for what we are to pray for others, and then responding by asking with boldness for those things He has clarified.

Desire to Become Involved

A further result of consistent intercessory prayer is that we are given a desire to become involved in the implementation of our prayers. When we have listened to the Lord to discover His strategy, often He gives us marching orders for practical assistance which we can be to the person for whom we have prayed. Armed with profound discernment we know what to do and say. All that we've been given of insight, wisdom, experience, and material resources can then be deployed to be the Lord's love in action.

A word of caution needs to be sounded about telling people the result of our listening prayers for them. When the Lord gives us wisdom on how to pray, we should be very thoughtful about going to a person to say, "The Lord has told me what you ought to do!" When that takes on the freight of our determination to gain control over a person it can be very dangerous. However, just as the Lord gives us guidance in how to pray for a person, He also will give us the signal of if and when to share an insight. We need to wait and watch for a receptivity in people. That usually is the result of our caring for them in very practical and supportive ways. Earning the right to be heard, coupled with the Lord's timing, is a winning combination.

The other day, I overheard a conversation. One man said to his friend, "I've been praying for you." The quick retort of the other man was, "Thanks, but tell me—what did you pray? Hope you're not like some of my friends who tell me they have a pipeline to heaven and tell God exactly what I ought to do. The problem is that they all have conflicting guidance. If I followed them I'd go off in all directions." Sensing the bristled spirit in the man, the intercessor said, "The conviction I get as I pray for you is that God loves you very much, knows the bind you're in, and will not leave or forsake you." I learned that later when the man was ready to talk, he called on this wise, sensitive and affirming friend. The faithful intercessor let him talk for a long time. When the troubled man got around to a possible solution which was close to what he had been led by the Lord to pray for, he gently responded, "I think you're on target. That fits with what I've sensed the Lord is trying to say in your need." I like that!

Of course, there are times when we are so convicted about a danger in another person's direction that we must share our concern candidly. But not without the preparation of becoming a loving friend. People resist those who try to straighten them out. There are people in my life who have communicated their faithfulness. I will listen when the Lord has guided them to intercede for me in a particular direction. Like most of us, I am put off by people who get into a power struggle with me and use the fact that they are praying for me as a hammer to tell me what to do. However, when they have become trusted friends, I seek their counsel which has been honed in prolonged intercessory prayer for me.

The issue raised about intercessory prayer is whether our prayers for others make any difference. Often we ask: Can our prayers change God's will for a person? Can our sincere wish alter the counsel of the Almighty? What I have tried to communicate in this chapter is that those questions indicate we are missing the purpose of intercessory prayer. The real question is: Can God implant in our minds the maximum expression of His will for another person? Can we cooperate with Him in the accomplishment of His will by praying for him or her? Yes! And when we receive that and respond in our prayers, we become essential agents for the Lord to pour out His blessings. Oneness with Him and the persons for whom we pray will result. We can stop worrying and start living!

Note

1. Author unknown.

Chapter Six

THE QUESTION OF UNANSWERED PRAYER

Some time ago I gave a series of messages on prayer to my congregation in Hollywood, California. One Sunday morning, as I greeted the people after one of these messages, a woman pressed a carefully folded note into the palm of my hand. She held my hand firmly as I looked into her eyes long enough to know that whatever was written on the note was urgent and the expression of an honest need. I thanked her for it and assured her that as soon as I had finished with the greeting I would read it and respond.

When I reached my study and had a few leisurely moments to unfold the note, this is what I read: "Lloyd, I have appreciated all the positive things you have said about how to pray with power, but I must be very honest. This series on prayer has made me feel very lonely, even a bit angry at times. I look around me as you tell all the glorious things that happen when we pray and see everyone nodding in agreement and affirmation. Doesn't anyone feel the way I do about those times when prayer is unanswered? Here's my problem. For months now I've had the feeling that God neither heard nor responded to my prayers. I have gone from feelings of guilt that something must be wrong with me, to doubt about whether God cares. I just had to tell someone—to ask the lurking question—why are some prayers unanswered?"

Ever feel that way? Have you ever known an excruciating dry spell in your prayers when there seemed to be no answer to your prayers? Of course, we all have. Deep down inside of all of us are questions about why prayers sometimes seem like an endless monologue. In those times, the enthusiastic witness of others about answered prayer seems to mock our impatience with God. We listen, not wanting to cloud the sunny skies of others with the thunderheads of our own doubt. But we do feel like Thomas Hardy once felt as he saw the joyous fellowship of praying believers.

> That with this bright believing band
>   I have no claim to be,
> That faith by which my comrades stand
>   Seem fantasies to me
> And mirage-mist their Shining Land
>   Is a strange destiny?[1]

There are some who have never had what they would call a definite answer to prayer. Others have known the ecstacy of sweet communion with the Lord in prayer and have also found that for some strange reason, prayer has suddenly become sterile and unrewarding. Still others are like this woman. You have prayed, waited, wondered, and become weary. And then there are others of us who wrestle with the bold promises of the Bible about prayer and are frustrated by the disparity of what is offered and what we seem to experience in our prayers. We follow Jesus' admonition to ask, seek, knock. We read that all we are to do is make our requests known and they will be granted. "If you ask anything in My name I will do it," He promises with assurance. Why then the problem of unanswered prayer?

Helmut Thielicke, the great German theologian and preacher, empathizes with us. "How often have we earnestly pled for something and haven't gotten it? All along the highway of our lives are there not the countless grave-markers of unanswered prayers? Have we not all known bitter disappointment and moments when no voice nor answer came as we ardently prayed, and when we remained alone and disappointed in the silence?"[2]

We answer with an honest "Yes!" But we need more than empathy or the comfort of a shared dilemma. We want to hear from the Lord about why He seems to be silent when we cry out to Him in petitions for the things we earnestly need.

And He is ready. He has dealt with the question before. He opens the way for us to pour out our frustration and then gives us more of an answer than we may have expected!

The other day I talked with a couple who were facing difficulties in communication. The man said, "How I wish I could express my feelings without my wife being defensive. If I could just get out what's happening inside of me in an atmosphere of complete acceptance, not of all that I say, but of me as a person, I know I'd get perspective and be able to change my attitude." That's exactly the kind of openness the Lord creates for us to be able to talk out our frustrations about seemingly unanswered prayer.

The Lord loves us very much. He wants us to express how we are feeling about those times when our prayers seem not to be answered. We don't have to protect His reputation—to ourselves or to others. The question from the deeps of our souls will be answered from the depth of His love. But while we are questioning Him, He may have some very crucial questions to ask us!

That's what happened to Job. The story of Job's suffering is a classic study of the problem of unanswered prayer. Job was a successful, prosperous man who lost everything—his wealth, children, cattle. Along with these, he also almost lost his faith in the righteous justice of God. His friends tried to convince him that he must have sinned in some way to have brought this punishment from God. They espoused the belief held at that time that suffering was the recompense of God for sin. Job protested his innocence. But most acutely he felt the absence of God when he cried out for vindication. He tried to maintain his belief in the righteousness of God and his conviction that, if he could only reach Him, he could question the Almighty about the injustice he was enduring, and why He would allow it. Most of all, Job wanted the Lord's presence and assurance. Listen to Job . . . ever felt as he did?

"Even today my complaint is bitter; my hand is listless because of my groaning. Oh, that I knew where I might find Him, that I might come to His seat! I would present my case before Him, and fill my mouth with arguments. I would know the words which He would answer me, and understand what He would say to me. Would He contend with me in His great power? No! But He would take note of me. There the upright could reason with Him, and I would be delivered forever from my Judge" (Job 23:1-7).

Finally, after a prolonged time of what seemed to be no answer from God to this prayer, Job borders on bitterness. The mocking question of Satan is, "Does Job fear God for naught?" But the real question is, "Does Job fear God for God?" When we understand the Old Testament usage of the word fear as awe and wonder issuing in adoration and praise, the question becomes ours. Do we love God for God or for what He will do for us? That's the real question we must ask ourselves in the time when our prayers seem to be unanswered.

But the time when we wonder about unanswered prayer is also God's time to question us. That's what He did to Job. He did not come in a calm, peaceful reassurance of Job's innocence, but in a whirlwind of disturbing questions. "Now prepare yourself like a man; I will question you, and you shall answer Me" (Job 40:7). The Lord faces Job with his arrogant pride which has questioned the purpose, power, and providence of the creator and sustainer of the universe.

Listen to some of the questions the Lord asked Job. "Where were you when I laid the foundations of the earth? Tell Me, if you have understanding. Who determined its measurements? Surely you know! Or who stretched the line upon it? To what were its foundations fastened? Or who laid its cornerstone, when the morning stars sang together, and all the sons of God shouted for joy?" (Job 38:4-7). Throughout the rest of chapters 38–40 the Lord mounts confrontive questions which expose Job's arrogant questioning of the Almighty. Who controls the sea? Who commands the morning and the cycle of day and night? Who sets the length of a person's life? Who gives the rain and snow in season? Who built the mountains? Who created the wonder of conception and birth? Who developed the species of plant, animal, and mammal life? All the questions of God reach a crescendo with the ultimate demand to one who demanded that He be accountable: "Shall the one who contends with the Almighty correct Him? He who rebukes God, let him answer it" (Job 40:2).

At last, in humble submission, Job surrendered his demand that the Lord justify Himself to him. In the last chapter of the book of Job, we witness how the Lord dealt with the sufferer. God answered Job's prayers not with any self-justifying explanation but with His presence. Then Job is able to pray, "I know that You can do everything, and that no purpose of Yours can be withheld from You. You asked, 'Who is this who hides counsel without knowledge?' Therefore I have uttered what I did not understand, things too wonderful for me, which I did not know. Listen, please, and let me speak; you said, 'I will question you, and you shall answer Me.' I have heard of You by the hearing of the ear, but now my eye sees You" (Job 42:2-5).

The question of unanswered prayer is not really our question at all, but the Lord's. What He asked Job, He asks us. "Who is this who hides counsel without knowledge?" Or put another way, "Who is this who withholds answers to our prayers without purpose?" The question forces us to think much more humbly about our audacious questioning of God. But the question also prompts the Lord's penetrating questions, not unlike the ones given to Job but with greater impact. In the context of the incarnation and Pentecost, the Lord reviews not only His creation but also His redemptive acts in Jesus Christ. It is at the foot of the cross, beside an empty tomb, in a Pentecost Upper Room, that He questions us about His readiness to answer prayer. "What more need I do?" And our response is, "Nothing, Lord, just give us your presence and all our questions will melt away!"

Job has taught us three crucial things about our dilemma with unanswered prayer.

All Prayers Are Answered

The first is that *all prayers are answered.* There is a great difference between unanswered prayer and ungranted petitions. Wishing is not real praying. We could have our wants granted and not have received an answer to prayer. The purpose of prayer is communion and conversation with God. The period of waiting for the granting of some request is often rewarded by a far greater gift than what we asked for. The Lord Himself. What is delayed or denied is according to a much greater plan and wisdom than we possess in our finite perception.

A dry spell, when it seems that the Lord has departed from us, is a sure sign that we are on the edge of a new level of depth in our relationship with the Lord. The purpose of unanswered prayer is to lead us from hearsay to heartsight. Job could say, "I have heard of You by the hearing of the ear, but now my eye sees You."

Oswald Chambers said, "Our understanding of God is the answer to prayer. Getting things from God is His indulgence of us. When He stops giving us things, He brings us into the place where we can begin to understand Him. As long as we get from God everything we ask for, we never get to know Him; we look at Him as a blessing machine. Your Father knows what you have need of before you ask Him. Then why pray? To get to know your Father. It is not enough to be able to say 'God is love.' We have to *know* that He is love. We have to struggle through until we do see His love and justice. Then our prayer is answered."[3]

> Thy gifts alone cannot suffice
> Unless Thyself be given
> Thy presence makes my paradise
> And where Thou art is heaven.[4]

It is during those periods of what seems to be unanswered prayer that we discover what Paul realized when his pleas for the healing of his "thorn in the flesh" appeared to be unheeded. Many have conjectured about what this physical malady might have been. Suggestions have been made that the apostle suffered malaria, poor eyesight, or energy draining infection. The word "thorn" in Greek really means "stake" which strongly supports the case for malaria which is often attended with excruciating headaches. Perhaps Paul felt like a stake was being driven into his cranium. The point is we do not know. Good thing! Our lack of specific knowledge of the diagnosis enables us to identify with whatever problem, perplexity, or person causes us pain—driving a stake of distress into our hearts. Then we can appreciate what the Lord said to Paul, "My grace is sufficient for you, for My strength is made perfect in weakness" (2 Cor. 12:9).

Like Job, the Apostle Paul had come to a place in his spiritual pilgrimage where he bordered on pride. There is no more debilitating pride than the misuse of prayer as a manipulative device to get what we want when we want it. Prayer becomes a substitute for the Lord Himself. In those times He delays what we think is best for us until we want Him more than an answer according to our specifications.

The personal and practical application to all this is that when prayers seem unanswered, take it as a signal that the Lord wants to help us discover our sufficiency in Him and not what He can give us in tangible blessings.

When I talked with the woman who had written me the note about what seemed to her to be unanswered prayer, I discovered that she was facing physical difficulties and a breakdown of communication in her marriage. She had asked the Lord for healing and a change in her relationship with her husband. The more we talked, the more I became convinced that she needed the Lord more than she needed physical health or the change in her husband's attitudes which she had delegated the Lord to pull off for her. Prior to these difficulties her relationship with the

Lord had drifted into vague blandness. Her physical and relational problems had shocked her into a realization that she needed God's help. But did she need or want God? That was the issue!

I asked a penetrating question. "What if you are not healed and your marriage fails? Will you still want God for God?" That alarmed her and prepared her for some deep conversation about allowing the Lord to be her ultimate and total security—for now and eternity. After several visits she was ready to surrender herself completely to the Lord's love and care. She told Him that she wanted a consistent and abiding relationship with Him more than the answer she had demanded. His Spirit entered her ready mind and heart.

Subsequently, prayers by me and the elders of the church for her physical healing were answered. The stress which had been hindering the flow of the Lord's healing Spirit was dissipated and she could receive what He had been willing to give all along. The woman was also ready to stop blaming her husband for all that was wrong in her marriage, and asked the Lord to change their marriage beginning with her. When she let up on her criticism and complaining, and became the Lord's person in her marriage, her husband was amazed at what was happening to his wife. Because she had surrendered him and his attitudes to the Lord, her efforts to change him were replaced by an effort to be to him the love and forgiveness the Lord was increasingly becoming to her. Eventually, when he could no longer blame his wife for the problems in their marriage, he was motivated to get help with his own attitudes. A Christian counselor put him through the paces of marriage counseling which resulted in a radical personality transformation. Though he had been a member of the church and active in the program, he too had not known the Lord personally. The counselor completed his program of helping him by leading him through a prayer of commitment and a willingness to receive the Holy Spirit as the power to implement what he had discovered about what it meant to love and care for his wife.

What the woman had called an unanswered prayer when she first appealed for help was really not a denial of her prayers but the Lord's wise delay. He did answer, but in so much greater way than she had dared to anticipate. The Lord answered first with Himself, then with spiritual healing of her soul, and finally a solution beyond her expectation.

Not Ready to Receive

This leads us to the second thing the Lord wants to teach us in times in which we feel He has not answered our prayers. The woman I've described asked for help but was not ready to receive what the Lord was willing to give. Now we must consider unanswered prayers for things which *may not be best for us or are not in keeping with the Lord's timing for us.* When I think of some of my "unanswered" prayers, I am filled with thanksgiving and praise! Looking back on some ungranted petitions I am gratified that the Lord said no. If I had received them they would not have been maximum for me or the people around me. Further, some of them were not consistent with the Lord's primary calling for my life. Reflecting on them, if I had received what I asked, I would have drifted into an eddy out of the main stream of His particularized will for me as an individual.

A good example of this in my life has been the way the Lord led me into a national television ministry. Seven years ago I thought I knew exactly what I should do. I devised a format for a program which featured interviews and performances by Christian stars and leaders with a very brief, closing meditation done by me at the end. Three pilot programs were completed featuring people like Jimmy Stewart, Carol Lawrence, and Dale and Roy Rogers. Not a bad billing for success! But efforts to raise money for a full series and syndication seemed blocked at every turn. Even though a large company in America offered to be sponsor, the networks were reluctant to run a "religious" program on prime time. Since the company only wanted a network program, that possibility was lost. Other schemes of syndication were tried with little response. Even those who turned down the program could not explain why.

All the time I was praying and disturbed by what appeared to me to be no answer from the Lord. Finally, I cried out, "What's wrong, Lord? Where have I missed in what I thought was your plan for me?" Silence for weeks. Then one day I received a series of phone calls from trusted friends. One of them articulated clearly the same thought all the others had tried to communicate. "Lloyd," he said, "you've spent all your life allowing the Lord to teach you how to preach the Bible for people's deepest needs. Don't spend time on television interviewing and featuring famous names. Just do what you do best—talk to people about their hopes and hurts and introduce them to the abundant and eternal life in Christ. I was praying about you this morning and aching over your period of unanswered prayer and suddenly I felt a rush of inspiration about your need. It was so strong, I wrote it down. What came to me is what I've just shared with you. I may be off base, but pray about it and see if the Lord confirms it in your own heart and mind."

That phone call led me into an experiment. I gave up the plans of the program I had wanted to do so urgently. I let go of it completely. A few days later, a man in my congregation went to the business manager of my church and gave him a check for a pilot for a very different kind of format. He said the money could be used only if I preached as the main focus of a half-hour format. His specifications perfectly matched the guidance my friend had shared on the phone. I exclaimed with assurance, "Sometimes the Lord gives and takes away, but in this case He took away and gave back—what He wanted all along."

The pilot production confirmed the new direction. Commitment to broadcast portions of the church's worship, including the sermon and music, was affirmed by the Lord in a gift through a will. The woman who had left the money had specifically directed that it should be used for expanding the Pastor's communication of the gospel. It was just enough for the first thirteen weeks' cost of production and airing on a local Los Angeles station.

Now years later, as the program reaches over three hundred cities in America, I look back at the goodness of the Lord in denying one prayer so He could give me a different strategy. When I was willing, He guided me each step of the way in how to talk to the nation about His grace. He showed me how to ask people to share their deepest needs, most urgent questions, and demanding challenges. People responded in hundreds of letters each week. What has resulted is that speaking on the program is like a conversation between friends. I know what people need from their own expressions and can respond with personal messages from the Bible.

This is no easy success story. Each week I face financial needs for the television ministry which press me into deeper trust and dependence on God. And He is faithful in helping me meet obligations through gifts from viewers motivated to help by Him. There's never a dime to spare.

And I must be cautious never to grasp what He has presently led me to do, and demand that He be faithful in only that direction. He may have other plans and a shift in strategy for the future. If so, when it is right in His planning, He will make it clear.

Not Play God

A final thing I want to say about what seems to be unanswered prayer is a word of caution. Like Job's friends, sometimes *we play God in other people's lives by suggesting that all unanswered prayer is caused by some sin in their lives.* This is simplistic and leads to defensive self-incrimination. The result is that people usually blame themselves and seldom seek the Lord Himself as the ultimate answer to all prayer. To be sure, God often delays an answer until He has prepared us to be ready for the blessing He has ready.

Our responsibility is not to accuse people of sin as an explanation of why their prayers seem not to be answered. Rather, if a person suggests that may be the cause we can ask, "Tell me, what do you think may be standing in the way?" If, in response, some sin is confessed, we are to help a person tell God about that and help him or her receive and know His forgiveness. Often that breaks the bind and he or she can be open to the Lord's answer.

The danger comes when we think we can ever be pure enough to deserve God's answers. That leads to pride. What's more, it becomes manipulation of the Almighty. We've all known times when the Lord has helped us when we least deserved it. And we know others whose lives are not spiritually impeccable who are graciously cared for by the Lord. Petulant perfectionism is boldly contradicted by those times when He uses us to help others know or grow in Him while we still have problems in our own lives. We can empathize with people's needs because we are acutely aware of our own. The result is that we lead people to the Lord and not to ourselves!

So when our prayers seem unanswered, yes, let's ask ourselves if there is a practice, habit, relationship, or misconception which may be blocking the flow of the Lord's Spirit in us. But also, let's never move beyond humble confession to attempts at haughty control. We will never be good enough to earn either salvation or the gifts the Lord longs to give us. If we could be, the cross would not have been necessary.

We are back to our central theme. Prayer starts with God. What seems to be unanswered prayer is also a part of His instigation and invitation to communion and conversation with Him on a deeper level. He wants us to know Him more profoundly than ever. When we feel our prayers are not answered according to our specifications and timing, that feeling is really a longing for God and not just for what He can give or do for us. Thank God for those times. By them we know we have been called into a much more intimate relationship than we've ever known before!

Notes
1. Thomas Hardy, "Impercipient", Gerald DeWitt Sanders and John H. Nelson, eds., *Chief Modern Poets of England and America* (New York: MacMillan Pub. Co., Inc., 1943).
2. Helmut Thielicke, source unknown.
3. Oswald Chambers, source unknown.
4. Source unknown.

PRAYER AND HEALING

This past week, I had a power failure in my home and in my life. The first became symbolic of the second. A violent storm cut the power lines which had fed electricity to my neighborhood. We were without electricity for hours. The lights and appliances were totally inoperable.

As I stumbled about in the darkness I was tempted to blame the lamps and light bulbs. That made me think about how absurd it would be to go up to the refrigerator and kick it saying, "You dumb refrigerator, why don't you work!?" It would have been equally unproductive to pound the stove saying, "Why you inefficient, inadequate stove, why don't you do what you were manufactured to do?" In the same way I could not lambaste the air-conditioning system when it did not produce throughout the long, powerless night. A whole section of Los Angeles was without the energy we take for granted with a flick of a switch.

That same week I experienced an overload of the circuits in my spiritual life. I took on too much. My own concerns, worry over people, and a humanly impossible schedule, broke the circuits. So much that I was attempting to get done was only what *I* had determined was crucial. Momentarily I forgot that there's enough time in any one day to do what the Lord wills us to do. Exhaustion set in. While doing a television taping I realized the overload was making me less than maximum. What was usually done with ease became arduous and difficult. Living on my own resources proved to be very inefficient. The business of the previous days had shortened my devotional time and the pressures had distracted me enough so that I didn't draw on the divine energy I usually find so sufficient through moment-by-moment prayer through each responsibility.

In the midst of the spiritual power failure the electricity failure occurred in my home. The parable was so pointed it made me burst out laughing at myself. The feeling of being out of power spiritually had prompted me to fall back into an old pattern of self-incrimination. "Lloyd, what's the matter with you!? You're a producer. You're supposed to pour out work—speaking, writing, pastoring, communicating on television. Now get with it!" Then, as I thought about the inadequacy of the light bulbs, refrigerator, stove and air-conditioning system without electricity, the Lord seemed to say, "My son, you were created to be a transmitter of me. You've blocked the flow of my spirit by attempting more in this week than I guided and set as priorities. You've had a power failure just like your house. To do my will effectively, you must depend on me and the flow of my power."

Ever have a day, week, or period like that? I suspect we all have. You may be experiencing a time of power failure right now as you read this. The solution, as I discovered repeatedly, is not to condemn ourselves but to reestablish the power hookup that profound prayer offers.

The night of the electricity failure I went to bed realizing what the deepest need in my life was. It was not to finish up all my tasks or get from under the burden of pressure. What I needed most of all was to open myself again to the power of the Spirit of the Lord. My prayer time before I went to sleep was a plea for the Lord to take over and do through me what He wanted done. I slept serenely and peacefully. My waking thought was amazing. It was so captivating that I got up and wrote it down. Seven words that helped me know that the power of the Lord was back on in my life: "Nothing has changed, but everything is different!" My desk was still piled high with demanding tasks, the schedule was still full, people's needs still concerned me. But *I* was different. In the flow of the Holy Spirit power I could prioritize, work with freedom, and enjoy being used by the Lord. The power failure was over!

A man shared with me a very moving experience he had in the sanctuary during the worship one Sunday evening. He said, "I had come to the service with a great need for healing in my spiritual and physical life. During the opening prayer I told the Lord how much I needed Him. I felt completely devoid of power. Then as you were finishing up the sermon, I felt a hand on my shoulder. I looked around to see if someone in the pew behind me was touching me or was trying to get my attention. The people behind me smiled but clearly indicated that they had not touched my shoulder. Then it happened again. After that I felt a warmth surge through my body. I felt the hand that had touched my shoulder was now connected to an arm that was joined by another arm to embrace me. I felt loved, accepted, cared about deeply. The Lord was answering the prayer I had prayed about my needs. I felt His Spirit surging through me. The tensions in my mind relaxed, my body felt calm, and my emotions were filled with joy. It was as if an electric current passed through every fibre of my being. Could it be that I received a touch from the Lord?"

It is important to mention that this man is a brilliant intellectual who is not highly emotional or spiritually expressive. He is a down-to-earth, practical, straightforward kind of man. In fact, he is reserved, sometimes very cautious, and genuinely scientific about the way he talks about evidence in any realm. When he went to his doctor the following week, the physical illness from which he had been suffering had radically improved. Subsequently, in the weeks that followed, he was completely healed. This was not in contradiction to the medical aid he was receiving, but a divine intervention which maximized what the medical profession was trying to do to help him. His prayer, "Lord, I desperately need you!" had opened the circuit.

As this man told me what happened, the melody and words of the gospel hymn flooded my mind and heart.

> He touched me, O, He touched me,
> and O, the joy that floods my soul;
> Something happened, and now I know,
> He touched me and made me whole.[1]

The Healing Touch

We should not be surprised when God touches a person. I've had it happen often. We should expect it when we gather for worship or are alone in the quiet of our own prayers. We all need the healing touch. The Lord is the source of all healing. When we are in need of healing spiritually, physically, emotionally, interpersonally, or in some problem of life, the Lord knows, cares, and wants to help us. The Church was meant to be a healing community and each of us is called to be an agent of healing. The healing ministry of Jesus Christ manifest so powerfully during the incarnation, is now entrusted to the Church. Prayer is our channel of power to pray for His healing in our own and others' lives. What happened to that man as he sat in church should be anticipated and gratefully expected. In sanctuaries, doctors' offices, operating rooms, hospitals, psychiatrists' counseling rooms, and in research laboratories searching for cures to virulent disease—the divine Healer is at work. He is seeking to release His healing power.

The Healing Power of Prayer

I want to consider with you the healing power of prayer. To do that I want to take James 5:13-16, one of the most incisive passages in the Bible, as a launching pad to consider other passages which deal with Christ's healing power. Before me are the urgent questions we all have about healing. What is spiritual healing? Is the Lord the source of all healing? Why are some we pray for not healed? When a person is not healed according to our timing and specifications, is that an evidence of lack of faith or some hidden sin in their lives? What about the effectiveness of healing ministries in the church or on television? How can we participate in spiritual healing in a biblically intelligent, and Christ-inspired way?

Keeping those questions before us, let's look at James's call to be a healing community. "Is anyone among you suffering? Let him pray. Is anyone cheerful? Let him sing psalms. Is anyone among you sick? Let him call for the elders of the church, and let them pray over him, anointing him with oil in the name of the Lord. And the prayer of faith will save the sick, and the Lord will raise him up. And if he has committed sins, he will be forgiven.

Confess your trespasses to one another, and pray for one another, that you may be healed. The effective, fervent prayer of a righteous man avails much" (Jas. 5:13-16).

This was written by James, the Lord Jesus' brother, around 50 A.D. In chapter 1, verse 18, he clarified the special calling of the early Christians, many of whom were facing severe difficulties living out their faith in a hostile secular world. Speaking of the Lord's plan and purpose for the Church, the new creation, he wrote, "Of His own will He brought us forth by the word of truth, that we might be a kind of firstfruits of His creatures." The evidence of the new age of the Messiah is the Messiah's people. As we said in the previous chapter, He seeks to do through us what He did in the incarnation. For James, a vital dimension of the Lord's continuing ministry through His people is healing of the manifold needs of people. The Lord had called His followers to a ministry of preaching the gospel, teaching His message, and healing the sick. This threefold ministry is ours today also.

The Meaning of Healing

To claim that, we need to understand what healing is in its full biblical meaning. James uses two very basic words for healing in this passage. In 5:15 he says that the prayer of faith will "save" the sick. This is the future active of the Greek word *sōzō*, to make well or whole. It also is a key New Testament word for salvation and wholeness as well as healing. In verse 16, "that you may be healed" the first aorist past subjunctive of *iaomai* was used in the New Testament for healing of both body and the soul.

The word *sōzō* is used for salvation and healing in Jesus' message and in the epistles. The noun form is *sōtēria* and it means "deliverance from danger, suffering, sin, and sickness" and was the primary word to describe the eternal salvation given to those who believed in Jesus Christ as Lord and Saviour (see Acts 2:47). In Jesus' assertion of why He came, He said, "For God did not send His Son into the world to condemn the world, but that the world through Him might be saved" (John 3:17). Again the word *sōzō* is used for His Aramaic word for "save." He came to deliver us from evil, sin, sickness, and death, but also to heal the whole person. He was concerned about our abundant life and eternal life. The Saviour's *(Sōtēr)* life, death, and resurrection was for our salvation *(sōtēria)* and the healing of all our brokenness spiritually and emotionally *(sōzō)*. Christ offered a salvation that encompassed the whole person. That's why He healed the sick as a sign that God was in Him to heal bodies, minds, and relationships as well as to suffer for the sins of the world on the cross.

The Source of Healing

There is one and only one source of healing. The Creator, Sustainer, and Redeemer of all creation is healing. This healing power dwelt incarnate in Jesus. When He touched the sick, deranged, or troubled, they were healed. The blind received sight, the lame walked, and the mentally disturbed were liberated.

After Pentecost, the Lord gave spiritual gifts to His followers for the healing of the varied needs of people. Paul lists these in 1 Corinthians 12. Particularly crucial were the gifts of faith, healing, and working of miracles. They equipped the Christians to dare to believe in the Lord's power to heal, actually pray for healing, and see miracles result.

The same healing power which had been revealed in the incarnation was unleashed through the early Christians. It happened just as Jesus promised. The early Church preached a salvation which included atonement for sin, reconciliation with God, and healing of the sick. Like their Master, the daring believers had a view of salvation that was inclusive of the whole person—physically, emotionally, and spiritually. There was no idea that the Lord only saved a soul for heaven and cared little for the body in which that soul lived. That came later in the Middle Ages when salvation was focused primarily on the soul and its future salvation in heaven. It is interesting to note that the anointing with oil for the healing of the sick was changed into the sacrament of extreme unction at the time of death.

The Healing Ministry of the Church

Today we have widely divergent views of the healing ministry of the Church. There are some who are convinced that the role of the Church is to preach eternal salvation and that the care of the physical needs of people is the exclusive responsibility of the medical profession. Others preach salvation but make a major emphasis on the healing ministry. Still others emphasize healing by prayer alone and deny the use of medicine or consultation of the medical profession.

I hold what I believe is a biblical view that we are to minister to the whole person—body, mind, soul, as well as everything which concerns a person's interpersonal and social needs. We are to lead people to Christ, introduce them to the abundant life in Him, expose the secret of power in His indwelling Spirit, and help them grow in Him in every area of life. Our calling is to affirm all means of healing of the mind and body. This involves support of the medical professions and cooperative efforts to minister to the whole person.

But in addition to that, I am convinced that we are called to a specific prayer ministry for the manifold illnesses and maladies of people. This should include prayer with individuals at times of sickness, prayer groups for intercession for the sick, and public services for prayer for the spiritual, emotional, and physical needs of people. Members and friends of our congregations need an opportunity to bring their varied needs for specific prayer.

James provides guidelines for this ministry of healing. Note the many kinds of needs enumerated in the passage we cited earlier. There were those who were suffering who needed to pray. Others were cheerful and needed to give thanks by singing psalms to avoid pride and self-sufficiency. Then there were the sick who needed prayer for healing and anointing with oil signifying the blessing of the Spirit of the Lord. But there were also those who had fallen into sin and were in need of forgiveness.

In any congregation gathered for worship all these needs and others suggested by these categories are present in our people. There are those whose deepest need is to receive Christ as Saviour and Lord of their lives. Others are facing problems in living the Christian life that need to be committed to the Lord. Still others have broken relationships which need reconciliation. Some have committed sins or known deep failure who need forgiveness and assurance of pardon. And then there are those who are distressed emotionally or under the grip of psychological problems. Finally, there are people who are ill, facing crippling diseases, grim prognoses, and debilitating physical pain. If we really care about people, some way must be devised to give individual and specific attention to these varied dis-eases and dis-tresses. A healing ministry is essential to bring people into contact and communion with the Great Physician.

In my church in Hollywood, we have followed James's admonition. The elders of the church have taken the biblical injunction seriously. They are not only the lay leaders of the spiritual life of the church and administrators of the program of the congregation, but they have been ordained to be channels of healing power through prayer for the manifold needs of the people. This is done periodically when a major portion of the Sunday morning service is set aside for prayers for the spectrum of physical, emotional, spiritual and relational problems people are suffering. After the morning message, they gather on the chancel steps to pray with people who come forward from the congregation. After sharing their specific need they are asked to kneel and the elder lays hands on them and prays for the release of the Lord's healing power in them. People come forward seeking to know Christ, others need assurance of forgiveness, some have concerns for loved ones who are ill or troubled. Many have physical illness and still others are facing challenges where they need the Lord's guidance and strength. The results of these prayers have been astounding.

So often in worship, the preaching, prayers, and music skim over the inner needs of people. The ministry of prayer for healing of the whole person gives an opportunity for people to respond to the Spirit and receive personal help.

Since it would be difficult to take a fifteen-minute section of every Sunday's worship for a healing service, we set aside specific Sundays throughout the year for this. But, because needs cannot be scheduled according to a church worship calendar, the elders come forward every Sunday during the singing of the concluding hymn. During that time and after the service they pray for individuals who have responded to the invitation to receive Christ or ask for prayer for a specific physical or spiritual problem. So the healing ministry, emphasized periodically with a special service, also takes place every Sunday at the conclusion of the weekly services.

The elders are not the only people who pray for the diversity of needs. Hundreds of members of the congregation have responded to the call to a ministry of intercession. A list of the needs of people is distributed weekly to those people for daily prayers. Sensitized by the emphasis of healing prayer throughout the life of the Church, people pray for one another one to one, in small prayer groups, and over the phone. The power of God is being released through His people! The Holy Spirit gift of healing is being claimed and exercised. No one elevates himself or herself to a permanent status of being a "healer." Rather the need presented by one brings forth the gift of healing in another.

The reason that the shared ministry of healing is so crucial is that at times of need often we are unable to pray for ourselves creatively. Problems, frustrations, and physical or emotional illness debilitates our capacity to hope and pray boldly for ourselves. That's when we desperately need to be able to share our disability with a sensitive, empathetic friend who believes that the Lord is able and all that He wills is possible.

When There Is No Healing

At this point in our consideration of prayer and healing we must face some of the hard questions we raised earlier. What about those for whom we pray and they do not get well? The temptation is to blame ourselves, our effectiveness in prayer, or the other person for resisting the healing. So often people say, "If I would have had more faith, my prayers would have been answered!" Or we subtly suggest that the person being prayed for does not have adequate faith or has some hidden sin or unconfessed rebellion against the Lord.

Surely there are times when we pray faithless prayers. And we've all known periods when we blocked the Spirit's way in us. Also we've observed those spiritual impediments in others. James confronts the problem head-on. "Confess your trespasses to one another, and pray for one another, that you may be healed" (Jas. 5:16). Note carefully that he did not say, "Your sickness is caused by sin. Therefore confess your sins to one another alarming each other with the danger of unconfessed sin." Helping another person honestly face anything which might debilitate healing must be done with tenderness and sensitivity. There are times when, after patient listening to another person share the area of need for prayer, I am led to ask one or both of these questions: "How do you feel about your need?" or "Now, before we pray, is there anything you know of that may be standing in the way of God's Spirit in your life?" I never ask either question without sharing my own answers in times of need in my life. In answer to the first question I share times when I have felt impatience, fear, or disappointment and longed for the Lord to intervene. I relate how I grew as a person in those times and how the Lord's answers were eventually given when the time was right. In response to the second question I can talk about times in the past when resentments, unhealed relationships, or unwillingness to act on guidance the Lord has given, kept me unwilling to receive what the Lord has offered to heal a problem or sickness. That usually primes the pump of honest sharing from a person for whom I am about to pray. Sometimes their response is "I don't know of anything." I take them at their word and proceed with the prayer for their need.

In our prayers for the sick, not all get well. The danger is that we think that either God did not hear us or that we didn't pray hard enough. The ministry of praying for others is often judged by our successes or failures. That's to play God. Or we stop praying for others because we didn't get what we thought was best when we thought it should happen. Our task is to be faithful and leave the results to God. His timing is perfect and His answers often come in ways we did not expect.

For example, I prayed for a man who was very ill. There seemed to be no physical change for months other than he felt the comfort of trusting God completely with his need. During the long illness, he came to know the Lord more intimately than ever before. He developed a closer relationship with his family and expressed love more profoundly than he had previously. Through this, his wife became a Christian and his joy in suffering was a mov‑ing witness to friends and fellow workers. Then the com‑bination of prayer and the skill of a Christ-guided physician restored him to health. The Lord had timed the recovery perfectly. So much more than the man's body had been healed.

What About Death?

But what about death? Have we failed in our prayers for healing if someone dies? Not if we believe that death for a Christian is only a transition in eternal life. Again we must trust the Lord. He has conquered over the power of death. We are alive forever when we belong to Christ. Of course we feel grief, that's an honest expression of a phys‑ical loss. But for a person in Christ, death is not a tragedy but a triumph. Heaven is the unlimited, maximized union with the Lord, and the unfettered experience of the love, joy, and peace of which we have realized in part during the years of life in the physical body.

Once we get free of judging the Lord for the results of our prayers we are liberated to pray boldly and leave the outcome to Him.

A surgeon friend of mine confessed that the most difficult transition he passed through in his healing ministry through surgery was when he realized that remorse over those who did not get well was not going to keep him from excellence in doing his best with God's help in his care for people. He said he made a covenant with the Lord to be the finest surgeon he could be, pray through each surgery, and claim God's healing power. "I decided that I was not going to brood over losing one patient and become ineffective in caring for hundreds of others." The same is true for all of us in our intercessory prayers for the healing of the needs of others. The Lord is in charge; our task is to become cooperative prayer partners in His healing.

We have come full circle to where we began. An awesome trust has been given to us to pray for healing. The power to do that is the Lord's and not ours. What is our responsibility is to keep the power lines open. When we overload or blow the circuits by running our own lives, we become ineffective transmitters of hope and courage to others. We live in a sick and suffering world. The gift of healing is offered to us for our prayers for people and their needs. Keeping the power lines open will make all the difference to the people whom the Lord will put on our agenda to pray for healing. James was right: "The effective, fervent prayer of a righteous man avails much." And that effectiveness and fervency comes from the Lord. He has made us right with Himself because He has decided to use human agents like us to accomplish His healing in the bodies, minds and spirits of His people.

THE NAME THAT CHARMS OUR FEARS

Just before I gave a prayer at a civic gathering, the chairman of the meeting said, "Lloyd, I hope you won't end your prayer in Jesus' name. This is a mixed gathering with several different religions represented and I wouldn't want anyone to be offended."

How would you have reacted to that? Would you have left out Jesus' name as you ended your prayer? If so, would the prayer have been less effective? What do you think about when you end a prayer in the Lord's name? Is that simply a rote habit or does it make any difference in the content and power of the prayer?

When I ended my prayer that day at the civic meeting, I said, "In the name that is above every name, Yahweh, and the one who was highly exalted and given that name, even Jesus Christ. Amen." When I returned to my seat the chairman was pleased. He thought I had followed instructions. That led to a deep conversation about why I had ended the way I did. Actually, what I had said was much stronger. After the meeting, we visited late into the evening about Jesus Christ and how to pray in His name. I was glad that I had held fast to my convictions.

Jesus told us to pray in His name. "Most assuredly, I

say to you, he who believes in Me, the works that I do he will do also; and greater works than these he will do, because I go to My Father. And whatever you ask in My name, that I will do, that the Father may be glorified in the Son. If you ask anything in My name, I will do it" (John 14:12-14).

That tells us several crucial things for praying with power. We are promised that we will be given authority to do what Jesus did. That means that the same power to love, forgive, heal, reconcile, and live out the kingdom of God we witness in Jesus' life and ministry can be done by us. Further, it tells us that Jesus wants to continue His ministry through us. Note that He forcefully claims that He will be the implementing agent. "I will do it" assures us that the risen Christ, glorified and reigning through the power of the Spirit, will undertake to accomplish prayers prayed in His name.

Jesus spoke that promise in the context of the Hebrew reverence for the power of the name. In Hebrew "the name" was synonymous with God. It was used for the character, authority, and power of God. The one name which no Hebrew ever spoke audibly was Yahweh. It was considered so sacred that the word *Adonai* was used. The name Yahweh was the name given Moses at the burning bush. I AM WHO I AM God told him. The phrase is the Hebrew causative verb "to be." It means "I will make happen." The new name given Moses by God was HAYAH, rendered YHWH, or Yahweh, the Lord. When Jesus said I AM in twenty-three crucial statements in His ministry, He was boldly claiming to be none other than Yahweh, God present in the Immanuel. Prayer in His name is able to unleash the power of God. Jesus Christ is the wisdom and power of God with us.

Now look at what Paul said about Christ in Philippians

2. We are told that we can expect to have the mind of Christ (v. 5). Then the apostle tells us whose mind it is that we can receive in our prayers. He tells us about the humiliation, obedience, and exaltation of Christ. Then he says an astounding thing. "Therefore God also has highly exalted Him and given Him the name which is above every name, that at the name of Jesus every knee should bow, of those in heaven, and of those on earth, and of those under the earth, and that every tongue should confess that Jesus Christ is Lord, to the glory of God the Father" (vv. 9-11). What is the name that is above every name? Jesus? Hardly. Though the name meant "Jehovah is salvation," there were many, both during and after Jesus of Nazareth, with that name. Christ? No, because that would put the name of "Anointed One," *Messiah,* above the name of God. There is only one name that is above every other name. *Yahweh!* The very name Jesus used when He boldly claimed that He was the light of the world, the resurrection and the life, and the way the truth and the life—plus all the other I AM assertions. Jesus the Christ is glorified to continue doing what He began in the incarnation, to impart the power of the essential verb, verve, and vitality of God. He is the Logos through whom all things were created and the living Word who recreated us through the atonement. Now as our living Lord, He is Yahweh with us to continue His re-creation in and through you and me.

Therefore Jesus' name is Yahweh. That's what is really meant by the words "in Jesus' name" or more accurately, "In the name given to Jesus, a name above every name, Yahweh." The God who makes things happen is with us and in us to make them continue to happen.

Pray in Keeping with What He Revealed
To pray in Jesus' name of Yahweh implies three things.

The first is to *pray in keeping with what He revealed in His life,* message, death, resurrection, and return in the Holy Spirit at Pentecost. We can be sure that the Lord will not contradict His message. Anything which denies His atoning death and perpetrates our self-justification will not be answered. He told us that we were to seek first the kingdom of God and His righteousness and to pray boldly in keeping with that sublime purpose.

Remember that "the name" represented the character of the one designated. The Lord wants to guide us in asking for that which is in keeping with His character and will further impute His character in us. The more we know of the Lord as revealed in Scripture and deepened in fellowship with Him, the more our prayers will express His will for us. Again we must stress the importance of listening as the major responsibility of prayer. Then we can test any request with this five-fold qualification: (1) Has what I am asking for been refined in meditative, creative listening? (2) If I received the request, would it enable me to grow closer to the Lord? (3) Does it seek the ultimate good of all involved? (4) Will it extend the kingdom of God, His reign and rule in my life and others'? (5) Is it something I can ask the Lord to enjoy with me if He grants it?

Pray in His Power

The second thing praying in Jesus' name, Yahweh, Lord, implies is that *it is accomplished in His power.* Ending a prayer in His name is not a perfunctory addendum. It is asking for the release of supernatural power for the fulfillment of what He has guided us to pray. He wants to continue His ministry through us as He promised. So often we pray for things we could do without His help. He wants us to dare to pray adventuresome prayers only He could accomplish. We are not meant to use prayer as a desire to get help to do our plan, but power to attempt His plans for us. What in your life could be done only through a supernatural intervention by the living Lord in you? Pray for that!

The power of Jesus Christ the Lord is offered us for the accomplishment of His will as He reveals it to us and for the confrontation of evil. We must consider both.

After the resurrection, Jesus promised that the disciples would be "endued with power from on high" (Luke 24:49). The word for "endued" in Greek is *endusēsthe* from the verb *endunō,* meaning clothed or to put on a garment. This would be done to the followers of Jesus. They were to wait in Jerusalem until it happened. We are reminded of the deeper implications of the Hebrew in the description of what happened to Gideon. "The Spirit of the Lord came upon Gideon; then he blew the trumpet" (Judg. 6:34). The words *come upon* really mean that the Lord clothed Himself with Gideon. This gave Gideon the courage to blow the trumpet and rally the forces of Israel against Midian and dare to go into battle in spite of impossible numerical odds. The image of the Lord entering a frightened man and actually clothing Himself with him is vivid and impelling. What happened through Gideon, and later through the disciples when they were endued— clothed—is exactly what we need when we pray for the challenges the Lord has given us. His work can be done only with His power. Our work done with our strength is humanism. The Lord's work attempted on our strength is religion. But the Lord's work done by His power is the abundant life.

When we pray in Jesus' name of Lord we call on the same power He revealed, the same divine energy that raised Him from the dead, and the same Spirit who entered the 120 waiting followers of Jesus in the Upper

Room at Pentecost. Jesus had promised exactly what happened, "If anyone thirsts, let him come to Me and drink. He who believes in Me, as the Scripture has said, out of his heart will flow rivers of living water" (John 7:37-38). John's comment on this in verse 39 is very pointed. "But this He spoke concerning the Spirit, whom those believing in Him would receive; for the Holy Spirit was not yet given, because Jesus was not yet glorified." The Lord's glorification took place when He ascended, having completed the incarnation, atonement, and resurrection. After His glorification He returned in the power of the Holy Spirit. He "clothed" Himself with His followers, indwelt them so that rivers of His power flowed from them, and they prayed and acted with divine strength beyond their human capacities. The same enduing and engendering is available to us as we pray.

Paul's prayer for the Ephesians reveals what is available to us. He prayed that, according to the riches of the Lord's glory, they would "be strengthened with might through His Spirit in the inner man, that Christ may dwell in your hearts by faith; that you, being rooted and grounded in love, may be able to comprehend with all the saints what is the width and length and depth and height—to know the love of Christ which passes knowledge; that you may be filled with all the fullness of God. Now to Him who is able to do exceedingly abundantly above all that we ask or think, according to the power that works in us . . . " (Eph. 3:16-20). There's a charter for powerful praying. The Lord lives His life in us to guide our prayers beyond what we would dare to ask or think possible. Prayer in His name is prayer by His leading and accomplished by His power. And He does exceedingly abundantly, far more, than we in our human reservations would imagine possible.

But that's not all. The power of Jesus' name enables us to confront and win over the evil powers in the world. Ephesians 6:11-12 in *Phillips* translation makes this very clear. "I expect you have learned by now that our fight is not against any physical enemy, it is against organizations and powers that are spiritual. We are up against the unseen power that controls this dark world, and spiritual agents from the very headquarters of evil." When we pray in Jesus' name we are armed with the one weapon that can defeat satanic influence in our lives and the people for whom we pray. Christ won the battle with Satan when He conquered through the blood of the cross. The Lord of Calvary is our power over Satan's diabolical invasion of situations and people. When we claim the power of the blood of the cross, we can command Satan to take his hands off the Lord's property. The one name he cannot resist is the name of Jesus Christ, the Lord, Yahweh. When our lives become hassled by evil influences we can boldly say, "In the name of Jesus Christ the Lord, leave this situation, person, or group." We do not need to be helpless victims of satanic influence. And further, when we give our lives to Christ and are filled with His Spirit we are sealed against the possibility of possession by Satan's negative, destructive, debilitating power. Persistent prayer in Jesus' name brings His authority and victorious presence that casts out Satan.

Prayer Overcomes Our Fears

That leads us to the third blessing of praying in Jesus' name. *It overcomes our fear.* We all have fears which rob us of the joy of living. We fear certain people, failure, pain, and inadequacy. Beneath all our fears is the fear of losing control and the ability to cope. At the root of this fear is the fear of dying.

Charles Wesley wrote beautifully about the power of the name to overcome our fears. "Jesus! the name that charms our fears, that bids our sorrows cease, 'tis music in the sinner's ears, 'tis life and health and peace."

How does Jesus Christ charm our fears? From my own personal experience He does it in several ways. First, He exposes them for what they are. He helps us ask, "Of what or whom am I afraid?" Then the Lord forces us to face the fear with a further question, "Does this person or situation have any power greater than Christ?" And then He lovingly asks, "Will you give me that fear and allow me to give you courage to overcome it?"

Fear is the outward manifestation of the feeling of insufficiency. We are afraid when we are unsure that we will have what it takes to live, face troubles, endure sickness, and die with assurance of eternal life. We worry over money because of previous shortages. We are troubled by certain kinds of people because of prior hurts by similar personality types. Failures in the past make us catatonic because we fear further failure.

Most of all fear is entangled with what has happened to us in the past. We need a healing of the memories in order to face the future unafraid. The secret of how the Lord does that is given us by the Apostle John. "There is no fear in love; but perfect love casts out fear, because fear involves torment. But he who fears has not been made perfect in love. We love Him because He first loved us" (1 John 4:18-19).

Remember that the one who wrote these words had faced persecution, imprisonment, and constant danger. The remedial remedy for fear he gives us is one he had experienced through long years of communion with the living Lord. He had been the beloved disciple of the Lord, had depended on His love in excruciating circumstances, and had found Him triumphantly adequate in his trials. Most of all, he had seen and heard Him say, "Do not be afraid; I am the First and the Last. I am He who lives, and was dead, and behold, I am alive forevermore. Amen. And I have the keys of Hades and of Death" (Rev. 1:17-18). Note the strong I AM, spoken with the authority of Yahweh. He is the beginning and end of all things. He has conquered death and overcome the forces of evil. John found that consistent oneness with the Lord cast out his fears. His love in each potential fear displaced the fear.

Fear can best be defined as the absence of love. The same emotional channel through which fear is felt and expressed is also the channel of experiencing and communicating love. The conquest of our fears happens through a love relationship with our Lord. The more we allow Him to love us, the more free we will be of fear. Fear is feeling unloved or being anxious about the consistency and faithfulness of people's love. Christ's love for us is unchanging, unlimited, and unqualified. He, divine love, fills us with His Spirit and fear is displaced. Anytime we feel afraid, it is a sure sign we need to surrender the memory, circumstance, person, or danger to the Lord.

But the ultimate conquest of fear happens when we accept that nothing or no one can ultimately hurt us. We are alive forever. Our destiny is sure. And anything in between now and heaven will be used by the Lord to help us trust Him more fully. We are indestructible! The Lord has taken up residence in us and our true inner person will reign with Him now and through all of eternity. That's the source of true courage for all of life's battles.

The name of Jesus is more than a title or descriptive designation of His nature. The name is really sacramental in that it is an outward sign of a limitless power, authority, and presence. The word "sacrament" comes from the

Latin *sacramentum,* a mystery. But it also was used for an oath or pledge of allegiance and obedience to Caesar by a Roman legionnaire. Ranking officers of the Roman armies carried a medallion of Caesar's authority. The idea conveyed was that wherever that officer went he could depend on all the authority and power of Rome to be marshalled in any conflict or battle. He had made his oath of obedience to Caesar and knew that the empire's power was available to be called forth.

His Name Gives Us Assurance

In a much more propitious way the name of Jesus Christ, the Lord, gives us greater assurance. Through His name, mysteriously the power of God is released for our needs, complexities, and fears. We are not alone. Our sacred symbol is the cross. The same victorious power revealed there and vindicated in the resurrection is ours. The faithful prayer in the name of the Lord brings the effluence of His Spirit, His wisdom for our decisions, His strength for our weaknesses, and His love for our fears. And in addition to that, He goes before us to invade our difficulties. He deals with people long before we meet them, and unravels problems long before we confront them. Our Lord is able!

The name of the Lord guides our prayers, gives power to implement the answers we are given, and makes us unafraid as we face the future. To pray without the name of the Lord is like trying to sail in a turbulent sea without ever hoisting the main sail to catch the wind. The wind of the Holy Spirit, the present, powerful Christ is available. Hoist the sail, open your heart, and allow Him to enable you to do what He's guided you to pray boldly.

Jesus said, "The things which are impossible with men are possible with God" (Luke 18:27). And the secret of releasing those possibilities is the name above every name, Yahweh. And His presence with us is One who has the authority to bring our impossibilities and His power together. In the light of that I don't want just to end my prayers with The Name, but begin, punctuate, and complete them in the fullness of all He promised He would do through us.

PRAYER IN THE VALLEY OF DECISION

A friend of mine called to arrange a visit over lunch. "I really need to talk with you," he said urgently. "I've got to make a crucial decision about a job offer I have. It could be the most important career decision of my life. My need is for an objective person to listen and tell me how to make a right decision." I told him I'd be happy to listen and share what I'd learned over the years about discovering God's specific will for particular decisions.

When we got together I quickly discovered that the young executive was very serious about wanting to know God's will for the important decision he had to make. He opened the conversation in earnest. "I don't want to make a wrong choice," he said. "But how do I know for sure what is God's will? I really want to take this job, but what if that's just my will and not the Lord's will for me?"

I replied with some questions. "Can you think of any reason the Lord would not want you to make this a yes decision? Will you be asked to do anything contrary to what you believe? Can you continue to put the Lord first in your life if you take this job? Will this opportunity bring you closer to your life goals professionally? Will it give you a chance to witness for your faith? Can you claim the Lord's presence and power as you do your work?"

He could answer all the questions affirmatively. "When do you have to give an answer to the offer?" I asked. He told me he had a few days. Then I suggested an exercise in prayer that has worked for me in making decisions. "It sounds like you really want to take this job. Why not try that on for the days between now and when you must respond. Live with a 'yes' decision. Ask the Lord to create a conviction of rightness or wrongness. Open yourself in prayer. Yield your mind to Him, surrender your will specifically for this, and ask Him to use everything—circumstances, people you trust, and the Scriptures—to affirm or negate your decision."

A few days later the man called me to tell me that he felt guided to take the job. "I was so concerned," he said. "I thought that because I wanted this, God was probably against it. I couldn't imagine that He would be for me in this!" I reminded him that the Lord was his friend and wanted what was best for him. He had guided the whole process. Because the man was open to allow the Lord to condition his thoughts, he had been given clear direction. In this case all signals were "go!"

Decisions, decisions. We all face them every day. Some are insignificant; others are crucial for our future. In all of them we want to make guided choices. We long to know and do the Lord's will.

The prophet Joel speaks of the valley of decision. "Multitudes, multitudes in the valley of decision!" (Joel 3:14). Times of making crucial decisions force us into that valley. The alternatives force us to make hard choices.

We Are Not Alone

We are not alone in that valley of decision. The Lord is there with us. His ultimate will for us is that we should know, love, glorify, and serve Him. He wills both abundant life and eternal life for us. Both salvation and sanctification are parts of His primary will. And within that awesome context, the Lord also has a personal will for each of us which is His plan for us—unique, particular, and specific.

That does not mean that the Lord's will is a rigid, inflexible set of sealed orders. Rather, the Lord has goals for us, work for us to do, challenges to tackle with His power. Our question is, How do we discover what He wants in each decision?

In every vital decision there is something the Lord does and then something He asks us to do. Let's consider both. The Lord really cares about us. He will not leave us in a quandary when the decisions we face will determine our effectiveness as persons or affect our relationship with Him.

What the Lord Does

Here's what the Lord does to help us in our decisions. Two specific promises from Scripture give us assurance. In Philippians 2:12-13 Paul tells us, "Work out your own salvation with fear and trembling; for it is God who works in you both to will and to do for His good pleasure." This promise refocuses our central theme: God is the initiator of prayer and is the prime mover in the revelation of His will for us. Why would He go to the extents He has to love, forgive, reconcile, and empower us to be His persons, and then leave us without help in making decisions that will shape our destiny? When Paul suggests that we are to work out our own salvation with fear and trembling, he is not suggesting that we can save ourselves by our own self-justification or righteousness. What he is saying, it seems to me, is that we are to live out our salvation in all of life with deep concern that all which we decide and do enables us to grow in that salvation and express its power in all aspects of our life. And the Lord doesn't leave us on our own to do that. He loves us so much that prior, during, and after the major decisions of our lives, He takes the responsibility to work in us a clear conviction of what we are to live out.

He Liberates Our Wills

In the consistent communion of prayer, the Lord works to liberate our wills. The will is the implementor of thought and desire. Thus the Lord's task in us is to clarify His will, condition our thought around His ultimate and specific desires for us so that our wills can function properly with the right goals and plans. The wonder of it all is that He can and will enable us to desire what He desires for us. He gives us an eager mind, desirous of discovering His strategy for our lives. Our thoughts are purified by prolonged and repeated times of prayer. We become expectantly alert to the implanting of the Lord's long- and short-range goals for us. These give us the beginning basis for discerning His will in specific decisions. Added to that, the Lord uses all our faculties to create an assurance of the best choice.

So often we feel we are solely responsible for our decisions. When a big one comes along we think that we should check in with the Lord to get help. Then soon we forget our need of His continuing guidance and live on our own ability. That's to miss the hourly and daily direction He offers.

The Lord knows the future. He foresees the decisions that are ahead of us. The essence of the promise Paul made the Philippians is that, long before the decision must be made, He begins His preparation in us. He uses everything in and around us to condition our thoughts and will in anticipation. The habitual communion of prayer and Bible study gives us the convictions, ideas, and values which will affect our understanding at the time of the decision. Repeated relinquishment of our will makes us ready and receptive. As a result, our wills will not be an impediment, but an implementor of the clarified direction when the decision must be made.

The question I'm asked most often is, How can I know the will of God? The question exposes people's inconsistent communion with the Lord. My answer is not to give people a set of rules to finding God's will but to explain His promise to work in us constantly so that we are ready for the choices of life. That leads to the discipline of prayer, not just for crises, but in daily times of listening and constant communion through the day. That's often more than people bargain for who raise the question about how to know God's will.

Over the years, I have discovered that the Lord does not distribute cheap grace and guidance. He created us for a consistent companionship and redeemed us to live in close oneness with Him. Those who rush to Him only when a decision demands His help are often made to wait. He uses the time of indecision to draw us closer to Him and establish a profound relationship which will prepare us for decisions in the future.

I have a friend who calls her doctor only when she has an illness. She talks to him on the phone and wants a prescription of some miracle drug for whatever malady she has. Consistently, she has resisted general checkups and the doctor's desire to help her with an overall plan of diet, exercise, and health care which would avert her repeated illnesses. Recently he refused to give quickie remedies on the phone and told her she must submit to his comprehensive program of remedial care for her long-range well-being. That would necessitate more than a phone call in crises. The doctor cared too much for this woman's health to continue as a telephone prescription service. How much more the Lord wants to maximize our spiritual lives. He is up to momentous things with us. In His master plan for the kingdom in our time, He has plans for each of us which fit into His overall will. The people around us, the churches of which we are a part, the places we work, and the communities in which we live are dependent on our seeking the Lord's will consistently so that His maximum in every area can be accomplished. When we are out of touch with Him, we make wrong choices, develop unguided programs, and head in directions that are less than He envisions for us. We and others, as well as situations in which we are involved, are cheated.

Hebrews 13:20-21 sounds a trumpet call giving the same promise as the Philippian verses we quoted a few pages back. "Now may the God of peace who brought up our Lord Jesus from the dead, that great Shepherd of the sheep, through the blood of the everlasting covenant, make you complete in every good work to do His will, working in you what is well pleasing in His sight, through Jesus Christ, to whom be glory forever and ever."

The continuing ministry of Christ, God with us, is the focus of this triumphant benediction. Through Him we are participants of the new covenant in His blood. A covenant is a promise. We are covenant members of the new Israel through Christ. Our relationship is based on the grace offered us through the cross. The Lord has called us to be His people and will not let us go. As He took responsibility for our redemption, He assumes the initiative role in "making us complete." The word for "complete" in this stirring passage is *katatisai,* from *katartizō,* meaning "to equip." The Lord equips us to do His will. As indwelling

Lord living in us He gives us whatever we need to know and do His will. He wants us to do what is "well pleasing in His sight." But He does not leave that for us to flounder about until we happen on it. He readily responds to our willingness and makes His will known for each situation, choice, and decision. To do that He equips us with the gifts of wisdom, knowledge, discernment, and vision.

What Is Our Part?

Now, in response to these awesome promises we must consider what our part is in discovering and doing the Lord's will in our decisions. There are three gifts we have to give: An open mind, a responsive will, and a faithful obedience.

An Open Mind

Prayer is the time in which what the Lord has been "working in us" is worked out in clarified thought. *An open mind is attentive.* What He has been developing in our thoughts about His specific guidance is crystalized. When we wait quietly in His presence, the Lord will reform our thinking around His plans for us. William Barclay said, "Here is something to ponder. We are so apt to think that prayer is asking God for what we want, whereas true prayer is asking God for what He wants. Prayer is not only talking to God, even more it is listening to Him."[1]

I find it helpful to say to the Lord, "I consciously yield my capacity to think, which you gave me to guide me in thinking your thoughts." That keeps me from falsely using prayer as a means of persuading God to do what I want. True prayer is intelligent, purposeful conversation with God in which our thinking is reoriented and redirected.

My good friend Paul Rees puts it this way. "If we are willing to take hours on end to learn to play the piano, or operate a computer, or fly an airplane, it is sheer nonsense for us to imagine that we can learn the high art of getting guidance through communion with the Lord without being willing to set time aside for it. It is no accident that the Bible speaks of prayer as a form of waiting on God."[2] But it is not waiting for God to hear, but waiting until our minds are quiet and receptive enough to receive what He has been waiting to communicate. Our task is to offer the Lord an open mind. Prayer is not seeking to convince the Lord of what we want, but the time of communion with Him in which He implants His thoughts in our minds. Our desires are transformed into His desires for us. He has created us to think clearly under the guidance of His indwelling Spirit in our thinking brain.

A Responsive Will

A responsive will is closely intertwined with an open mind. The will can be either an imperious sentinel guarding the door of a closed mind or a ready servant to carry out what the Lord articulates in our thoughts. The persistent prayer, "Lord make me willing to hear and desire what you want," is the key. Since He motivates the longing to pray that prayer, He is ready to answer it. The liberation of the will is one of the greatest aspects of God's healing Spirit we ever know. He does it by the power of love. Conditioned with the thought of His gracious care for us and repeated forgiveness of our failures, our wills become responsive to activating the guidance the Lord has given us. Then we can say with George Matheson:

> My will is not my own
> Till Thou hast made it Thine;
> If I would reach a monarch's throne
> It must its crown resign;

It only stands unbent
Amid the closing strife
When on Thy bosom it has leant
And found in Thee its life. [3]

A completely surrendered will opens the floodgate for the Lord to work in our minds "to will and do His good pleasure." We will not know His will or desire to do it until we ask for the miraculous healing of our wills. We will remain willful and stubborn until He sets us free.

A Faithful Obedience

Faithful obedience is the direct result of that freedom. The Lord progressively reveals His will to those who act on what He guides. Often we find it difficult to desire His will in a crucial decision because we have resisted acting on what He has clearly guided in other areas of our relationships and responsibilities. We get prepared for life's big decisions by following through with obedience in what we know He has asked us to do in daily faithfulness to Him. We need to ask Him, "Lord, is there any area where I have been unwilling? Give me courage to follow orders today so that you can trust me with guidance in the future." We do not know what demanding decisions are ahead. Preparation for them begins now.

I have found that journaling is a helpful discipline. Keeping a daily journal of what action steps have become clear in our prayers helps us remember what the Lord has guided and what we have done about it. Each day as a part of prayer and Bible study I try to log the insights I have received and steps of obedience I feel the Lord guides. It provides a good inventory when I return to my quiet time the next day. I can check off things which have been done and be reminded of unfinished orders. I also list specific petitions for the Lord's will under each day's entry. It is a great source of gratitude and praise to go back over a year's record of requests for guidance and realize how the Lord answered. I am filled with thanksgiving for what He has done and refortified for the future.

A friend keeps me fortified with bound books containing blank sheets for my prayer journaling. In affirmation of my Scots heritage, the covers are tartan, closely resembling the Ogilvie clan tartan! Several are filled each year with the records of my daily prayer pilgrimage. But any notebook will do. The important thing is the autobiography of growth in the will of the Lord that I record. Each day we can record guidance received, steps to be taken, and decisions pending the direction the Lord will crystalize in our thoughts, implement through our wills, and accomplish through our actions. Prayer for the will of the Lord in our decisions becomes an exciting adventure.

Abraham Lincoln puts an exclamation point on what I've tried to communicate about the Lord's guidance in our decisions. During the dark days of the Civil War, the Lord gave him direction and strength. One hundred and twenty years ago, the same year he reestablished a National Day of Prayer, Lincoln said, "I have been driven many times to my knees by the overwhelming conviction that I had nowhere else to go; my own wisdom and that of all around me seemed insufficient for the day." And then, explaining the Lord's answers, the president said, "I have had so many evidences of His direction, so many instances of times when I have been controlled by some other power than my own will, that I cannot doubt that this power comes from God. I frequently see my way clear to a decision when I am conscious that I have not sufficient facts on which to found it. I am satisfied that, when the Almighty wants me to do, or not to do a particular thing, He finds a way of letting me know. I talk to God, and when I do, my mind seems relieved and a way is suggested."

Notes

1. William Barclay, Daily Study Bible. 1 John (Philadelphia, Westminster Press, 1959.
2. Paul Rees, from a sermon.
3. George Matheson, "Christ's Bondservant", James Dalton Morrison, ed., *Masterpieces of Religious Verse* (New York: Harper & Row Publisher, 1948), p. 757.

WHEN YOU'RE TEMPTED TO GIVE UP

There are two very different ways of saying, "I'm finished!" One is the triumphant expression of the delight of completion. The other is the discouraged admission of defeat. So often it is the latter. Life is littered with unfinished tasks, uncompleted goals, unfulfilled assignments, and unhealed relationships.

Living is like a race with many laps. Each lap is made up of tasks given us to do. In His providential management of life, the Lord gives each of us challenges which only we can do. And in our efforts to accomplish His assignment, we are often tempted to give up before we are finished.

We've all known times when we were tempted to give up on people, prospects, and demanding opportunities. Perhaps we are breathlessly running one of those laps right now. We are not sure we are going to make it. We need a second wind, or what joggers call the "runner's high" when suddenly new strength is given and we are able to exceed our natural capacities.

He Provides Perseverance

In this final chapter, I want to focus our attention on how the Lord gives us a very special gift for completing each lap of life's race. He gives it to us through the consistent communion of prayer. Thus far we've talked about what the Lord can do when we prayerfully entrust our needs to Him. Now we must claim what He does when He entrusts a task to us. He provides perseverance. It is a balanced blend of our persistence and His power. The winning combination is hard work and the acceptance of supernatural strength. The Lord can accomplish magnificent things through people who invest all that they have and are to do His will and depend on His rejuvenating replenishment. Perseverance is the difference between life's pressures finishing us and our finishing the task of each lap by God's grace and for His glory.

Think about the particular challenge of the lap you're running right now. You felt the urge to pray about a concern. You turned it over to the Lord. Then He gave it back to you with guidance for what you were to do according to His strategy and strength.

What is it for you? Perhaps it's some person in your life the Lord has called you to help. You've prayed prayers of intercession and the Lord has made you part of the answer by telling you what He wants you to be and do with that person. Or perhaps it is a project you feel called to tackle. Prayer has given you a vision of what needs to be done. You know you can't do it without the Lord's ever-present guidance and divine energy to follow through faithfully. Maybe it is in your church, or in some aching social problems in the community. You feel the burden to do something. Then the Lord shows you what He wants you to do.

We are all called to extend the kingdom, communicate love and grasp the opportunities the Lord gives us. Every Christian is responsible to be a contagious witness to individuals and to become involved in some area of society where people suffer or are debilitated by social injustice.

And in our churches we are to be cooperative, willing participants in the Lord's renaissance of the parish. He is on the move today, bringing churches back to basics and renewing them to be Spirit-empowered, Bible-centered laboratories of new life. There's a new wind blowing in the Church today. These are the most exciting days since the first century. When we pray about our congregations the Lord helps us to set goals only He could help us accomplish. Then He calls us to be partners with Him in reviving religious members who need a fresh experience of His power and in restructuring the Church to be a place where people can meet Him, grow as vital Christians, and become equipped to live out their faith in the tensions of the world.

It is after we've accepted our particular assignment and worked hard to accomplish it, that often we grow weary. Sometimes we face resistance which drains our enthusiasm. Things take longer than we expected. We become impatient with ourselves, others, even God. Discouragement sets in. We wish we could be free of the responsibility; resign from the Lord's assignment. We are tempted to give up!

The Lord Understands

The Lord understands. He's been dealing for centuries with people who feel they are finished before they finish. He is for us: He waits to give us exactly what we need to finish our present lap so we can get on to the next lap He's planned for us. He uses prayer not only to clarify our assignments but also as a channel for the flow of His perseverance each day. Prayer is not only for what the Lord does for us, but also for what He wants to do through us.

In order to claim how He gives perseverance I want to reintroduce you to one of the heroes of the Old Testament who was given an awesome task to do and show how he did it through the power of prayer. His life is a stirring example of perseverance—what it is and how we can receive it.

The patron saint of perseverance through prayer is Nehemiah. You may have anticipated that I would cite Moses, Job, or Elijah. But in my observation Nehemiah is a model for perseverance not only in difficulties, but in finishing what the Lord gave him to do. How he endured to the finish of a lap of the race of his life gives us a basis of drawing together the promises of God for perseverance.

In the year 445 B.C. Nehemiah was called to spearhead the rebuilding of the wall of Jerusalem. When the work was nearing completion and his enemies threatened his life, a false friend pleaded with him to come down off the wall being reconstructed and flee to a safe hiding place in the Temple. For Nehemiah that was tantamount to quitting when he was near reaching the goal the Lord had given him. What he said in response was to ask two questions and make a flat statement. "Should such a man as I flee? And who is there such as I who would go into the temple to save his life? I will not go in!" (Neh. 6:11). That could be the motto of those who refuse to give up and who receive perseverance from the Lord to finish.

A man such as I. What kind of person was Nehemiah? There are five things that occur to me as I study the book that bears his name. Each gives us a window to look into his character—and all in order provide us a progression for a perseverance profile.

Greatly Favored by God

First of all, Nehemiah was a person greatly favored by God. He was a second generation Hebrew in the Persian exile. By God's grace he had risen to a position of power as the cupbearer and advisor of King Artaxerxes in Shushan. But Nehemiah never forgot that he was a Hebrew and that his God was Yahweh. Through his growing years he was given training in the law and an exiled heart that had reverence for Jerusalem as the Holy City. The Lord guided his development as a man of strong character, faithfulness, and determination. One of the most crucial aspects of the Lord's favor is the healthy development of our wills. The balance between willingness and willfulness can be tipped so easily. The Lord wants us to grow as clear-thinking people guided by His Spirit with wills open to respond to His direction. His care for Nehemiah built a strong-willed man who could hear and obey Him and not falter under pressure.

Clearly Called

That leads us to the second aspect of his perseverance. Nehemiah was a person clearly called. We can have determination to finish when we know we have been appointed and deployed by God to do a particular task. His call began in a concern which grew into a conviction.

Some Hebrews from Judah told Nehemiah about conditions in the city of Jerusalem. The city had been destroyed in 586 B.C. when the Babylonians razed the city and carried off most of the population into exile. The Temple, the wall and the buildings of the city were left in rubble. In the spring of 458 B.C., through a decision of Cyrus, then the Persian emperor, Ezra led an expedition of Jews back to Jerusalem. They began reconstruction of the Temple and rebuilding of the wall. Then suddenly the work on the wall was stopped through conflict with the local Persian overlords. The report brought to Nehemiah was that the despicable condition of the city was matched by the dejected spirit of the Jews who were living in worse circumstances than they had known in exile. When Nehemiah heard this sad news, he felt a warrant in his soul to rebuild the walls of Jerusalem.

He fasted and prayed. His prayer was one of praise and the specific petition that he would be given favor in the king's sight. Nehemiah knew that only the Lord could move the heart of the king to release him. And the Lord was faithful. When He gives us an assignment, He clears the way for us to do His will.

The Lord answered Nehemiah's prayer in an astounding way. When the cupbearer and advisor to the king appeared to serve him, his face was downcast. The king inquired about the cause of this uncustomary sadness in the Hebrew. Nehemiah relayed the burden on his troubled heart. "Why should my face not be sad, when the city, the place of my fathers' tombs, lies waste, and its gates are burned with fire?" (2:3). The king asked a crucial question, "What do you want me to do?" Before Nehemiah answered he prayed and then asked to be sent to Judah to rebuild Jerusalem. The Lord was guiding each step of the conversation. The response of the king was not only to give Nehemiah permission to go but he willingly granted his request for letters from the king for safe travel from Persia to Judah and for cooperation from the local leaders over the area. He would need timber from the king's forest to make beams for the gates, but most of all he would need the king's blessing and authority as leverage with the leaders who would probably resist any rise of the Jews to patriotism and power. All that Nehemiah asked was granted by Artaxerxes and he set off for Jerusalem. The Hebrew was clearly called and the Lord who called him confirmed His guidance in the miraculous opening of Artaxerxes' mind and his willingness to affirm his servant's mission.

Richly Blessed

Third, we see Nehemiah as a person richly blessed. The Lord had equipped him through the years with great leadership ability and the impelling gifts of a leader. He had charisma, the capacity to impart a vision, the skill to organize people, and the enthusiasm to work with them until the task was finished.

When he arrived in Jerusalem he saw the walls in shambles and felt the depleted hope of his people. The Lord not only wanted Nehemiah to rebuild the walls but to reconstruct a new confidence and self-esteem in His discouraged people. With Spirit-birthed urgency in his voice, Nehemiah rallied the people. "You see the distress that we are in, how Jerusalem lies waste, and its gates are burned with fire. Come let us build the walls of Jerusalem, that we may no longer be a reproach" (2:17). He told the people that the call to do that had come from God. Their response was inspired by His Spirit. "Let us rise up and build" (v. 18). The Lord gives a vision and then gives us people who are ignited with the same vision in order to help us accomplish our assigned task.

But great work for the Lord is seldom done without opposition from both enemies and friends. Nehemiah had both. How he dealt with that reveals him as a person who consistently prayed and was repeatedly strengthened. We see a man who faced impossible odds with the perseverance received in prayer.

Nehemiah's enemies were the local Persian overlords who saw him as a threat to their positions. These were joined by the Samaritan leaders. They feared the rising unity and vigilance of the Jews. When they observed Nehemiah's charisma for leadership and saw the response of the people to rebuilding the wall, first they laughed with scorn and then were gripped by hatred. Their power was being threatened. A power struggle is usually behind most negative criticism and eventually turns it into open hostility.

In spite of the opposition, Nehemiah marshalled the Jews to action and the work of reconstruction of the walls began. He divided the wall and its gates into sections and assigned the various parts to families in Jerusalem and teams of Jews from nearby cities. The work proceeded with perseverance inspired by the leader's prayers for strength.

Every means was used by the hostile enemies to debilitate Nehemiah's determination. Rumor, intrigue, and finally, organized armed attacks made the work of rebuilding perilous.

The progress was further crippled by dissension among some of the Jews whose equivocation was threatened by Nehemiah's courage and determination. We all know what that means. Sometimes our most difficult antagonists are the very people we are trying to help. Few things contribute more to our temptation to give up than that. We border on saying, "What's the use? The very people the Lord has asked me to help don't want Him or the task He's given us to do together." I hear that from discouraged church leaders often when they take themselves too seriously and don't take their need for moment-by-moment replenishment of His strength seriously enough. And yet, if we ask the Lord for fresh perseverance, He provides it. He is more concerned about our finishing the lap than we may be! He doesn't give up and doesn't give us the luxury of giving in to people's attitudes. As leaders we can accomplish God's assignments only when we draw security from Him, and not those He's given us to lead. Nehemiah had that single-minded determination. "The God of heaven Himself will prosper us;

therefore we His servants will arise and build" (v. 20). And rise up and build is what they did. The reason was a dynamic mixture of trust in God and loyalty to Nehemiah.

A Man Greatly Admired

The fourth thing we observe about the dynamic leader is that he was a man greatly admired. The people trusted him because of his prayer-saturated vision that they could finish the rebuilding. People long to rise to the finest we dare to picture they can be. When we communicate that we are for them and not against them, they will give their utmost. That also requires working with them in the accomplishment of the dream. Nehemiah did not administrate the rebuilding from an aloof director's office, sending out impersonal memos of what he wanted done. He was there on the wall laboring night and day with his fellow Jews. Certainly, Nehemiah directed the work and depended on the follow-through of others. But all the people could see and feel the impact of his indefatigable commitment to finish the task by giving the people himself as well as his vision. That's why he could not flee and take refuge in the Temple.

When the rebuilding was nearing completion, Nehemiah's enemies conspired together and threatened to raise up an army to stop the work. He devised a plan for half of the Jews to stand guard while the other half held spears to protect them. In addition each worker held his own sword and trumpeters were stationed to sound the alarm in case of attack. Nehemiah's watchword was, "Our God will fight for us" (4:20).

When threats of attack did not dissuade Nehemiah and the builders, other tactics were devised. The enemies of the leader tried to distract him with conferences to talk. They tried to get his attention with false accusations that he and the Jews planned to rebel and that he was grooming himself to be king of Judea. He flatly denied the charge and refused to stop work for disputations with them. Prayer was Nehemiah's secret weapon. And what did he pray for in the pressure? Perseverance. Listen to the courage in his voice when he responds to the challenge to stop the work to consult with his enemies. "I am doing a great work, so that I cannot come down. Why should the work cease while I leave it and go down to you?" (6:3). That courage came from the quality of Nehemiah's prayers. "But now, O God, strengthen my hands."

That led his enemies to try one further method of discrediting the great leader. He went to visit one of the Jews who was confined to his home. Again we see Nehemiah's personal care for individuals. The man's name was Shemaiah. What Nehemiah did not know was that the man was an informer. Strange twist. The man had pretended sickness to get Nehemiah to visit him so he could plead with him to flee from the wall and find safety in the Temple. The plot was to expose him as one who was frightened. Shemaiah's plea was drenched with factious concern for Nehemiah. "Let us meet together in the house of God, within the temple, and let us close the doors of the temple, for they are coming to kill you . . . at night" (6:10). Nehemiah's response to this beguiling concern for his welfare reveals the fifth and final thing I want to underline about his perseverance. He was a person courageously unafraid. That enabled him to make the statement we quoted earlier which has given courage to so many who have noted it in tight places through the centuries. "Should such a man as I flee? Who is there, that, being such as I would go into the temple to save his life? I will not go in" (Neh. 6:11, *ASV*).

Feared No One

Nehemiah feared no person. His relationship with the Lord through prayer gave him the freedom to want to please Him and not people. People-pleasers will always be afraid. They are taking their signals from the wrong source. Repeatedly in the Old Testament we are admonished to fear the Lord. The Hebrew word means "awe and wonder." That quality of reverence is the antidote to our fears. It produces daring and boldness. When our only concern is to know and do the Lord's will, we need be afraid of no person or group.

Note that Nehemiah did not think of the Temple or worship as an escape from danger. So often we think of getting out of difficulties into the comfort of prayer. That's not authentic prayer. Prayer gives us the fearlessness to stay in the battle. Dr. Alexis Carrell in *Man, the Unknown* said, "Prayer is the most powerful form of energy that one can generate. In prayer we link ourselves with the inexhaustible power that spins the universe. Prayer is a force as real as terrestrial gravity. The influence of prayer on the human mind and body is as demonstrable as that of secreting glands. Its results can be measured in terms of increased physical buoyancy, greater intellectual vigor, moral stamina, and a deeper understanding of the realities underlying human relationships. Only in prayer do we achieve that complete and harmonious assembly of body, mind, and spirit which gives the frail human reed its unshakable strength."[1]

That's what prayer did for Nehemiah and can do for us when we are tempted to give up. In prayer we give in to the inflow of the Lord's power so that we do not need to give up to the desire to be safe. Prayer is not a retreat

from danger; it is the secret source of courage to finish.
People of unshakable vision and indefatigable perseverance are those who have been with the Lord long enough,
consistently enough, and deeply enough to know that He
delights to help us accomplish the impossible dreams He
gives us.

Nehemiah finished the building of the wall to the glory
of God. The Jews were amazed and their enemies were
discouraged. Here are Nehemiah's own words of triumph.
"So the wall was finished on the twenty-fifth day of the
month of Elul, in fifty-two days. And it happened, when all
our enemies heard of it, and all the nations around us saw
these things, that they were very disheartened in their
own eyes; for they perceived that this work was done by
our God" (6:15-16). There is no limit to the perseverance
the Lord will give when we are willing to give Him the
glory. He is pleased to astound the people around us with
the resiliency and resoluteness He gives to those who
refuse to give up.

The greatest temptation had come to Nehemiah to flee
and not finish the work when he was close to completion.
That often happens. Our exhaustion is most excruciating
as we are nearing the end of the lap. That's when we need
an inflow of supernatural power. The Lord says, "Don't
give up. I am with you. Press on. Victory is within your
grasp!"

It is in prayer that we put our roots down deeply into
the limitless reservoir of God's strength. When we tell the
Lord we are tempted to give up, that we are dangerously
close to being engulfed with our problems, then He gives
us the stamina to keep on steadfastly.

A clergy friend of mine was tempted to quit. He was
drained and depleted. In despair, he went to a spiritually
sensitive older friend. She empathized, and then put her

finger on the raw nerve. "You are like a pump unconnected to a well. People have pumped you dry. Your greatest need is to reestablish contact with the Lord. People need Him, not your knowledge, adequacy or cleverness. Instead of quitting, take a week off for silence with the Lord. Allow Him to heal your hurts and meet your needs. Stop working for the Lord and let Him work through you."

The man was stunned by the woman's directness. The Lord was at work and gave him the honesty to accept the piercing advice. He secured a retired pastor to fill his pulpit the following Sunday and went into the mountains for a full-week retreat of silence. Exhausted in body and soul, he slept for the first full day and night. Then he began to allow the Lord to refocus his life's purpose and goals. That was followed with long walks in which he asked the Lord to show him what He wanted him to do to complete the lap of his life in the parish he was serving. Most of all, he allowed the Lord to meet his own needs for replenishment. He returned to work a new man. With his priorities redefined, he reestablished his own time of daily prayer and meditation which had previously been edged out by busy-ness. The greatest gift he could give his congregation was to do more than say his prayers; to spend prolonged time in prayer. He began living in the stream of the Lord's power. The result was that he now had an indefatigable supply of inspiration and wisdom as well as joy and hope to give to his people. He is finishing the lap of renewing his present parish. After that the Lord will have another lap for him to run. He told me that his fondest hope is that he will never forget what he's discovered in this lap of the race.

Winston Churchill said in dark days when his countrymen were tempted to become discouraged, "Never give in! Never give in! Never, never, never—in anything great or small, large or petty—never give in except to convictions of honor and good sense." To take and apply that admonition we need more than human pertinacity; we need God-given perseverance.

James reminds us that faith without works is dead. So too, prayer without work is ineffective. But equally so, work without consistent prayer will wear us out. The Lord never assigns us more to do than we can accomplish with His replenishing power. He guides the task, gives the strength to do it, and keeps us going until we finish. Don't give up!

We are back to where we started our journey together in search of the secret of praying with power. Prayer starts with God. He is the initiator of the challenges of each lap of the race of life. And He never gives up on us regardless of our failures and weakness. With that assurance we can ask Nehemiah's question. "Can a person like me flee?" No! What the Lord did for Nehemiah through prayer, He will do for us and so much more. We live on this side of Calvary. Christ endured the cross for our forgiveness. When He completed the atonement for us, He cried, "It is finished!" Because of that we never need say in despair, "I'm finished!" We are never finished sharing the love and hope we have in Christ and working in His strength to accomplish each lap of the race. In a way, our confidence of eternal life enables us to run each lap with the assurance that we've already won the race!

Note

1. Dr. Alexis Carrell, *Man, the Unknown* (New York: Hillman-Mac-Fadden, 1961).

THE HEALING CHOICE

Finding God's Grace in Discouragement, Conflict,
Mistreatment, Illness, Loss, Loneliness, Failure,
Inferiority, Doubt and Fear

Ron Lee Davis

with

James C. Denney

Guideposts®

CARMEL • NEW YORK 10512

Library of Congress Cataloging-in-Publication Data

Davis, Ron Lee.
  The healing choice.

  Bibliography: p.
  1. Christian life—1960–   . 2. Spiritual
healing. 3. Consolation. I. Title.
BV4501.2.D387 1968   248.8′6   86–1558

To *Paul John Davis,*
my only brother, my best friend,
who taught me so much
about how to live,
and then about how to die;
who in life and in death
continually made
The Healing Choice.

Contents

Prologue

Do You Want to Be Healed?

God permits us to go through deep waters, not to drown us, but to cleanse us.

—Anonymous

Now if we are children, then we are heirs—heirs of God and co-heirs with Christ, if indeed we share in his sufferings in order that we may also share in his glory.

—Romans 8:17

It was a Monday evening in July 1985, and I had just flown to Dallas for the Christian Booksellers Association Convention. The first draft of this book was nearly completed, and I was planning to discuss this material with my publisher and friend, Ernie Owen of Word Books. As I walked into the Hyatt-Regency Hotel where the Word Books reception was being held, my mind was focused two states away, consumed with thoughts and prayers for my brother Paul. For several weeks, he had been experiencing abdominal pains, and all the noninvasive medical tests had failed to yield a diagnosis. So now, at the same time I was in Dallas, my only brother and best friend was undergoing exploratory surgery in a Denver hospital.

I met Ernie Owen at the reception. We chatted briefly, agreeing to meet for breakfast the next morning to discuss details of the book. During the rest of the evening, I repeatedly left the reception and went to a pay phone in the lobby, placing call after call to the hospital in Denver. No one at the hospital could tell me anything about Paul's condition. I prayed and waited and continued calling until about 10:30 P.M., when a nurse finally told me Paul was out of surgery. She had orders, however, not to give out any other information over the phone.

More anxious than ever, I called Paul's home, hoping to speak with his wife, Jan. There was no answer. So next I called Marty Asbury, a good friend of Paul's. I knew Marty and his wife had stayed in the waiting room with my sister-in-law throughout Paul's surgery. "Jan just left a few minutes ago, but I can tell you what the doctors found," Marty told me. "Ron, Paul has cancer."

Cancer. The word penetrated like a knife. I tried to speak, but I couldn't. Instead, I found I was weeping. *I should have been there,* I thought. *I should have been with Jan and the boys when the doctors gave them the news.*

Marty went on, "It apparently began in the appendix, which is very rare, and it's spread to several other organs. The doctors think there's cancer in the liver, but they won't know for sure until the tests are in tomorrow. I'm sorry, Ron, but the doctors just aren't very optimistic. They only give Paul about six to twelve months."

My next call was to the airlines; I booked a 6 A.M. flight to Denver. The next morning, a few minutes before my departure, I called Ernie Owen from the airport and broke our breakfast appointment. Telling him I was going to Denver to be with my brother, I briefly explained the situation. Ernie graciously offered a prayer for our family over the phone and assured me that he and others at Word Books would be praying for Paul in the days ahead.

I landed in Denver and took a cab to the hospital, arriving just a few minutes before Jan. She and I were both with Paul when the doctor came in and explained to him that he had an advanced cancer. Paul took the news with amazing steadiness and replied that he was ready to fight it any way he could. He asked simply, "What do we do now?"

In the weeks that followed, I made several more trips between Denver and my home in California. During one of those trips to Denver, I stayed day and night in Paul's hospital room while he underwent chemotherapy immediately after his completion of five weeks of radiation treatments. During those difficult days and long nights, whenever the pain and nausea of the chemotherapy would subside, Paul and I had many opportunities to talk. We reminisced about growing up together in a small town in Iowa; and we talked of life and death and how Paul's faith in Christ was carrying him through this crisis.

He shared very openly with me his fears regarding the future and his concern for his wife and two teenage sons should this cancer take his life. We wept and prayed together many times, and I never felt closer to Paul than I did in those hours.

During those weeks, I watched Paul—who for over twenty years had been a coach to hundreds of young men, conducting basketball clinics around the country, active in the Fellowship of Christian Athletes—as he reached out from his hospital bed to touch the lives of young men whom he had already influenced powerfully for Christ. I saw tears streaming down the lean, tanned faces of rugged athletes as they dropped all their "macho" pretenses and wept openly at Paul's bedside.

It was only two months after Paul's cancer was first diagnosed that he suddenly began to develop serious complications. When we received the news, my mother flew to Denver from Iowa, and I again flew back from California. In his hospital room, my mother was able to tell Paul how much she loved him and what a wonderful son he'd been. I stayed through that night beside Paul's bed as he alternated between sleep and wakefulness. When he was awake, we talked, sharing thoughts and memories and prayers. During those long midnight hours in that darkened hospital room, Paul was as close to God as I had ever seen him.

At 8:00 the next morning, Jan and I hugged him and prayed with him as he was wheeled down the hallway to surgery. We stopped at the door that led to the operating room, and I kissed Paul on the neck and told him I loved him. He told me he loved me. Then he and Jan had a few precious moments together, and at last Paul was taken into surgery. That was the last conversation Jan and I had with Paul in this life. Despite the doctors' best efforts, the surgery was unable to extend Paul's life any further. The next morning, my brother— my closest friend—passed from this life into eternity.

The God of all mercy and comfort

As I write these words, it has only been a few weeks since Paul's death. There are a lot of things I still have to sort out, understand, and accept about Paul's suffering with cancer and his death at the age of forty-one. I know that time will never fully heal this sorrow I feel for the loss of my brother.

I know this is true because there are still many times when I feel the loss of my father as keenly as if it were yesterday, even though it has been twelve years since he died. Time *doesn't* heal all wounds. I expect the grief I feel for Paul to recur again and again as long as I live—and that's as it should be. When we love someone deeply, it hurts us deeply to let him or her go.

Still, despite the sorrow, the unanswered questions, and the trials and tears that continue in my life, I know peace. And while Paul's death is still too close and too painful for me to understand all the reasons for it, I believe I do have at least a faint and partial glimmer of one reason for some of the tragedy that comes into our lives. I'm convinced that our own grief and pain give us something authentic to share with others who are going through trials. By some process I don't fully understand, God is able to take the wounds and scars of our lives and transform them into a source of healing in the lives of others.

In 2 Corinthians, the apostle Paul tells us that God is

> the source of all mercy and comfort. [And he] gives us comfort in all our trials so that we in turn may be able to give the same sort of strong sympathy to others in their troubles . . . Indeed, experience shows that the more we share in Christ's immeasurable suffering the more we are able to give of his encouragement. This means that if we experience trouble it is for your comfort and spiritual protection; for if we ourselves have been comforted we know how to encourage you to endure patiently the same sort of troubles that we have ourselves endured (1:3–6, PHILLIPS).

More than ever before, I'm coming to realize that God gives us His comfort in our trials to make us His ministers of healing to others in their trials. So I've felt a need in this book to be very open with you about my own hurts—not because I'm prepared as yet to make any profound applications from this experience, but to let you know as you are reading this book that I hurt along with you.

As I've talked with many people over the years about their problems and trials, I've found ten particular forms of trial to be the most difficult hurts of life: discouragement, conflict, mistreatment, illness, loss, loneliness, failure, inferiority, doubt, and fear. From time to time, I've personally wrestled with *each* of these areas in my own life. I struggle with some of these hurts even as I'm writing these words. So I hope you'll find in this book not only some encouragement and insight for your time of trial, but some consolation in the simple fact that these words are written by someone who can identify— at least to some limited degree—with your hurts.

In these days, I know what it means to hurt deeply over the death of a brother, of a close and irreplaceable friend. At the same time I've also been watching my mother, who has recently come to live with us, as she has been grieving over the death of a son. In all this I'm reminded of the fact that we have a God who also knows what it means to hurt over the death of a Son, Jesus Christ. God's love far exceeds any human love, and so if to love deeply means to hurt deeply in times of loss, then God who loves *perfectly* must have known the greatest pangs of loss and sorrow ever felt. This same Father, the God of all mercy and comfort, is alongside us in our trials, hurting along with us, mingling His tears with our own.

The pulse of pain

I suppose we could not find any more real pulse of mankind than the pulse of *pain*. The Word of God throbs with the pulsation of human pain. The words of David: "Many are the trials of the righteous." Job: "Man's days are short-lived and full of turmoil." Jesus: "In this world you shall have tribulation." Paul: "No one should be unsettled by these trials for you know quite well that we were destined for them." Peter: "Do not think it strange concerning the fiery trial which is to try you."

Trials are inescapable. In this life, we will encounter hurts and trials that we will not be able to change. We're just going to have to allow them to *change us.* In times of trial God has our undivided attention. We are aware of God and of our own limitations and powerlessness. But the question is: Are we teachable? Are we attentive to the way He wants to touch us, to the lesson He wants to show us? Trials call us to make a response to God.

There's a choice we have to make: We can decide to cooperate with God in our trial and seek His healing—if not a healing of the trial itself, then at least a healing of our attitude and emotions and character. *Or* we can choose bitterness, resentment, and self-pity.

Do you really want to be healed? When I'm counseling others or facing a rocky time in my own life, I am often reminded of the way Jesus penetrated one man's self-pity with this question. The story is found in John 5. Picture the scene with me:

A man lay by a large public pool. Helpless and paralyzed, he had been an invalid for thirty-eight years. He was one of scores of blind or crippled people gathered around this pool because of a local legend that an angel periodically came down, stirred the water, and imparted healing power to the pool. This man was waiting, passively and self-pityingly, without hope, without expectation.

A shadow fell across the paralyzed man where he lay. He looked up and saw that a man stood over him, piercing him with His gaze. "What do you want with me?" asked the paralyzed man.

The man eyed him levelly, "Do you want to be healed?"

At first glance, this might seem an astoundingly insensitive question. Who would be so cruel as to go up to an invalid and ask, "Do you want to be healed?" But in the original language of this Scripture passage, this is a much more penetrating question than that. What Jesus really asked this man was, "Do you *will* to be healed? Do you *choose* to be healed? Are you actively *committed* to the process of your own healing?" It was a question of the man's commitment to becoming whole.

This same question confronts you and me today. It's a question I raise all the time in my counseling with people who are struggling with deep depression, with self-pity, with a low sense of self-worth, with conflict in their marriage or other relationships: Are you actively *choosing* to have healing and maturity come forth in your life? Or do you just want my approval for your actions? Or do you just want someone to sympathize with all your woes?

I believe the reason Jesus asked this question of the paralyzed man was that He knew this man was filled with a blame mentality. When Jesus asked him, "Do you choose to be healed?" the man replied not with an answer but with an excuse: "No one will help me into the pool—and when I try to get in myself, someone else pushes ahead of me." But Jesus wasn't interested in this man's excuses.

The blame game is the oldest one in the world. In Genesis 3, immediately after the first sin in Eden, God confronted Adam with his sin. And Adam's reply was a masterpiece of blamesmanship: "The woman *you* put here with me—*she* gave me some fruit from the tree, and I ate it." In one finely tuned excuse, Adam managed to shift the blame two ways—onto Eve, who gave him the fruit, and onto God, who gave him Eve.

You may not have caused the trial you are experiencing. In fact, the circumstances of your trial may be completely unfair. But just as God wasn't interested in the excuses of Adam, just as Jesus wasn't interested in the excuses of the paralytic, neither is He interested in our excuses today. There was nothing fair or just about a man spending thirty-eight years of his life in paralysis and neglect—yet Jesus didn't ask him, "How has life been treating you?" but rather "Do you want to be healed?"

God is asking you and me the same question today. And if our answer is "Yes, Lord, I *choose* to be healed according to your will," then the next words He speaks to us are like those Jesus spoke to the paralyzed man by the pool. "Get up!" He tells us. "Quit making excuses! Make a *decision* to become whole! Get up out of that trough of self-pity and *start walking!*"

The cost

Do you want to be healed? If your answer is a bold, honest, courageous *Yes,* then here is how you must begin: Don't blame others anymore. Don't blame circumstances. Don't blame God. Get rid of your excuses. Commit yourself to doing whatever is necessary in partnership with God to find His chosen form of healing in your life. *Shoulder your responsibility for becoming whole.*

You may say, "I can't do that. It's going to hurt too much." Yes, there's *pain* involved in the process of gaining growth and wholeness. That's why so many of us shrink from that process. We would rather live with our brokenness, our neurosis, our emotional, spiritual, or relational disease than to *deal* with it decisively and courageously. We endure the throbbing ache of our disease because we fear the sharp, surgical touch of the Great Physician's healing scalpel. And so we *choose* to be tragically less than God wants us to be!

So this is *The Healing Choice* for all the hurts and trials of life: "Do you *truly* want to be healed?" To say "Yes" to this question will mean pain—the pain of honest self-appraisal and confession, the pain of taking responsibility for our own lives. To say, "Yes, I *choose* to be healed," is going to be costly.

But to say "No" will cost us even more.

1

Healing the Hurt
of Discouragement

There can be no rainbow without a cloud and a storm.

—J. H. Vincent

We are pressed on every side by troubles, but not crushed and broken. We are perplexed because we don't know why things happen as they do, but we don't give up and quit. We are hunted down, but God never abandons us. We get knocked down, but we get up again and keep going.

—2 Corinthians 4:8–9 (LB)

My friend John Huffman, the pastor of St. Andrew's Presbyterian Church in Newport Beach, California, recently shared a story with me that was told him by his long-time friend, Bertha Spafford Vester. Mrs. Vester, who passed away a number of years ago, was the daughter of a wealthy Chicago businessman named Horatio Spafford, and the story she told my friend John was one that took place in her family before she was born.

In late 1873, Horatio Spafford saw his wife, Anna, and their four children aboard the ocean liner *Ville du Havre,* bound from New York to France. Spafford had some business affairs to conclude in the States before he could rejoin his family in Europe. The journey of the *Ville du Havre* proceeded smoothly until sometime after midnight on November 22, when the vessel was rammed broadside by another vessel, the *Lochearn.*

As the wounded *Ville du Havre* settled heavily into the midnight sea, violently rushing waters separated Mrs. Spafford from the three oldest children. She still clutched her youngest child, little Tannetta, as the swirling water swept her into the cold Atlantic. Suddenly, the child was torn from her grasp. Mrs. Spafford frantically sought her only remaining child in the darkness, caught the hem of her gown for a moment, then lost it. She fell unconscious and was later pulled from the water by sailors from the *Lochearn.* Her four children were drowned.

A few days later, Horatio Spafford received a telegram stating that his wife had been saved from the sinking of the *Ville du Havre,* but all four of his children had been lost at sea. Spafford fell into an unrelievable gloom. In New York, he boarded a ship for Europe to join his wife. At a certain point in the voyage, the captain of the ship announced that they were passing the site of the wreck of the *Ville du Havre.* Spafford stood at the rail and peered into the depths of the sea that had shipwrecked his family and swallowed his four children. Then he returned to his cabin and began composing the opening lines of one of the most moving hymns ever written:

> When peace, like a river, attendeth my way,
> When sorrows like sea billows roll,
> Whatever my lot, Thou has taught me to say,
> It is well, it is well with my soul.

Spafford well knew the meaning of the words "sorrows like sea billows." Yet burdened as he was with depression and grief, he was able to find a kind of inner peace. He was learning to say, even in the depths of his discouragement, "It is well with my soul."

Shipwrecked!

The hurt of discouragement takes varied forms in different lives: The estrangement of friends, parents, or children. The ruin of one's reputation. Financial failure. A failed marriage or a love relationship that has grown cold. Inability to build good habits or to break bad ones. Stress at work or in the home.

Whatever form your trial of discouragement takes, it almost always involves a sense that life has let you down. It's the feeling described in the motion picture *The Natural* when the story's aging baseball player, Roy Hobbs (played by Robert Redford), looks back on his life and grimly observes, "Life hasn't turned out the way I thought it would." It hurts to go on, and you feel defeated and worn down. You had set out in one direction, but the storms of life have arisen and tossed you the other way. Now you feel you've been beached on an obscure island, far from the course you charted for yourself.

The apostle Paul knew that feeling. The closing chapters of the Book of Acts tell us that Paul was determined to take the gospel of Jesus Christ to the very pinnacle of the Roman empire, the city of Rome—even if it meant going as a prisoner in chains. Confined in Roman custody, Paul was placed on a ship with other prisoners, bound for Rome. But along the way, hurricane winds rose up, driving their ship relentlessly across the angry Mediterranean. After two weeks of being tossed about by the storm, most of those on board despaired of ever being saved. Finally the ship ran aground and broke apart, spilling Paul and his 275 shipmates onto a cold and windy beach on the island of Malta.

As I've considered this story, I've wondered what was going through Paul's mind as he pulled himself out of the surf and dropped in exhaustion onto the beach. His plans, his timetable had been dashed to pieces. Now he was drenched, cold, hungry—and he had a choice to make: he could either yield to the discouragement and defeat of this catastrophe, or he could make the healing choice, the choice to become God's man for the crisis.

Acts 27 records the decision Paul made. He saw that there was a vacuum of leadership, so he *emerged* in leadership. He gave encouragement to his 275 discouraged fellow-castaways. He told them to take courage because God was with them. He urged them to take nourishment, and then he gave thanks to God, broke bread, and ate it. His shipmates began to follow his lead, drawing encouragement from his example. In the midst of discouraging circumstances, Paul refused to be defeated. Rather, he made the choice to be an encourager to the discouraged, an example to those in despair.

Paul knew how it felt to be shipwrecked, and perhaps you know the feeling too. In your career, your ministry, your family, or your schoolwork, you have certain goals. And for a long time you believed God was drawing you toward those goals. But you've fallen into discouraging circumstances. You feel as though God has led you to a dead end. You're confused about His will and discouraged about your life. You feel ship-wrecked.

I've known that feeling myself. In my own life and in the lives of others, I've noticed a tendency which I believe may be at the root of much of our discouragement: We sense that God is calling us to some new adventure, and then *we* decide how we're going to get there, how long it's going to take, and what route we're going to travel. But somewhere along the way, it dawns on us that God's timetable doesn't coincide with ours. His schedule for us includes some layovers, some setbacks, some storms, some things we never anticipated. The inevitable result is discouragement, and we even begin to doubt God's plan and His love for us.

But God *does* love us and He *does* have a plan for our lives. Why, then, does His plan often permit us to undergo trials of discouragement? I believe one of the principal reasons God allows us to be tried is that He wants us to learn to have *His perspective* on both the good times and hard times of our lives. As Peter Marshall once wrote, "It is a fact of Christian experience that life is a series of troughs and peaks. In His effort to get permanent possession of a soul, God relies on the troughs more than the peaks. And some of His special favorites have gone through longer and deeper troughs than anyone else." This is the same truth expressed by David in Psalm 119:71—"It was good for me to be afflicted so that I might learn your decrees." We learn about God and His truth through the discouraging times of our lives.

Now, you may feel you don't even *want* God's perspective. All you really want is for your discouraging circumstances to go away. That's understandable; when we've been deeply hurt, we all want an anesthetic much more than we want a lengthy process of healing. Yet we have to acknowledge that when we find ourselves powerless to alter our circumstances, we're going to have to alter our *response* to those circum-stances—and that means we're going to have to find God's perspective for our discouragement.

In my own trials of discouragement I often recall the words of F. B. Meyer: "If I'm told I am to take a hard and dangerous journey, every jolt along the way will remind me I'm on the right path." Trials, perils, setbacks, and delays may discourage us—but viewed correctly, from God's perspective, these discouraging circumstances are actually the very reminders that we are on the *right* path, the hard path of following Jesus. That's the Christian life. It's your life, it's my life, and it was Paul's life too.

Paul looked discouragement squarely in the face—and then he made a choice to be God's man for the crisis. That's a choice we can all make, no matter what our circumstances may be. We can always make the healing choice to be God's person in a crisis of discouragement. Like Paul, we can acknowledge that God is with us, even in our deep discouragement, and He is still working out His plan in our lives. That's the bottom-line promise that runs throughout all of Scripture: God is with us. Psalm 23:4—"I will fear no evil, for you are with me." Jeremiah 1:8—"Do not be afraid . . . for I am with you." Matthew 28:20—"Surely I will be with you always, to the very end of the age."

Whatever our circumstances, God is with us. God was with John Gunther in the suffering and death of his little son, Johnny. In his book *Death Be Not Proud,* Gunther writes,

During Johnny's long illness I prayed continually to God. Naturally, God was always there. He sat beside us during the doctor's consultation, as we waited the long vigils outside the operating room, as we rejoiced in the miracle of a brief recovery, as we agonized when hope ebbed away and the doctors confessed there was no longer anything they could do. They were helpless and we were helpless. But God in His infinite wisdom and mercy was standing by us.[1]

That's what the presence of God is like amid our sorrows, our disappointments, our discouragements: He cries with us and He hurts with us. In the presence of the God of all comfort there is encouragement for all our discouraging circumstances. And we can then take that encouragement and pass it on to others in the same way—by offering our presence to those who hurt, crying with them, hurting with them, being with them just as God is with us.

The apostle Paul once wrote that God comforts and encourages us so that we are enabled to "comfort those in any trouble with the comfort we ourselves have received from God" (2

Cor. 1:4). But do any of us ever really feel *adequate* to comfort someone else during their trial of grief or discouragement? We think, *I don't know what to do! I don't know what to say!* So all too often our response to someone else who is going through a period of discouragement is to do nothing and to say nothing.

Yet there's a very simple and effective ministry of comforting others that *everyone* can practice—a ministry of *simple presence* coupled with *practical encouragement.* You don't have to be able to deliver a comforting sermon or quote passages of Scripture. In fact, usually the most helpful thing you can do for a down-and-out friend is to simply say, "I want to spend some time with you. Would you like to go out for lunch?" It sounds too easy, but it's absolutely true: the most comforting thing you can do for a discouraged person is to offer your presence and some practical, everyday encouragement—encouragement such as:

"Have you been getting any sleep? Why don't you just go home early tonight and get eight solid hours of sleep?"

Or, "Could we just take your kids tonight? We know you've been going through a lot lately. Why don't you and your spouse go see a movie or just spend the evening alone together?"

Or, "You know, I'm a pretty good listener. I'd be glad to just stop by if you need somebody to talk to."

That's called *practical encouragement.* That's the kind of encouragement Paul gave to his discouraged shipmates after they had been storm-tossed for two weeks. "For the last fourteen days, you have been in constant suspense and have gone without food," he says in Acts 27:33–34. "I urge you to take some food. You need it to survive." Then he set an example, giving thanks for the little bread they had, breaking it, and eating it with them. A few hours later, their ship ran aground, and all hands were saved, perhaps in part because they had been strengthened by the practical encouragement of the apostle Paul.

Marie Rothenberg, in her book *David,* describes the ordeal of her six-year-old son David, whose father intentionally left him in a burning motel room in southern California in 1983.[2] Though he received third-degree burns over 90 percent of his body, David survived.

During the first few days of David's hospitalization, while

Marie was facing the agony and discouragement of watching her little boy suffer and struggle to live, she was approached by a Christian couple, Ken and Judy Curtis. Ken himself had discovered the presence and comfort of God during his recovery from an industrial accident in which he had been severely burned. Now he and his wife offered that same presence and practical encouragement to Marie, inviting her to stay in their home so she could be near the hospital where David was being treated.

Late one night, Marie returned to the Curtis home, angry and crying. Ken and Judy met her in the kitchen. "What happened?" they asked her. "Is Davie okay?"

"His ear fell off," Marie answered, "and I had to be the one who discovered it."

How did Ken and Judy Curtis respond? Ken offered her a chair: *practical encouragement*. Judy poured her a cup of tea: *practical encouragement*. Ken took her hand, offering no words, just a touch: *practical encouragement*. Judy prayed for her, simply and briefly: *practical encouragement*. And in her book Marie describes her response to the presence and practical encouragement of her friends, Ken and Judy: "As Judy prayed, I felt relieved . . . and I was grateful for Ken and Judy, who waited through the night to comfort me." [3]

When someone you know is feeling defeated, discouraged, depressed, and you don't have any words of comfort to offer, there is still something you can do to bring comfort and encouragement. You don't have to quote Scripture. You don't have to explain why God allows trials in our lives. All you need to do, and perhaps all you *can* do, is simply to offer down-to-earth, practical encouragement—a word of support, a touch, a brief prayer, a cup of tea, simple presence.

Why am I shipwrecked?

Anyone who has ever had to endure trials of deep discouragement would probably like to ask God some questions, such as, "Why does it seem there is so much trouble in the Christian life? Why do committed Christians so often find themselves disheartened, discouraged, and shipwrecked?" Let me suggest a few possible answers—partial answers, even just *glimpses* into the answers—which may help you come to a place of inner peace about your discouraging circumstances.

First of all, I'm convinced that one of the principal reasons we encounter trials of discouragement is because of the influence of Satan in this fallen world. The apostle Paul recorded several occasions in which he experienced the active opposition of Satan to his plans and dreams. For example, in 1 Thessalonians 2:18 he writes, "we wanted to come to you . . . but Satan stopped us." Paul was a man who knew the power of the resurrected Christ to change lives, and Satan continually sought to neutralize his effectiveness.

How should we respond to satanic attempts to discourage and deter us? The apostle John gives us the key: ". . . the one who is in you is greater than the one who is in the world" (1 John 4:4). God in us is greater than the evil god of this world. We will face hindrances and opposition, yet we can and will overcome all these evils because God is in us and with us. He is greater than our trials, greater than our discouragement—and the knowledge of His presence strengthens us to stand firm in the faith.

A second possible reason God allows trials of discouragement in our lives is He wants us to be involved in the lives of others. Whether we are aware of it or not, we continually influence those around us, either for good or ill—and it's in the storms of life that our influence on others is distilled and concentrated. People look to our example and watch how we respond under pressure. The choices we make when we are hurting and discouraged—including our choice of *attitude*—will have a profound impact on friends and loved ones, fellow Christians and non-Christians, and most of all on our families.

Paul made the healing choice to be a positive, encouraging influence on those who were shipwrecked with him. He took his crisis and turned it into an opportunity for witness and ministry to others. Instead of cursing his bad luck, he led, he prayed, and he exhorted. In his trial of discouragement, Paul made the choice to offer himself as God's channel of blessing and healing to others. You and I can make this same choice as we face our discouraging circumstances.

After her husband and four other missionaries were murdered by Auca Indians in Ecuador, Elisabeth Elliot made a decision to bring good out of a seemingly senseless tragedy. Courageously she chose to offer her trial of grief and discouragement to God so that He could transform it into ministry to others. After many weeks in prayer, she sensed that God was leading her to go to the Aucas who had killed her husband, Jim Elliot, and carry on his work among them.

Months later, Elisabeth Elliot stood in the Auca village which had been her husband's objective, sharing the gospel with the same men who had murdered the five missionaries. Touched by her forgiveness and love, these men gave their hearts to Jesus Christ and were later baptized in the river where the slaughter had taken place. Next, the Aucas themselves baptized the children of Jim Elliot and the other slain missionaries. That day, the waters that had once flowed with the blood of martyrs became a river of healing and forgiveness.

But the story doesn't end there. The Auca Christians were so transformed by the forgiveness and love that had been modeled toward them that they decided to go to an enemy tribe downstream and tell them of the love of Jesus. They set off into danger—armed only with the gospel of peace.

The Aucas arrived at the encampment of the other tribe and were met by fierce warriors armed with arrows and spears. The Auca Christians offered no resistance, only love and forgiveness. One of them, named Tona, stood in his boat saying over and over to his enemies, "I forgive you! I forgive you! I am dying for your benefit!" Those were his last words before he was slain.

But even this is not the end of the story. This fierce downriver tribe, like the Aucas before them, ultimately yielded to the forgiving love of Christ. On and on, the gospel spread through this remote region of Ecuador, just as the gospel has spread throughout Christian history. God uses people like you and me, even in our most painful and discouraging circumstances, to influence others and work out His plan. We are to demonstrate to a watching world what Christian men and women are really like away from the safety of the harbor.

Another possible reason God allows trials of discouragement in our lives is that He wants to make us more mature, more like Christ. As Paul tells us in Romans 8:28–29, God works "in all things"—even our trials and discouraging circumstances—so that we might "be conformed to the likeness of his Son." He is building Christlike maturity into our character.

You may wonder, "Will I ever get to a place in life where

it's all smooth sailing, and God won't have to allow these trials in my life anymore?" Probably not. Trials and discouragements will always be with us. Look at Paul: Though he was approaching the end of his life and was full of faith, courage, and character, God allowed him to be shipwrecked. Why? Because Paul still had some lessons to learn about Christian maturity. So do we.

Daniel Poling, the former editor of *The Christian Herald,* had only one son. During World War II, Poling and his wife committed their son to God's care when he went to the South Pacific as a chaplain. The Polings and their son had a strong bond between them, and they exchanged letters often. In one of her letters to her son, Mrs. Poling wrote, "Son, I pray every day for your safety."

One day the Polings received a letter from their son which read in part, "Mom, don't just pray for my safety. Pray for my maturity." And that was the last letter the Polings received from him before he was killed in action.

What do we pray for in our own prayer life? Yes, we pray for safety—but do we also pray for maturity? Do we only pray for a painless life—or do we pray even more for a *productive* life? God's goal for our lives is *Christlikeness*—conformity to the character of Jesus Christ—and He often uses stormy trials and shipwrecks to achieve His plan in us.

We know that God's strength is often perfected in our lives when we are at our weakest. In 2 Corinthians 12, Paul tells how he prayed repeatedly that God would remove from him a troubling physical affliction, a "thorn in the flesh." God answered Paul's prayers, "My grace is sufficient for you, for my power is made perfect in weakness." Many of us would be discouraged and tempted to give up in the face of a "No" answer to our prayers—but Paul made the healing choice to respond, "I delight in weaknesses, in insults, in hardships, in persecutions, in difficulties. For when I am weak, then I am strong."

Ultimately, as we are trying to understand why God allows trials of discouragement in our lives, we have to acknowledge that we will never fully know all the reasons. That's hard for many of us to accept. We feel that God should have given us those answers in the Bible, but what the Bible tells us is that "the secret things belong to the Lord our God" (Deut.

29:29). God is greater than our understanding, and in Him there are deep mysteries we are unable to penetrate in our lifetime.

During the time he was going through treatments for Hodgkin's disease, my friend Gid Adkisson told me, "I don't know what lessons I've learned from this, but I know God is with me and He is sovereign." Though lacking all the answers for his discouraging circumstances, Gid was still able to trust in God. He experienced the presence of God and received practical encouragement from many of his Christian friends—but there were mysteries and questions that would have to go unanswered, and he accepted that by faith. He was living by the truth of 1 Corinthians 13:12—"Now we see but a poor reflection; then we shall see face to face. Now I know in part; then I shall know fully, even as I am fully known."

Someone believes in you

Some time ago, my friend Bruce Larson was vacationing in the Bahamas. One day as he was walking along the beach, he saw a crowd gathered on a pier. He went closer to investigate and found the focus of attention to be a young man preparing for a solo around-the-world journey in a homemade sailboat. All of those who crowded around the pier were trying to discourage the ambitious young sailor:

"The sun will broil the skin right off of you!"

"You'll run out of drinking water!"

"That little boat will never make it!"

The boat pushed away from the pier and began moving out across the blue Caribbean waters, followed by jeers and ridicule from the shore. Bruce was suddenly seized by an irresistible impulse to offer some encouragement to the young man, so he began running along the pier, waving his arms and shouting, "Bon voyage! We're with you! We believe in you! You can do it!" The young man smiled and waved back at Bruce, then continued on until he was out of sight over the horizon.

Like that young man in his frail boat, we're on a journey through life. There may be storms and delays ahead. There may even be a shipwreck in our future. Sometimes we feel there are more people waiting for us to fail than there are people cheering us on. We need to know someone is pulling for us, believing in us. The young voyager in the tiny sailboat had only one supporter the day he set sail—but he eventually made it completely around the globe.

Where are you on your voyage today?

Even though you may feel as though you're ditched on an obscure beach, God has promised to be with you. He's piloting you to a safe and secure harbor. Whatever your storm or shipwreck right now, God is pulling for you, cheering you on, and He wants to give you His healing for your hurt, His strength for your weakness, and His courage for your discouragement.

2

Healing the Hurt of Illness

Healing in Scripture does not refer to becoming as you were; it is becoming what you should be.
—Charles Farr

Heal me, O Lord, and I will be healed; save me and I will be saved, for you are the one I praise.
—Jeremiah 17:14

When Richard, a close friend of mine, was diagnosed as having a terminal illness, he and his family began to pray to God for healing. According to the medical literature, the diagnosis was practically a death sentence. As his condition began to worsen, Richard and his family began to seek out the help of several of the most famous faith healers in the country. Many of them promised without qualification, "Jesus wants you to be healed"—in effect, an unconditional guarantee that Richard would be delivered from his disease.

It was just a short time ago that Richard died at the age of thirty-two. Until just a few days before his death, Richard and his family were certain that God was going to physically heal him. But God *didn't* heal him—at least not in the way they sought. Richard's faith ran deep, and he made the hard adjustment from believing God was going to deliver him from his illness to the painful truth: the only way out of this illness was through the door of Death itself.

Shortly before Richard's memorial service, I was talking and praying with his father and his young widow. When the subject of the inscription on Richard's headstone came up, his father suggested a few lines from Scripture. "No!" Richard's grieving wife interrupted, "How can we put a Scripture verse on Richard's headstone? If we can't believe what the Bible says about healing, then how can we believe any of it?"

If you had been me, how would you have responded? Prominent faith healers had given Richard and his wife false assurances about healing, and the shattering of those illusions shook her faith and deepened her grief. Miraculously, her faith survived. She has accepted God's will for Richard, and says that his being at home with the Lord is "the ultimate healing." She continues to work through her questions toward deeper trust in God. But how many people have actually had their faith completely broken by a misunderstanding of God's healing for the hurt of illness?

A few years ago, Carol, a young woman in the Midwest, became a Christian following an accident which left her a paraplegic. From her wheelchair she wrote:

> Someone told me just after I became a Christian that God would heal me. This seemed too good to be true. I didn't know if I dared believe it. But I began to hope, and then to believe. Day after day, I prayed to be healed, but I remained a paraplegic.
>
> I began to realize that God had the power to heal me, but that He wasn't going to heal me. I became increasingly bitter. I would read about healing in the Bible, then accuse God of holding the promise of healing before me like a piece of meat before a starving dog. He taunted me by showing me the potential, but never quite allowing me to reach it. Then I would feel guilty because I know the Bible says God is a loving God and answerable to no one.
>
> My conflict deepened, and my mental state became precarious. I've considered suicide many times. Over and over I have asked God why He refuses to heal me, but I get no reply.

How would you respond to the plea of this physically and spiritually wounded young woman?

Blaming the victim

Many of us feel very confused about the hurt of illness. Where is God when sickness enters our lives or the life of

someone close to us? Do miracles of healing still happen—
or are they just something we read about in the Bible? In
an article in *Christianity Today*, surgeon Paul Brand frankly
assesses the failure of the church to deal realistically and forth-
rightly with these questions:

> God neither protects Christians with a shield of health
> nor provides a quick, dependable solution to all suffering.
> Christians populate hospital wards, asylums, and cancer
> hospices in approximate proportion to the world at large.
> Many Christians who roll in wheelchairs, or awake each
> day to the scarred stumps of amputated limbs, or undergo
> the debility of spreading cancer have prayed for healing.
> Some have attended healing services, felt a sudden rush
> of hope, and kneeled for an anointing of oil; yet still they
> live unhealed. For them, divine healing is the cruelest
> joke of all. At the precise moment when they most need
> support from the church they receive instead a taunting
> accusation that in spiritual as well as physical health they
> do not measure up.[1]

It is one of the most common tragedies in the church today:
a Christian who is already struggling with the hurt of illness
has his suffering compounded by accusation and guilt. "It's
never God's will for Christians to suffer," say some advocates
of divine healing, "so your suffering must either be due to
unconfessed sin in your life or lack of faith to let God heal
you." In effect, the victim is *blamed* for his disease.

In an article she wrote, Kathryn Lindskoog describes the
remarks she has endured during two decades of suffering with
multiple sclerosis (MS), a chronic disease that gradually weak-
ens and paralyzes the body. A few typical examples:

> "You must really like to be sick; you bring so much
> of it on yourself." That from a nearby relative who never
> so much as sent a get-well card.
> "The reason I have perfect health is that I think right;
> nobody gets sick unless he thinks wrong." That from a
> relative who seems to feel insecure about all his good
> luck in life. . . .
> "Dear, if your faith is sincere, tell everyone right now
> that God has healed you completely." That from a friend
> who couldn't wait to report such a claim to her Bible
> study.

"I know just how you feel about being crippled; I had
a bad case of tennis elbow last month." That from one
of the local country club crowd. . . .

"God must cherish you to trust you with this burden."
That from people who would rather die than to be cherished by such a God.

"Your present improvement is just wishful thinking."
That from people who are very rigid about sticking to
current medical orthodoxy.

"I know you fake your limp to try to get attention."
An entirely serious remark from my pastor after a dozen
years of seeing me hobble around our large church com-
plex. That's the one I haven't gotten over yet.[2]

These statements reported by Kathryn Lindskoog may seem
bizarre, but I would affirm that they are not at all unusual.
While my brother Paul was being treated for cancer and following his death, I received many comments from people who
clearly meant well, but who were simply no comfort in that
time of trial. In particular there were two things people said
to me that I found were not at all helpful: "Time heals all
wounds," and "God will use greatly only those He has hurt
deeply."

Some people feel awkward in the presence of a suffering
person and simply feel a need to fill up the silence. Others
genuinely want to offer comfort but don't really know what
to say. My own experience is that often the greatest comfort
is offered in the fewest words. Simple presence, a touch, an
embrace, a brief prayer: these can be the greatest comfort of
all in a trial of illness.

The miracle of prayer

Our deep need in times of illness is to grasp firmly what
His healing really means in our lives. We approach the Great
Physician as unique individuals, and His prescription for your
health and mine will vary according to our individual need.
We may need emotional and spiritual healing even more than
we need bodily health. But what if He chooses to heal us
physically? Does that mean we should be looking for a miracle?

Unfortunately, in our fascination with the miraculous and
the sensational, we often fail to recognize the everyday miracles

God engineers throughout our lives. Properly viewed, *every* recovery from illness or injury is a kind of divine miracle. The human body has been marvelously engineered to protect and repair itself. It contains elaborate, intricate systems for fighting off infection, repairing lacerated tissue, mending broken bones, and repairing diseased organ tissue—and the actual mechanism by which these systems keep us healthy is either incompletely known or totally hidden to medical science.

In an episode of the television series *M*A*S*H*, Army surgeon Hawkeye Pierce (portrayed by Alan Alda) expressed amazement over the self-perpetuating, self-repairing human body. "How does it all work?" he wondered. "I've held a beating heart in my hand. I've poked into kidneys and crocheted them together again. I've pushed air into collapsed lungs like beat-up old pump organs. I've squeezed and probed and prodded my way through hundreds of miles of gut and goo, and I don't know what makes us live! I mean, what keeps us in motion? What keeps the heart beating without anybody rewinding it? Why do the cells reproduce and then re-re-reproduce with such gay abandon? What force brought us together in such fantastic complexity? I've seen a lot of bodies, and it never ceases to amaze me." Or as the Psalmist more succinctly put it, we are "fearfully and wonderfully made."

In *The Road Less Traveled,* Dr. M. Scott Peck observes that the so-called "normal" biological systems that keep us alive and give us our resistance to disease and injury are, in fact, completely *miraculous*. He writes:

> In the ordinary course of things we should be eaten alive by bacteria, consumed by cancer, clogged up by fats and clots, eroded by acids. It is hardly remarkable that we sicken and die; what is truly remarkable is that we don't usually sicken very often and we don't die very quickly. . . . There is a force, the mechanism of which we do not fully understand, that seems to operate routinely in most people to protect and encourage their physical health even under the most adverse conditions.[3]

This dimly understood "force," Peck suggests, is actually God's sustaining *grace* in our lives. God's grace to us, which we so often take for granted, is nothing short of miraculous—or, as one hymnwriter termed it, *amazing;* " 'Tis *grace* hath brought me safe thus far," he wrote—and it's true: God's amazing grace protects us, nurtures us, and heals us in ways that we tend to overlook. Healing, then, is not usually an *event;* rather, it is most often a process. The process of healing takes time—but it is through our time of healing that we gain a greater sense of God's grace and His presence with us.

There is another miraculous dimension to the healing process: the miracle of *prayer.* God gives us immediate access to Himself any time, any place, for any reason. We can call upon the sovereign God of the Universe, and know He has the power to heal—and that gives us hope. That is why Hebrews 4:16 tells us, "Let us then approach the throne of grace with confidence, so that we may receive mercy and find grace to help us in our time of need."

How, then, should we pray for healing?

First, we have to acknowledge that there is no formula, no ritual, no magic word to coax God into healing us according to our will. The sovereignty of God calls us to humility: if He is truly Lord, then it is *His* will that must be done, not our own. Yes, we raise our honest petitions before Him in prayer, and we ask Him to heal—and then we listen for His answer: *Yes.* Or, *No.* Or, *Wait.*

We know that when we pray for healing, we must pray in faith. But we wonder, "How much is *enough* faith?" In Matthew 17:20, Jesus says all we need is "faith as small as a mustard seed." The tiniest particle of faith is sufficient. A distraught father once brought his son to Jesus for healing, and his prayer to Jesus was, "Take pity on us and help us!" Jesus told him that all things are possible to those who believe. At that the father cried, "I *do* believe! Help me overcome my unbelief!" That is a mustard seed prayer, and God has promised to honor that prayer.

Sickness is hard on faith. A crisis of pain can quickly become a trial of doubt. Job was an upright man who walked closely with God, yet his trial of illness pressed his faith right to the wall. This is only natural. If illness is causing you to doubt and cry out to God, don't feel as though you've lost your faith. The mustard seed of your faith is still there, even though hemmed in by pain. God is still at work in your life, answering your prayers.

The Bible gives us a pattern for prayer when we find ourselves in a trial of illness. This is not a formula for manipulating
God, but a means of prayerfully preparing *ourselves*—body,
mind, and soul—to receive God's healing touch in our lives.
God doesn't want to merely remove our symptoms, but to
heal us in a thorough, integrated way. He doesn't just want
to make us feel better; He wants to make us *whole*. So as
I've studied the Scriptures, I've found this biblical pattern for
prayer in times of illness:

1. *Worship.* This is the first and foremost aspect of *all*
prayer. Worship is honest acknowledgment of God's holiness,
power, and complete sovereignty. Worship is not just our duty
toward God; it's our *joy!* As we worship God, we become
aware of His authority over all things, including disease—and
that gives us hope.

2. *Confess and be forgiven.* Prayer is hindered by sin in
the life of the one who prays, so confession and forgiveness
are always a vital part of effective prayer. Since God desires
not just our physical wellness, but our *wholeness* in body,
mind, and spirit, we find a close linkage of healing and forgiveness in the Bible. Thus James 5:15–16 (NASB) says, "The prayer
offered in faith will restore the one who is sick, and the Lord
will raise him up, and if he has committed sins, they will be
forgiven him. Therefore, confess your sins to one another, and
pray for one another, so that you may be healed."

3. *Listen for guidance and wisdom.* As we pray, we seek
to think God's thoughts after Him, not tell Him what to do.
It takes a lot of wisdom to discern God's answer to our prayers
because His answers often differ from our expectations. James
1:5 tells us, "If any of you lacks wisdom, he should ask God,
who gives generously to all without finding fault, and it will
be given to him." Unless we continually seek God's wisdom for our trial of illness, we risk missing the answer he
gives us.

4. *Petition.* We must ask God for healing. This seems obvious—yet we all too often treat prayer as the final act of despera-
tion when all else has failed. The simple truth of James 4:2
is "You do not have, because you do not ask God." In times
of trial, prayer should be our first impulse, not our last resort.
Listen to the prayer of David in Psalm 6:2–3, "Be merciful
to me, Lord, for I am faint! O Lord, heal me, for my bones

are in agony! My soul is in anguish! How long, O Lord, how long?" A time of illness calls us to lay our honest feelings, our pain, and our plea for healing before the throne of God's healing grace.

5. *Request the prayers and anointing of the elders.* "Is any one of you sick?" says James 5:14. "He should call the elders of the church to pray over him and anoint him with oil in the name of the Lord." One way we can demonstrate our desire to make the healing choice for our illness is to take the initiative to call the elders to come and pray for our healing.

Notice, too, that the oil mentioned in James 5:14 was the common, accepted medical treatment for most ills in the first century—not a magical potion. In this passage God calls us to cooperate with the best medical expertise available in order to bring about our healing; the oil is merely a *symbol* of our commitment to seek God's chosen form of healing.

6. *Request the prayers and encouragement of others.* The pain of illness can often cloud our ability to pray effectively to God. But we're not alone in our illness. God has given us Christian brothers and sisters to love us, encourage us, and uphold us with their prayers. As Rev. Charles Farr, pastor of the Church of the Epiphany in Denver, said,

> We often mistakenly assume that faith has to come from the sick. The faith of anyone who is suffering is likely to be diminished. We would never expect a child who is sick to get up, prepare his own food, and nourish himself. Why do we expect hurting people to heal themselves with exemplary faith?
> Remember the story of the paralytic in Scripture? . . . The man's friends took him to the housetop, removed the tiles around the hole where the cooking fire was vented, and with ropes they lowered the man on his pallet into Jesus' presence. Jesus, seeing "*their* faith," not the man's faith, told him to take up his bed and walk.[4]

James 5:16 tells us, "Pray for each other so that you may be healed." It was never intended we suffer our illness alone. We need each other in the body of Christ.

7. *Wait upon God.* When you have prayed, when others have prayed for you, when everything medically possible has been done, then *wait*. Allow God to work. Give Him time

to answer. And be open to His answer—whatever it is. Paul Tillich once wrote that prayer gives us access to "a power that shakes us and turns us, and transforms us and heals us. Surrender to this power is faith." So as we pray for healing, we need to surrender to God, by faith allowing Him to heal as He chooses.

The ultimate form of healing

I believe God always heals—but we have to be open to whatever *form* of healing God chooses to bring into our lives. He may touch us through a sudden miracle or through a lengthy healing process or by giving us His sufficient grace to endure a trial of illness that won't go away.

The ultimate form of healing that every believer faces one day is physical death and bodily resurrection. Paul, in Romans 8:18 and 23, shares his strong assurance, "I consider that our present sufferings are not worth comparing with the glory that will be revealed in us. . . . We ourselves, who have the first-fruits of the Spirit, groan inwardly as we wait eagerly for . . . the redemption of our bodies."

Charles Farr put it this way: "God wants us to be healed even if that means dying well. Health is being at peace with God and at peace with yourself." This is a *biblical* definition of health; it agrees with the witness of Scripture: "Heal me, O Lord, and I will be healed; save me and I will be saved, for you are the one I praise" (Jer. 17:14). And Isaiah 53:5 tells us that Christ suffered and died to purchase our *peace*— peace with God, peace with ourselves—"and by his wounds we are healed." Healed—even in our trials, even in our pain, even in death itself. We can live well and die well, at peace with God, filled with the healing assurance of eternal life.

Can we believe in miracles of healing? I believe the answer to that question is an emphatic *Yes!* I've seen God dramatically heal. My friend Ruth, a woman in her early fifties, was conclusively diagnosed as having an advanced form of cancer that is usually fatal. So Ruth did what any of us would do: she prayed and asked God to give her a miracle of healing.

She followed the admonition of James 5: She first made sure to follow her doctors' advice and was scheduled to begin treatments almost immediately. Then she called me and asked that I call some of the elders of our church to her bedside to pray for her and anoint her. We went to her home that evening, and as I was about to lead in prayer Ruth said, "Ron, I want to be healed, and I know God *can* heal me. But what I really want you to pray for is that God will heal me the way He thinks best. Pray that I have the strength to learn whatever He wants to teach me through this trial."

We honored her wish and prayed for her in the way she asked us to. We anointed her with oil as a symbol of her commitment to seek God's form of healing. A short time later, when Ruth went to the hospital for treatment and tests, the doctors were astonished to find that her cancer had completely disappeared. That was almost ten years ago, and Ruth is alive and well today. But the most important thing about Ruth's story is the demonstration of her faith in God: she humbly submitted herself to God's will for her life—even if the way to freedom from cancer led right through the Grave itself.

David Ireland, in his book *Letters to an Unborn Child,* described the attitude with which he faced his incurable neurological disease:

> I have often asked myself, and have on occasion been asked by others, "Do I believe in faith healing?" I have never taken the matter lightly. On one occasion I asked a former bishop of the Methodist Church to lay his hands on me. Later I attended the service of a nationally known faith healer, not as an observer, but as one open to whatever God might will. In neither case did my failure to undergo a miracle in any way affect me negatively.
>
> Today when I'm asked, "Do you believe God will heal you?" my response is a question, one I have asked myself. "Do I really need to be healed?" It's a genuine question, not a mere defense to avoid the issue. . . . My faith is in the genuineness of God, not in whether He will do this or that to demonstrate His goodness. I don't need acts of benevolence or wondrous words to prove it to me. That's not the nature of my relationship to God.[5]

Which attitude takes more faith: To believe that God is going to miraculously take us out of all our problems and pain or to believe that God can take us *through* our trial? If your faith in God depends on seeing Him perform a miraculous healing in your life, then perhaps your faith needs some stretching.

When the leper came to Jesus for healing in Luke 5, he threw himself humbly to the ground before Jesus and prayed, "Lord, if you are willing, you can make me clean." And this must be our attitude before God as we go to Him in prayer for healing: "Lord, *if you are willing,* please heal me!" God is sovereign, and our prayers to Him must always reflect His absolute sovereignty.

Health—a state of mind?

In his book *The Call to Wholeness: Health As a Spiritual Journey,* physician Kenneth L. Bakken cites research by the American Academy of Family Physicians which shows that "two-thirds of office visits to family doctors are prompted by stress-related symptoms." He explains:

> Stress is known to be a major contributor, either directly or indirectly, to coronary heart disease, cancer, lung ailments, accidental injuries, cirrhosis of the liver and suicide—six of the leading causes of death in the United States. . . . The three most prescribed drugs in this country—Tagamet for peptic ulcers, Inderal for high blood pressure, and Valium for anxiety—offer a sad commentary on the way we have chosen to live as individuals and as a society.[6]

Norman Cousins, former editor of *Saturday Review* and noted author, wrote a book about his encounter with a massive, near-fatal heart attack, *The Healing Heart.* There he writes of the overwhelmingly important role such positive mental and emotional qualities as "hope, faith, love, laughter, and a strong will to live" had to play in his recovery. He concludes:

> A weak body becomes weaker in a mood of total surrender. The mechanisms of repair and rehabilitation that are built into the human system have a natural drive to assert themselves under conditions of illness, but that natural tendency is deferred or deflected by an erosion of the will to live, or by the absence of confidence in one's physician or in one's own ability to play a vital part in the attack on disease.

Obviously, it is absurd to suppose that there is no illness that can't be reversed. But it is also true that under conditions of extreme illness we need all the help we can get. . . . Since the human body tends to move in the direction of its expectations—plus or minus—it is important to know that attitudes of confidence and determination are no less a part of the treatment program than medical science and technology.[7]

In my book *Gold in the Making,* I told about a dear friend of mine, Diane Schmidt, and the battle she was then undergoing with cancer.[8] When the doctor first informed Diane of the diagnosis of her disease, she replied, "I want you to know, first of all, that I'm a Christian. My life is in God's hands, and I know that even if this cancer ends my life, I will live on with Him in eternity."

The doctor then listed for her the various options for treatment, the best of which seemed to be immediate surgery. She said, "That's fine, let's do the surgery." The next day, Diane was in surgery for ten hours. During that time, I waited with Diane's mother and sister. Finally the doctor came out of the operating room and said, "In all the years I've practiced medicine, I've never seen anyone face cancer with the courage and character Diane has."

Diane came through surgery and recuperation with good humor, trust in God, and a strong will to live. The doctors felt certain they had completely eliminated the cancer from her body. During and after her recovery, Diane was able to use the experience of her own cancer to encourage and minister to others who were afflicted with the disease.

Since *Gold in the Making* was published, doctors again found cancer in Diane's body, and it was spreading rapidly. Again she underwent a series of treatments, but this time the prognosis was very bad. The doctors didn't tell Diane at the time, but they felt she had only a few more months to live at most. In fact, however, she survived almost two more years. Indeed, she did far *more* than survive; she *lived* her life. Until just a short time before her death she remained actively involved in her church, in the athletic pursuits she'd always enjoyed, and in the lives of her friends.

Her doctors can only offer one explanation for the extra,

full years she was able to live: her positive, affirming, *Yes* attitude to life. She trusted God, and refused to give in to resentment or self-pity. She kept her sense of humor. Despite enormous suffering, she maintained a strong will to live, yet she was ready to die. She had peace with God. And all of these factors together enabled her to have a richer, longer life—even through the trial of terminal cancer.

Medical science is becoming increasingly aware that it's not enough to simply treat symptoms. Even in a disease of purely physiological origin, there are powerful mental, emotional, and spiritual factors that must be addressed if there is to be true healing. This truth is at the heart of the holistic approach to healing—an approach that has become something of a media fad packaged in best-selling books, touted on television talk shows, sold as big business. A fair one-line summary of extreme holistic philosophy is, "You're as healthy as you think." It is often as simplistic—and as wrong—as that.

What I'm suggesting here is an approach to health that is truly *whole*-istic. That is, we should deal with illness from the point of view that man is not merely a physical being, but a mental and spiritual being as well. We should not seek to merely cure disease, but to make people *whole*. This doesn't mean (as some holistic advocates suggest) that "health is just a state of mind." We can't forget that a virus is a *physical* organism—and so is a human being. Thus, some of our illnesses have purely physical causes, and all the "good thinking" and "positive attitude" in the world are simply powerless to prevent us from catching some of these diseases.

Kathryn Lindskoog voices concern over some of the excesses of the holistic extremists:

> Much of the insight of holistic medicine rings true because we always knew it. Is it news that we are what we eat, and we are what we think, and worry wears us out? Is it news that people die of broken hearts, that no man is an island, that the whole is more than its parts? Is it news that we are more than machines, that our bodies are the temple of the Holy Spirit, that a merry heart doeth good like medicine? Eternal news, maybe.
>
> The sick side of holistic medicine is that it promotes a blame-the-victim attitude toward people hit by serious disease.[9]

This blame-the-victim attitude usually takes the form of telling the sick person there is some direct connection between his sickness and some *sin* in his life. Certainly from a biblical point of view, *all* sickness and death is the result of original sin. As Romans 5:12 tells us, "Sin entered the world through one man [Adam], and death through sin." Too, there is sometimes a *direct* relationship between personal sin and illness. In Psalm 32, David says that when he allowed his sin to go unrepented and unconfessed, his body wasted away—a biblical expression of the relationship between the spiritual, the emotional, and the physical aspects of our being.

But sometimes there is *no* relationship between personal sins and sickness. There are moral laws operating in our world, which often cause painful consequences to follow sinful actions—but it's not as simple as $2 + 2 = 4$. In this fallen world, evil sometimes goes unpunished and good sometimes goes unrewarded.

Why, then, do we get sick?

Aside from the simple fact that our physical bodies are naturally susceptible to disease or injury, we have to understand that God sometimes chooses to *use* our illness to achieve a greater purpose. In John 9, Jesus and His disciples are passing by a man who has been blind since birth. His disciples ask Him, "Who sinned, this man or his parents, that he was born blind?" Notice the uncaring fatalism of the disciples' question, an attitude which says, "If you're sick, it's because of your sin, or your family's sin. You've gotten what you deserve from God. You'll get no help from us."

But Jesus' reply cuts through the fatalism of the disciples' question; He says that this illness is not due to anyone's sin, but "so that the work of God might be displayed in his life." Sometimes the hurt of illness strikes us so that the work of God might be displayed in our lives, so that He can make us more mature, more Christlike, or so that He can equip us to be wounded healers, able to use our pain to heal the hurts of others.

The scriptural prescription

Is God interested in our physical health? Yes, of course He is. Many of the warnings He gives us in Scripture—warnings which many people think harsh and restrictive, warnings against sexual sin or harboring anger, for example—are really God's guidelines for health. God doesn't want to hurt us. He doesn't desire our pain. In His Word, He gives us a plan for living as happy and healthy a life as possible. As surgeon Paul Brand notes,

> Scientists have verified that positive choices can have a salubrious effect on the physical body. A spirit of gratitude, inner peace, love, hope, happiness, support from friends, joy—these qualities can have far greater effect than any injection I could give. A body that is at peace and surrounded by loving support quite literally heals better. In view of this fact, the Old Testament Levitical laws and the New Testament prescriptions for spiritual health also translate into an accurate formula for physical well-being.
>
> The list of qualities mentioned above bears a striking parallel to the fruit of the Spirit outlined in Galatians: love, joy, peace, patience, kindness, goodness, faithfulness, gentleness, self-control. Such characteristics of growth in the Spirit can have a powerful effect on healing by properly aligning the orientation of mind and body. I am convinced that the Creator designed the mind and body to flourish when under the control of the Spirit.[10]

God *does* care about our physical health—but He cares even *more* about our spiritual health, our maturity, our growth, because these add up to *eternal* health, a quality of wholeness that lasts long after the physical body has fallen to dust. God is sovereign, and I cannot demand that He give me a life of health or comfort or success if that is not His choice. It has taken my whole life to learn that truth—and I'm still learning it.

I have to confess that until a few years ago the sovereignty of God was little more than just another doctrine to me. But I have known a man to whom the sovereignty of God was not just a doctrine, but the passion and obsession of his life—and I want to share with you something of what he taught me.

Two ways to live on

I came to know Rev. Theodore Lyons in early 1983, when he joined the pastoral staff of our church. During that year, he became a close friend, and even a spiritual father to me. At sixty-four, Ted was a wise, generous man with a warm sense of humor and humility. I also came to know him as a man of courage, a man who was battling cancer.

Ted staked his life on the claim of Romans 8:28–29: "And we know that God causes all things to work together for good to those who love God, to those who are called according to his purpose. For whom he foreknew, he also predestined to be conformed to the image of his Son" (NASB). Christlikeness was the goal of Ted's life. He understood that God in His sovereign wisdom could use even the ravages of cancer to accomplish His good.

We talked together of this truth during the final weeks of Ted's life. He was lying in his hospital bed and tears were welling in his eyes as he told me, "I'm just trusting in Romans 8:28 and 29, Ron, and however God wants to work out the details is okay with me." I knew he was telling the truth, but I knew it was a hard truth. I knew he was in terrible pain, and that it hurt him deeply to know he was scheduled very soon to leave his wife, his three children, and his many friends who would remain behind. And yet, despite the pain and grief he felt, there shone through it all an amazing confidence and assurance in his Lord.

Throughout his battle with cancer, Ted used his suffering to discover his identification with Christ. "Ron," he once told me, "this cancer is teaching me just a little bit more about the suffering and humiliation of Christ on the Cross." Through his pain, Ted was becoming more and more like Christ. The process continued day by day throughout his illness, right up until that moment on a sunny autumn morning in 1983 when God called Ted Lyons home to be with Him.

There are two ways that a Christian lives on after death. One way is by living on in eternity with Jesus. The other way is by living on through the lives of those in whom we have invested ourselves—those we've encouraged, affirmed, and built up to be like Christ. Ted lives on in both of these ways. Today, he is healed and free from pain, a joint-heir with Christ in eternity. But he also lives on in me and in many other people he taught and encouraged through his example.

Don't you want to live and die like that? Don't you want

to live on and on, both in eternity and in the lives of others around you?

God doesn't always engineer miraculous physical cures in our lives. He never promised to. This is a hard truth—but it's also a glorious truth, because we know He is able to bring about even *greater* miracles of true healing—healing of the spirit, healing of the soul, healing of others—even through the tough process of our deepest pain.

3

Healing the Hurt of Loss

God mourns with us. He sits down beside us and mingles His tears with ours.

—Theodore Lyons

Just as the sufferings of Christ flow over into our lives, so also through Christ our comfort overflows.

—2 Corinthians 1:5

If you were to walk into my office and look at my desk, you would find (somewhere amid the clutter) a polished rock. It's not a gemstone by any means, yet to me it's very precious. My office is filled with mementos and reminders, and this bright and shiny rock is a reminder of a boy name Corey.

About seven years ago, my wife Shirley and I had the opportunity to go to Austin, Texas, where I spoke during a week of meetings at the church pastored by my friend, Gary Dennis. We stayed with Gary and Sarah Dennis, and during every spare moment I would go outside with their eight-year-old boy, Corey. We talked, laughed, and played ball together. In that short week we built up a great friendship. I remember telling Shirley at the time, "Corey is the greatest little guy! What a joy he must be to his mom and dad."

When it was time for us to go, Corey's tears just rolled down his face. It hurt me to say good-bye to him. At the last moment before we pulled away, Corey dashed into the house. Moments later, he came back outside with a small polished rock in his hands. "Oh, that's Corey's favorite rock!" said Sarah, as Corey placed his precious gift in my hands—the polished rock I keep on my desk to this day.

One Friday night a few years ago, we received word that Corey Dennis had died of cancer at the tender age of eleven.

All human life is short. It hangs by a slender thread. The loss of a loved one may come at any time. And when it comes, the trial of loss stabs us deeply. Loss touches our lives in many ways. It may come through the death of a loved one, but the pain of loss often comes to us in other ways as well.

In 1963, Brian Sternberg was named Outstanding Athlete of the Year by several sports periodicals. He held the world record for the pole vault at 16′ 8″. As part of the intense training he was undergoing for a dual track and field competition between the United States and the Soviet Union, Brian was working out on a trampoline. A split-second's misjudgment brought him down the wrong way, injuring his spine. From that instant on, Brian has been paralyzed from the neck down.

Brian continues to live with almost intolerable pain every day of his life. At a Fellowship of Christian Athletes conference a few years ago, I saw a crowd of young athletes weep openly as they listened to the testimony of Brian Sternberg, speaking from his wheelchair about the love of Jesus Christ that he has experienced—even through the tragedy of his loss of health.

Brian once told me that his favorite passage of Scripture was Philippians 3:7–8—"Whatever was to my profit I now consider loss for the sake of Christ. What is more, I consider everything a loss compared to the surpassing greatness of knowing Christ Jesus my Lord, for whose sake I have lost all things. I consider them rubbish, that I may gain Christ." As a deeply committed and competitive athlete, Brian prized his health and vitality above almost everything else in life. He hates his paralysis. He doesn't understand why God would allow such a trial of loss in his life. Yet, compared with the surpassing greatness of knowing Christ, Brian Sternberg is learning to write off everything he once had, including his health, as a *loss*.

Some of us experience the hurt of loss in the area of our finances and material security. Mr. Foster was a friend of mine, an executive of a major corporation in the Midwest. He was a respected and successful family man. But as he ascended the corporate ladder, he began to learn more and more about the way his company operated, with unethical and often illegal practices toward employees, clients, and the government.

Because Mr. Foster sought to live his entire life under the lordship of Jesus Christ, he realized he could not be a part of the highly placed corruption in his company, nor could he remain silent about what was happening around him. So he began to challenge those illicit practices—and it was made clear that he would have to "play ball" or face removal. So Mr. Foster resigned. He lost his job, his handsome salary and benefits, his pension, and his financial security during a time when jobs were hard to come by. But in the midst of this deep loss, he had maintained his integrity.

John White, in his book *The Golden Cow,* observes that Jesus calls all of His followers to this same kind of self-sacrificing integrity. He explains:

> To give up everything for Christ consists of an *internal* relinquishment of all our possessions. . . . All of us are to have a contract with Christ that whenever obedience to Him means sacrifice of any degree, even to losing everything we have or to facing prison and death, then obedience is what matters. The obedience will be all the easier if we daily relinquish to Him all we possess.
>
> All Christians are called to be disciples. All Christians at any time, under any circumstances, are to be ready for new sets of instructions from headquarters which might mean total material loss.[1]

Some of us face loss in the form of lost hopes and dreams. This was the hurt of loss suffered by George Matheson, a young man living in the mid-1800s. Afflicted by an incurable disorder that gradually robbed him of his sight, Matheson found himself increasingly avoided by family and friends. Finally, there was only one person who stood by him: his fiancée.

But as the day of their wedding grew closer, she began to be less affectionate, less spontaneous with Matheson. He knew something was troubling her, so he asked her what was wrong. At first she said nothing, then, with her own beautiful eyes averted from his gradually failing eyes, she blurted, "I'm sorry. I just can't face a future of caring for a blind man." With that, she left him—forever.

George Matheson had lost his sight, his friends, his family, and the love of the only woman he ever cared for. All his

plans and dreams for the future were dashed. And it was in
the depths of this terrible loss that Matheson sat down at
his desk and wrote the lines of that great hymn,

O Love that will not let me go,
  I rest my weary soul in Thee;
I give Thee back the life I owe,
  That in Thine ocean depths its flow
May richer, fuller be.

Because the hurt of loss can come into our lives in so many
ways, I want to broaden the definition of loss beyond the experience of losing a loved one. We experience the pain of loss
when friends and family members move to a distant city. We
feel loss when we reach a realization that some lifelong goal
or ambition will never be fulfilled. We know the hurt of loss
as we grow older and our health and vitality begin to wane.
We suffer a loss as deep and painful as the death of a loved
one when our marriage begins to break down.

Holding on—loosely

"Life is like an onion," wrote Carl Sandburg. "You peel
it off one layer at a time, and sometimes you weep." That's
a great truth: in life, sometimes you weep. The problem is,
deep down, most of us really don't believe it. We tend to see
life as an idealized journey of our own making, without any
hills or unexpected turns. We plan for the future and we build
up unrealistic expectations of what life should be like. Deep
down, we all expect to keep our health, our loved ones, and
our possessions throughout our lives.

But loss is inevitable in life. We don't anticipate that fact;
we don't even want to think about it. We fool ourselves into
believing we have every right to expect a life without loss—
and so we begin to take life and health and loved ones for
granted.

Before my brother Paul became ill, I never gave much
thought to the possibility I might lose him so soon. The urgency
of the diagnosis of cancer focused and concentrated my mind
on my relationship with Paul, and indeed on all my relationships with family and friends. Since then, every meal I

take with my family is like a sacrament to me, a holy meal. But I often wonder, why did it take having to face the loss of my brother before I stopped taking him for granted, before those daily moments with my family became so precious?

I don't ever want to take life and the ones I love for granted. I don't ever want to live my life as if it's just another day. I want to keep gaining more of God's perspective on the *gift* of life we have as we share it with the ones we love.

But there's a paradox here. For while we need to gain a deeper appreciation of God's gifts to us, He never intended for us to clutch them to ourselves. All God's gifts are for us to enjoy and to care for while we have them—but a time will come when God will have them back.

Corrie ten Boom was fond of saying, "I have learned to hold on to everything loosely." That has been hard for me in the loss of my brother, and in the loss of my father and so many close friends over the years. It's not easy for me to hold loosely the ones I love deeply, and I'm certain it's not easy for you either. But I am slowly learning that the hurt of loss calls us to a response: Will we simply resent our loss as a great unfairness—or will we be open to God's sustaining grace so that we can *grow* through the hurt of loss?

God's truth for our lives often springs at us unbidden, delivered in a package we are unwilling to receive. It's only natural to want to reject the *pain* of loss, but by God's grace we can make the healing choice to accept the *lessons* of loss. As Benjamin Franklin said, "Those things that hurt, instruct." Similarly, Paul in Romans 5 tells us, "Suffering produces perseverance; perseverance, character; and character, hope." As followers of Christ, we want to gain all the lessons and growth to be found in our trial of loss—or else we will have suffered for nothing.

C. S. Lewis understood very well the hurt of loss. Almost every book he wrote is a pleasure to read, but there is one book by C. S. Lewis that is filled with pain and questioning. In *A Grief Observed*, Lewis bluntly recorded his feelings of anguish over the loss of his wife to cancer. "Her absence is like the sky," he wrote, "spread over everything." [2] And, "Where is God? . . . Go to Him when your need is desperate, when all other help is vain, and what do you find? A door slammed in your face, and a sound of bolting and double bolting on the inside. After that, silence." [3] For Lewis, it was many months before the silence ended and he was able to hear God's voice again.

Let's not kid ourselves: the hurt of loss is universal. While the Christian has the blessed assurance of God's presence in times of loss, the *pain* of loss afflicts Christians and non-Christians alike. If we're honest, we have to confess that our times of loss are often times of questioning, of anger, as we demand of God, *Why?* C. S. Lewis recorded all these emotions and painful questions in *A Grief Observed*—yet he ultimately came to a place of acceptance of his loss. So may you and I.

Martin Luther was a great man of faith: the founder of the Protestant Reformation, the author of the powerful hymn "A Mighty Fortress Is Our God." Yet when Luther's beautiful fourteen-year-old daughter Magdalena died, Luther was torn by a despairing sense of loss. Almost as troubling to Luther as his grief was the fact that he was unable to set aside the normal human reaction to loss. To him, the loss of a daughter became a crisis of faith. "How strange it is to know that Magdalena is at peace, and all is well," he said, "and yet to be so sorrowful!"

Luther went through many long months of depression, questioning, and inner struggle. He wrestled deeply with the pain of his loss. But Luther ultimately emerged from his struggle with a deeper understanding of how a father's love for a child is like our Father's love for us.

Maturity in Christ does not enable us to feel the hurt of loss less keenly. We are human, and so we will grieve. This is why Paul writes, "Brothers, we do not want you to . . . grieve like the rest of men, who have no hope" (1 Thess. 4:13). He acknowledges that, yes, we will grieve—but *not* like those who have no hope! The Christian experience of loss does not entail absence of sorrow, but of *hopeless* sorrow.

Our hope is Christ, who wept in grief over the loss of his friend Lazarus. And our hope is in God the loving Father, who has known the death of His only Son. God knows the hurt of mourning, and He mingles His tears with our own. His grief sanctifies our own human sorrow.

Responding to loss

No one can go through an experience of loss unchanged. Whether our hurt is due to the loss of a loved one, a loss of health, a financial loss, or some other cause, this trial will inevitably produce a set of responses within us. The first response will be a normal, human reaction, involving some combination of shock, denial, anger, guilt, and depression. There is nothing sinful or unhealthy about such a reaction to loss. However, if this initial reaction is not worked through, it can deepen into a lifetime of bitterness. So it's very important that we make the healing choice to couple our normal *human reaction* with a *divine reaction.*

The divine reaction enables us, after a normal period of pain and grief, to say to God, "I accept this loss in my life. While I may not understand it, I submit to it. While it's painful, I see it as reality. Lord, please teach me your lesson in this loss, and help me to grow more like Christ because of it." That's not a natural response; it's a *supernatural* response, and it's the kind of response God ultimately wants to achieve in us.

This is a supernatural reaction because it goes completely against the way we feel. The hurt of loss is still there—but as we open ourselves to what God wants to teach us in our hurt, the pain takes on the nature of a healing act of surgery, not merely a scarring wound.

A truly deep loss—the loss of someone close to you or the breakdown of a marriage relationship—is going to hurt for a long time. And even after the pain has subsided, and you are able to get on with your life again, there will be moments when the pain will come back, seemingly as deep and sharp as the first moment it was inflicted. Expect the grief process to take time. Don't let it throw you; you're going to come through.

The grief process took a long time for Job. Here was a man who had everything—and lost it all. At the beginning of the book of Job, he is pictured as an amazingly rich man— rich in many ways. He is described, first of all, as "blameless and upright; he feared God and shunned evil." In other words, Job was a genuinely authentic man of God, rich in spiritual assets. And he had seven sons and three daughters; Job was rich in family. He had enormous holdings of land, livestock, and servants; Job was rich in possessions. He was, according to Job 1:3, "the greatest man among all the people of the East"; Job was rich in reputation and respect.

But this godly, respected, affluent man was soon to be plunged head-to-heels into the deepest trial of loss anyone could possibly imagine. Job's losses came suddenly and mounted rapidly. First, enemies attacked his fields, slaughtering servants and stealing oxen and donkeys. A fire from the sky destroyed his sheep-flocks and killed more servants. Next came the loss of his camels and the rest of his servants. Finally Job's ten children and oldest brother were killed.

One moment, Job was "the greatest man among all the people of the East." The next moment, he was bereaved of almost all his family. He was financially wiped out. Notice, too, that Job's trial was not the result of any wrongdoing in his life. He was blameless before God. The losses Job suffered were enormously unfair.

How, then, did Job respond? Job 1:20 records, "At this, Job got up and tore his robe and shaved his head. Then he fell to the ground in worship." Job reacted, first, with grief. That's a normal, human response. Job was not stoically indifferent to his loss, nor did he take masochistic pleasure in it. He grieved, and he displayed his grief openly.

But then Job went a step further. He coupled his normal, human response with a *divine* response: he *worshiped.* He bowed his face to the ground in a gesture of adoration toward his God. And in Job 1:21 he demonstrates a divine response to loss still further, saying, "Naked I came from my mother's womb, and naked I will depart. The Lord gave and the Lord has taken away; may the name of the Lord be praised." This incredibly rich man had learned to hold on to everything loosely.

And Job 1:22 adds, "In all this, Job did not sin by charging God with wrongdoing." Reading this, we might think, "Well, that's Job. He was some kind of super-saint, a legendary man of God." But no, he was simply a human being who had made a choice to so closely link himself to God that he didn't get derailed by the hard places of life. In *Pain's Hidden Purpose,* Don Baker observes,

Screaming "ouch" when you stub your toe is not cursing God.

One of the tragic interpretations of Job has encouraged people to suffer in silence. It has heaped guilt upon them when they dared to ask God a question or to suggest to God that they would like some relief. . . . Tears are therapeutic and talk is therapeutic. God has given us tear ducts and tongues, and they become a very real part of the relief process when we hurt. And Job employed both.[4]

The message of Job is not, "Here is a legendary saint of unattainable faith," but, "Here is a flesh-and-blood man who knew deep trouble, and he ultimately responded with God's perspective." Job coupled his human reaction to a divine reaction: he *wept* and he *worshiped*. That's a choice you and I can make as well, no matter how the hurt of loss touches our lives.

On the ash heap

What more could happen to Job?

But more *did* happen. Job 2 records that he was afflicted "with painful sores from the soles of his feet to the top of his head." Job experienced the loss of his health. At this point his wife turned against him in rage. "Are you still holding on to your faith in God?" she cried. "Why don't you just curse God and die?" Job then found himself shut out of his house and left to die on a heap of ashes, the ancient equivalent of a garbage dump. There, amid the filth and flies, he picked up a shard of broken pottery, shook the dust from it, and began to scrape the accumulating corruption from his stinging flesh. At this point Job became the most miserable and degraded man on earth.

Then three of Job's friends—Eliphaz, Bildad, and Zophar—heard of Job's troubles and made the journey to offer him comfort. Approaching him, they found him a disfigured, disease-ridden derelict sprawled on an ash heap at the edge of town. Immediately they cried out, tore their robes, and wept over him. Then they sat on the ground with him for seven days and seven nights. For a whole week, no one said a word to him, not even to quote Scripture. They simply offered the comfort of their presence. If only they had left it at that.

But at the end of that week, Job's friends began to offer "advice"—and at that point they ceased to be of any further comfort to Job. Eliphaz and Bildad accused Job of hiding sin in his life. When Job protested his innocence, Zophar presumptuously claimed to speak for God, calling Job a liar. Finally Job cried out in frustration, "Miserable comforters are you all! Will your long-winded speeches never end?"

Here is a sharply etched illustration of two ways to stand by people in a time of loss: one, a ministry of quiet presence with the sufferer; the other, a reckless and judgmental intrusion into the sufferer's misery. When someone is going through a trial, he probably doesn't need to hear more words, not even words from the Bible. He just needs a friend who will offer simple presence and practical encouragement. In God's own time, he may gain a divine perspective on his trial, but that perspective can never be imposed on him from without, especially during the very worst depths of his suffering.

Loss transformed

At the conclusion of his time of trial, Job is able to say, "My ears had heard of you but now my eyes have seen you" (Job 42:5). In other words, Job was saying that before his trial of deep loss he had only heard of God—but now, with his own eyes, he had seen God powerfully working in his life. That's what the hurt of loss often does to our lives: our trials enable us to *see God* in new and meaningful ways. All the things we've heard about God, all the doctrines and sermons and books about God are completely transcended by the reality of God's presence through our pain and loss—and we emerge from our trials with the knowledge that we have *seen* Him at work with our very own eyes.

In so many ways, we discover that God is able to take our trial of loss and radically *transform* it. This happened in a tangible way in Job's life: "The Lord made him prosperous again and gave him twice as much as he had before" (Job 42:10). Yet this verse is being misused and distorted in many quarters of the church today. God doesn't promise that if you lose a $20,000-a-year job this month, then he'll give you a $40,000-a-year job next month. The way God transforms our loss is up to Him, not us.

God's blessings are not always material blessings. He often takes what is tangible and gives what is intangible: deeper faith, stronger character, compassion for others, and peace that passes human understanding.

Why?

A young woman, only eighteen years old, was driving alone on the freeway, headed back to college after a visit home with her family. On the way, she ran into mechanical trouble, carefully pulled as far off the pavement as she could, then got out of her car to open the trunk. Just then, a drunk driver steered his car over the center divider of the freeway, across several lanes of traffic, and directly toward the unsuspecting young woman. In an instant, her life was over.

"We prayed together as a family the night before she left," this young woman's father told me. "We prayed *specifically* that God would protect our daughter, but He *didn't!* And I want to know why! If God is all-loving and all-powerful, He could have deflected the path of that car just eighteen inches, and my daughter would be alive today! *Why* didn't He?"

I don't know why. Certainly, there are *partial* answers, such as the fact that this drunk driver's actions were a matter of human free will, not an act of God—yet such philosophical niceties mean little in the face of real human tragedy. The fact is that a father's prayer was answered *No,* and if we're honest with ourselves we have to echo this father's haunting question: *Why?* Indeed, faced with God's mysterious *No* to our prayers, we may well be tempted to cry out, "Why, then, should we pray? If we are powerless to influence God's actions and to obtain His protection for our lives and loved ones through prayer, then *why pray at all?*"

I want to encourage you not to despair in the face of God's unsearchable *No.* I can testify that a prayer prayed humbly before God is the positive power to change things, to move mountains, to radically alter lives. I've seen many situations when the only thing that stood between life and death, success or failure, salvation or hell, was the prayer of one of God's faithful servants.

At the same time, we have to concede that it's the One who *answers* prayer—not the one who prays—who is sovereign. God's will is not always going to coincide with our will.

Sometimes God must allow us to be hurt in order for us to be healed, and our only assurance at such times is the fact that God is sovereign. When His will has been made clear to us, and His will is clearly not our will, His way not our way, then we must pray anew, asking God to teach us His lesson through our trial of loss.

One hymnwriter put it this way:

> *What He takes and what He gives us*
> *Shows how precious His love is for us.*

Notice, the author of these lines had the courage to write "what He takes" first. It's true. Very often, it is what He *takes* from us that shows how precious His love is for us. That's the lesson of a lifetime—a lifetime spent seeking God's perspective on the hurt of loss.

It's terrible to go through the tragedy of a loss, but it's even more terrible to suffer the hurt of loss and not even learn anything from it. In the final analysis, life is a process of learning and preparation. We are preparing ourselves for that one form of loss we all face: the loss of our earthly lives, by which we will one day gain all of eternity.

4

Healing the Hurt of Loneliness

Alone, alone, all, all alone.
    Alone on a wide, wide sea.
                    —Samuel Taylor Coleridge

I will be with you always.
                    —Jesus Christ, Matthew 28:20

Rupert Brooke—that great, sad poet of England who died in World War I—was a very lonely man. One day, Brooke boarded a steamship sailing from Liverpool to New York City. He stood at the rail, surrounded by throngs of people—but totally alone. There was no one to say good-bye or shed a tear.

On an impulse, Brooke left the rail and ran down the gangplank. On the dock he found a young boy about ten years old. He knelt and looked the boy in the eyes and asked, "Young man, would you like to earn sixpence?"

"Indeed I would, sir!" said the boy.

Brooke took some coins from his pocket and pressed them into the boy's hand. "Then, lad," he said, "would you wave to me as the boat goes out to sea?"

Alone.

It's perhaps the most desolate word in the world. You can't buy your way out of loneliness. You can't wish it away. "Loneliness," as Thomas Wolfe observed, "far from being a rare and curious phenomenon peculiar to myself and a few other solitary men, is the central fact of human existence."

Every human being of every age and culture, says psychologist Erich Fromm, is confronted with one question: "How to overcome separateness, how to achieve union, how to transcend one's own individual life and find at-onement." He explains,

> Man is gifted with . . . awareness of himself, of his fellow man, of his past, and of the possibilities of his future. This awareness of himself as a separate entity, the awareness of his own short life span, of the fact that without his will he is born and against his will he dies, that he will die before those whom he loves, or they before him, the awareness of his aloneness and separateness, of his helplessness before the forces of nature and of society, all this makes his separate disunited existence an unbearable prison. . . .
> The deepest need of man, then, is the need to overcome his separateness, to leave the prison of his aloneness.[1]

Here is a surgically precise diagnosis of the loneliness of the human condition—a condition to which Jesus Himself was no stranger. From the cross He cried out one of the most stark expressions of loneliness and alienation ever uttered: "My God! My God! Why have you forsaken me?" Jesus, the Son of God, was alone, separated from God the Father as the moment of His death approached. There He took our deepest hurt of loneliness and crucified it forever. The "at-onement" that Erich Fromm said every human being seeks is found through the *atonement* Christ purchased for us on the Cross.

In Revelation 3:20, Jesus says, "Here I am! I stand at the door and knock. If anyone hears my voice and opens the door, I will go in and eat with him, and he with me." Jesus waits outside the door of your heart, wanting nothing more than to come in with you, break bread with you, and end your loneliness.

Death by loneliness

Everyone knows the terrible 3 A.M. loneliness that comes with insomnia, often mixed with worry about the problems of the day or the dread of death. The shadows of our fears loom especially large in the middle of the night, when we have no one to talk to.

But loneliness doesn't come only in the pit of night or in times of solitude. The hurt of loneliness often stabs us when we are surrounded by people. As Lloyd Ogilvie observes,

> Loneliness . . . lurks under many a jolly mask, and pulses in the hearts of the most gregarious and outgoing. It's there beneath the busy adequacy or pretended assurance of the popular, the famous, and the attractive people we admire.
> One of the most crucial discoveries I have made over the years, working with and listening to people, is that loneliness has little to do with the absence of people. We can feel lonely in a crowd, among friends, in a marriage, in the family, at a sorority or fraternity house, and in a church.[2]

I met Helen at the back of the church following the worship service. She accepted my hand, smiled bashfully, and nodded as I greeted her. I chatted with her for a few moments, but she volunteered very little information about herself. She hardly said anything unless encouraged to speak. She was obviously a very lonely woman.

Helen continued coming to church. My wife and I invited her into our home several times, and I slowly began to learn more about her. She had no family and no close friends. She liked coming to church because the people there were friendly. They smiled, she said, and many spoke to her.

I tried to help Helen find a group where she could experience deeper Christian fellowship than she was receiving on Sunday mornings. But she just didn't seem to connect with any of the groups in our church.

One evening, just a few days before Christmas, Helen was found dead in her small downtown apartment. In one desolate act, completely alone, Helen had taken her life. Seven people, including myself, stood at the graveside as the plain wooden box was lowered into the earth. Though some of us had tried, none of us had really gotten to know Helen very well.

Since then, I've often asked myself, Why? How could a woman die of loneliness in a church filled with joyful, outgoing Christians?

And yet I believe Helen's tragedy is not really so unusual after all. Surely, the marks of a lonely soul were very plain on her life and death; most of us keep our loneliness—and, indeed, all our deepest feelings—hidden from view. Not many people will act on their feelings of loneliness as Helen did— but there are many lonely people in every church, and each is a silent tragedy.

An epidemic of loneliness

In 1983, the California State Department of Mental Health studied seven thousand adults from ages thirty to fifty-nine. One of the dynamics under investigation in this study was the correlation between *friendship* and *health.* The researchers found that people without long-term friendships have from two to five times the normal mortality rate for their age group, and experienced higher than normal incidences of cancer, heart disease, circulatory disease, and other ailments.

Certainly, that is not to say that people with few friends will inevitably get sick, or that those with deep friendships are immune from illness; there are many factors that contribute to the state of our health, either good or ill. But this study does seem to establish a statistical connection between loneliness and a tendency toward decreased health and vitality.

At the same time, we are increasingly becoming a nation of strangers—rootless, friendless, and alienated. This is the age of modular relationships and disposable people. The average American moves fourteen times in a lifetime, uprooting acquaintances before they have a chance to blossom into friendships. Loneliness is an epidemic. It's stealing our happiness. It's even *killing* us—silently and slowly as it steals our health, or swiftly and shockingly, as it killed Helen.

A *Newsweek* report following the death of actor William Holden began, "William Holden was a very private man, and he died a very private death. Alone in his apartment in Santa Monica, California, he bled to death from a gash in his forehead caused by a drunken fall against his bedside table. It was four or five days later that his body was found." [3] Holden's films had captivated millions of viewers for decades—yet when he died, four or five days passed and no one even missed him. Why? The closing lines of the article suggest a possible reason: "Holden guarded his privacy with increasing vigilance." A fitting analogy, I think, for many of us.

Why are so many Christians dying inside, even though surrounded by other Christians? One reason, perhaps, is self-imposed isolation—not physical isolation, perhaps, but distance and guardedness in our relationships with one another. We vigilantly guard our privacy. We're afraid to let anyone into our lives. We smile because we're expected to smile, and behind the smile our loneliness deepens. And it will continue to deepen until we make the healing choice to become transparent to a few trusted friends, to let ourselves be known.

No one can exist in a vacuum. In Genesis 2:18, God said, "It is not good for man to be alone." That's why God gave Adam, the first lonely man, a *family*. And God has given you and me a family as well. Even if you have no spouse, no parents, and no children, you have a family indeed, and that family is the church.

Biblically, the church is not a building or an institution or a religious organization. The church is to be our Family of Faith, a place of healing, belonging, and joy. Have you found your place in the Family of Faith? I don't just mean a church to attend on Sunday mornings, but a place to truly *share your life*—your hurts, your doubts, your fears, your joys—with a few other Christians.

Walking in the light

In John 3:21, Jesus commands us to live not only righteously, but *openly,* to "live by the truth," to "come into the light" so that our lives and deeds may be known. First John 1:7 tells us that "if we walk in the light" then "we have fellowship with one another." The Christian who chooses privacy and isolation from deep relationships, who chooses self-reliance and self-sufficiency, has chosen *darkness* and *loneliness*. Isolation is the black hole of the soul; withdrawal from vulnerable, open relationships will suck all the light and warmth out of your life.

In *There's a Lot More to Health Than Not Being Sick,* Bruce Larson confronts us with the question, "How are you fixed for friends?" He writes:

> The question "How are you fixed for friends?" could
> be phrased in more psychological or spiritual terms. You

could ask, "Is there a group of people to which you really belong?" or, "Are there people who know you totally, warts and all?" or, "Do you need to account for yourself, your time to anyone else?" The point is that it is hard to be a whole person without at least a few friends with whom you are free to be yourself, to whom you are accountable. To know and to be known is a vital ingredient for physical and spiritual wholeness.[4]

That's how the Family of Faith functions in the life of the individual who chooses belonging over aloneness, community over isolation, light over darkness. Our fellow Christians let us truly be ourselves, affirming us in an atmosphere of unconditional acceptance. At the same time, they watch our lives and help us to become more like Christ, supporting us in prayer and opening their lives to us.

For me, all of this takes place in several ways, but especially in a setting which, in our church, we call "house churches." We meet in homes, study the Bible together, apply the truth of the Bible to our lives, openly share our joys and sorrows with each other, and uphold each other in prayer. In my own house church there have been people of different ages, background, education, and economic status; people struggling with unemployment, marital stresses, the pain of divorce, guilt and doubt, financial problems, and the loss of loved ones. Whatever our individual differences, we have learned one thing together: the ground is level at the foot of the Cross. We all struggle and hurt—and we all need each other.

In my role as a pastor, I continually lead meetings and counsel other people. In my house church, however, I'm just another fellow-struggler. For a couple of hours a week, I don't have to lead; I can simply *belong*. I can ask others to counsel me, to pray for me, to forgive me, and to hold me accountable. Close Christian community in small groups of caring, Scripture study and prayer is the best way to transcend the lostness we often feel in our churches, large or small.

A few years ago, a young friend of mine called me on the phone. His voice quavered as he told me that his girlfriend had suddenly broken up with him. She had dropped out of school, left the church she was attending, and joined a cult. "You know, Ron," he told me, "the thing that's so amazing is that she can't even explain to me what the cult believes."

"Well, do you know why she joined?" I asked.

"She said she joined because she found a kind of acceptance and caring in this cult that she never experienced in her church—and now she's not lonely anymore."

The cults are beating us at our own game! They've discovered a distinctive dynamic that the twentieth century church has largely lost, but which *energized* the life of the early New Testament church: intense community and fellowship. When Christians in the first century church said "fellowship" (*koinonia* in New Testament Greek), they meant the disclosure of the deep recesses of their lives to other believers, sharing their possessions with others in need, and celebrating together in prayer, praise, and worship. This same kind of *koinonia*-fellowship can be ours today as we begin to walk together in the light, sharing our lives together, confessing our hurts and failures to one another, and *liberating* each other from loneliness.

Making connection

Some time ago, AT&T, the nation's largest long-distance telephone company, spent $60 million dollars to find just the right phrase to move people out of their chairs and over to the phone to make a long-distance call. The result of all this expensive research, testing, and creative development was a simple five-word slogan:

Reach out and touch someone.

Everyone knows these familiar commercials, with their scenes of distant loved ones making connection across the miles, old friends reminiscing and sharing their deepest feelings, parents telling their kids they're sorry for some thoughtless outburst, and kids telling their parents, "Hey, that's okay." And each of these scenes is tagged, *Reach out and touch someone.*

I admit it: I'm a pushover for these commercials. Why do they manipulate our emotions so effectively? Because they touch a real longing in each of us to be reached, to be touched, to be known deep within. These commercials offer *connection* and *intimacy* with someone outside of ourselves. They offer an instant bridging of the distance between two people. The underlying message of all these mini-dramas is that the cure for loneliness is just a phone call away.

Reach out and touch someone. This would be an excellent

slogan for the church, for any church, even though AT&T thought of it first. How are we doing at the job of reaching out, touching human need with the love of Christ, and helping lonely people feel less alone?

I made a surprising discovery a few years ago. I found that roughly *half* of all adults who joined our church during one given year were single—either unmarried, widowed, or divorced. In fact, this trend is really indicative of the American church at large.

Yet at the same time, we are seeing the emergence of some very hurtful and unbiblical teaching regarding single people in the church. Let me quote the recent words of two leading Bible teachers. One wrote, "Since the family is the place where God ultimately builds character, you will never become fully mature in Christ so long as you are unmarried." The other said, "If you are unmarried, you are incomplete."

Frankly, I get angry when I hear statements such as these—not only because they are unbiblical, but because they assign a kind of second-class status to unmarried Christians, a view the Bible never endorses. And such statements inflict greater pain on people who have already been hurt by life, people who struggle with the pain of loneliness.

Paul, writing in 1 Corinthians 7, states that the single condition, far from being any kind of second-class status, is a *special* condition. He says of the unmarried that "it is good for them to stay unmarried, as I am." In verses 32–35, Paul states that there is a definite benefit for those who are single, in terms of their service for Jesus Christ: their interests are undivided; they do not have to be burdened with the problems of caring for a family; they can serve the Lord with undivided devotion.

Some people think there could be nothing worse than remaining single for life—but there is: being married to the *wrong* person for life. John Denver's beautiful, evocative song, "Seasons of the Heart," tells of a husband and wife who have been together for many years, and yet have become strangers to each other. One sad line in the song tells it all: "When I'm lying right beside you is when I feel the most alone of all." Marriage is no cure for loneliness. Some of the loneliest people in the world are married people.

Yet I don't want to be misunderstood: Marriage is a beautiful gift of God. I don't want to downgrade marriage, but to upgrade the status of single Christians. Everyone in the church has first-class status in the kingdom of God. If you're single, don't wonder why you've missed God's best for your life; rejoice that you *have* God's best, and then use your gift of singleness for God's glory.

Victims of divorce

In 1 Timothy 5:3, Paul tells us we are to give special honor and concern to those who are bereaved. And I believe Paul has given us a principle here that applies not only to those who have been widowed, but to divorced Christians as well. Psychologists tell us that the depth of sorrow that accompanies divorce is second only to that which accompanies the death of a loved one. That pain is often compounded by the ordeal of court trials, the bitterness and anger of spouse vs. spouse recriminations, and the self-righteous accusations and judgments of many in the church.

People often quote verses such as Malachi 2:16, " 'I hate divorce,' says the Lord God," seemingly unaware that it's divorce itself—not divorced *people*—he hates. God hates divorce because it's such a tragic and destructive thing in human lives. But God unconditionally loves *people,* including divorced people. It's true that people often enter into divorce for sinful reasons, such as selfishness, infidelity, or lack of commitment. But many people are truly *victims* of divorce—people who have been abused and discarded by an uncaring or hostile spouse.

The victims of divorce have gone through years of misery in an unhappy marriage. Now they're alone and seeking to rebuild their lives. They've been told by their spouse that they're unwanted. Their self-esteem has been cruelly wounded. Now they come to the church and just ask for a place of belonging and refuge, and maybe just a friend or two to say, "You're going to be all right. We're your friends and we're going to help you get better."

But how does the church all too often respond? "Divorced? Sorry, you're all washed up. You're second-class." I've seen it happen again and again: people who have been victimized once by divorce are made victims again—victims of self-righteous, unloving people in the church.

People who have just experienced the sorrow of either divorce or bereavement have a long process ahead of them. There is an authentic, long-term grief process—and we need to be sensitive to that process as we stand by the victims of loss or divorce. But grief also has a tendency to turn to a kind of destructive self-pity in the life of a lonely person if he or she is never directed outward, toward God, toward others, away from self. Today there is a growing convergence of agreement on this biblical truth among physicians, psychologists, sociologists, and theologians.

The apostle Paul understood this fact well. He knew that only a cause greater than ourselves can ever truly rid us of loneliness. So he established a plan to care for the needs of those who were alone—in particular, for widows—in the early church. We see that plan in 1 Timothy 5:3–16, where Paul outlines the duties and qualifications of a special order or registry of widows who were cared for by the early church, and who in turn were given responsibility for a ministry of service in the church. You see, Paul was a master psychologist. He was well aware of the tremendous therapeutic value that Christian *servanthood* can have when someone is going through grief and loneliness.

Hundreds of times, I've heard statements like: "I've got to become whole first; I've got to get rid of this loneliness first. *Then* I'll serve." I've found that statement almost always *not* to be true. Certainly it may be true for people with especially deep emotional problems. And certainly the person who has recently suffered a deep loss or trial will need some time to heal before getting back into active service. But I'm convinced that, in general, the therapy for loneliness is to get *out* of yourself, to lose yourself in service to God and others. The self-fulfillment philosophy of our culture says, "Get into yourself, get in touch with yourself, fulfill yourself." This philosophy saws across the grain of the Christian gospel.

There's one saying of Christ which is recorded in all four Gospels: "Whoever finds his life will lose it, and whoever loses his life for my sake will find it." I've seen the truth of that statement proved again and again: those who introspectively try to "find" themselves, who try to get "into" themselves, almost always end up sinking deeper into alienation, emotional turmoil, and loneliness. But those who get out of themselves and lose themselves in service to Christ and others almost always find themselves. In the excitement of discovery, as they begin to find new character, wholeness, and strength through service, they simply have no room for self-pity.

In the aftermath of a bloody battle during the Korean War, a war correspondent paused to watch a young Army nurse who was caring for some of the wounded. Standing over her shoulder, he leaned forward for a closer look just as she was removing the bandage from the leg of a badly injured soldier. He was caught off-guard by a glimpse of the gaping, oozing wound and the stench of blood and infection. He had to turn away to avoid becoming sick.

Thinking no one could hear him, the newsman muttered under his breath, "I wouldn't do that for a million bucks!"

"I wouldn't either," said the nurse, looking kindly up at him. "I do it for Jesus Christ."

Intrigued by her response, the correspondent began to talk with this nurse. He discovered she had lost her husband in an accident some months earlier. Her grief and loneliness seemed too much to bear. But during this time she made a choice to offer her nursing experience to God. This led her to service in Korea, just a few miles from the battlefront. "Once, all I cared about was financial security, a nice car, a nice house. Now I'm surrounded by all this blood, pain, and devastation—but I've never been more fulfilled. If I was home right now, I'd be clean and comfortable, but awash in self-pity. Here, my life has meaning." This nurse had learned one of the most important lessons in life: Christlike servanthood is the healing choice for the hurt of loneliness.

The great homesickness

I was twenty-one years old, hitchhiking across the beautiful Welsh countryside on a holiday from my studies at the University of London. My journey alternated between high exhilaration and deep loneliness. I sometimes reflected on all the miles that separated me from my family and friends in Iowa, and at times I even felt out of touch with God. Near the close of one day, feeling very homesick, I sat down on one of those green Welsh hillsides, shrugged off my backpack, and began to read from Psalm 139.

Where can I go from your Spirit?
  Where can I flee from your presence?
If I go up to the heavens, you are there;
  If I make my bed in the depths, you are there.
If I rise on the wings of the dawn,
  If I settle on the far side of the sea,
Even there your hand will guide me,
  Your right hand will hold me fast.

As I was reading those words, I felt a quiet assurance wash over me: God Himself was with me. Though I was halfway around the world from home, He was beside me—and I no longer felt alone.

The human heart is afflicted with a longing, a homesickness that is so deep and so vast that only something very much larger than ourselves can fill it. "Loneliness is none other than homesickness for God," Lloyd Ogilvie once wrote. "Intimate communion with Him is our home."

All our human relationships, as important as they are, are *horizontal* relationships. Our relationship with God is of a different dimension: it is *vertical.* God reaches down to us in our loneliness and lifts us up toward communion with Him. The wonderful paradox God offers us is that in order to escape the prison of our loneliness, we must learn the discipline of *solitude.* We are homesick for God, and freedom from loneliness can only come as we become increasingly intimate with God. This is what Jesus was telling us by the example of His life, as He spent many hours—and even entire nights— alone in prayer.

Intimacy with God is our home, and no matter where we are, He is never far from us. When we have a vital love-relationship with Him, how can we possibly feel alone? God is far greater than all the longings of our hearts, and when we lose ourselves in the love and wonder of His presence, we have true freedom from loneliness.

5

Healing the Hurt
of Failure

Be valiant in the attempt, yet not ashamed to fail.
—Samuel Johnson

The race is not to the swift,
   nor the battle to the strong.
—Ecclesiastes 9:11 (KJV)

One day, not long ago, the parents of a college student received a letter from their daughter which went something like this:

Dear Mom and Dad,
Just thought I'd drop you a note to clue you in on my plans. I've fallen in love with a guy named Jim. He quit high school after the eleventh grade to get married. He's been divorced now for about a year. Jim and I have been going steady for two months and we plan to get married in the fall. Until then, I've decided to move into his apartment.
By the way, I think I might be pregnant. At any rate, I dropped out of school last week, although I'd really like to finish college at some time in the future.

This young woman's parents hastily turned to page two of their daughter's letter and read:

Mom and Dad, I just want you to know that everything I've written so far in this letter is *false*. Not a word of it is true. But Mom and Dad, it *is* true that I got a C– in French and I flunked math.
I just wanted to put things in their proper perspective.

85

How we need the proper perspective on the times of setback and failure that are inevitable throughout our lives.

Richard Haydn, a comedic character actor of the 1940s and '50s, was noted for his highly original interpretation of a poem by Edgar A. Guest, *It Couldn't Be Done*. Haydn—the perfect image of a fogeyish professor in black bow tie and pince-nez—would stand stiffly, with his hands behind his back, and stuffily recite:

> Somebody said that it couldn't be done,
>   But he with a chuckle replied
> That "maybe it couldn't," but he would be one
>   Who wouldn't say so till he'd tried.
>
> So he buckled right in with a trace of a grin
>   On his face. If he worried he hid it.
> He started to sing as he tackled the thing
>   That couldn't be done—
>
> *And he couldn't do it.*

Edgar A. Guest, of course, wrote about a man who "tackled the thing that couldn't be done, and he *did* it"—a poem about effort, a positive attitude, and *success*. Haydn turned it into a story of failure—though he *never* failed to draw laughs from audiences who identified with the man who "couldn't do it."

We all know what it is like to try and fail. The Bible acknowledges that all of us, despite our best efforts, will know the hurt of failure. Ecclesiastes 9:1 reminds us that the race is not always to the swift, nor the battle to the strong. Time and circumstances sometimes overwhelm our dreams. Yet, if we're honest with ourselves, we have to admit that failure is not nearly so much what happens to us, but what happens *within* us. We fail outwardly because we have been inwardly negligent or undisciplined.

Keys to success

Accomplishment is never an accident. It requires thought, diligent planning, effort, and strength of character. I believe the first key to success is goal-setting, which is simply the hard work of *thinking* our way through to a direction in life.

If you go to a successful person and ask him what his goals are for the next year or five years or ten years of his life, he can probably tell you without pausing to think. His goals are clearly before him all the time.

Say you want to see improvement in your physical fitness over the next several years: First, you can sit down and plan out where you want to be in terms of your weight, heart rate, and blood pressure at certain intervals in your life. Then you can decide what you will need to do to achieve those goals: a diet program, an exercise program, a schedule of checkups with your doctor.

You can develop a similar set of goals for all the areas of your life: professional and financial goals, educational or intellectual goals, and most importantly, spiritual goals. Our plans should not be rigid and inflexible, lest unforeseen circumstances derail and discourage us. But we need always to keep our goal before us, even if we have to take a few detours along the way; if we aim at nothing, then nothing is exactly what we are most likely to hit.

The second key to success is to set priorities. It's easy for most of us to allow the most "urgent" things to crowd out those things that are truly the most important. We can end up spending so much time "putting out fires" that we never get to accomplish the things we truly feel God is calling us to do. That means we're going to have to learn to say "No" to some good things so we can say "Yes" to the best things.

An example of the failure to set proper priorities would be the successful businessman who becomes the envy of his colleagues at the same time his family life is crumbling. He has been so ambitious in his career that he has neglected his family—and one day he awakes to realize that he has failed as a husband and father. Another example: the pastor or Christian layperson who diligently performs years of Christian service, only to discover that his faith has become hollow and the God he's tried to serve has now become a stranger to him; it's easy to allow our relationship with God to be squeezed out by Christian "busy-ness." Unless we periodically take time to sort out our priorities, we will never reach our most important goals.

The third key to success is to accept complete personal

responsibility for our problems and failures. In *The Road Less Traveled,* Dr. M. Scott Peck writes,

> We must accept responsibility for a problem before we can solve it. We cannot solve a problem by saying "It's not my problem." We cannot solve a problem by hoping that someone else will solve it for us. I can solve a problem only when I say, "This is *my* problem and it's up to me to solve it." But many, so many, seek to avoid the pain of their problems by saying to themselves, "This problem was caused me by other people, or by social circumstances beyond my control, and therefore it is up to other people or society to solve this problem for me. It is not really my personal problem." [1]

As long as our focus is on making excuses or shifting blame, we will continue to experience failure because we will fail to learn, to grow, and to change. But as we accept responsibility for our lives and make the healing choice to truly *learn* from our failures, then we can begin to transform the failed patterns of the past into new patterns of future success. This learning process can continue throughout our lives, turning our everyday existence into a lifelong *adventure.*

The pressure of failure

Shortly after I was ordained a pastor, I started a young people's singing group in our Minneapolis church. Called The Children of Hope, this group performed around the Midwest, sharing about Christ in song and testimony. Following one concert, I gave a ten-minute message, after which we greeted people in the back of the auditorium. One woman came up to me, put her hand on my arm, and said, "Young man, I see real potential in you. I think you could be a good speaker some day, maybe even a preacher! Now, what you need to do is to go on to college and take some speech courses, and then you should go on to seminary—"

"Excuse me, ma'am—" one of the boys in our group interrupted. "He's already been to college and seminary. You see, he's our preacher and—well, that's the best he can do!"

An example of one woman's good-intentioned attempt to give encouragement—an attempt which failed. On a more serious level, many of our failures are like that; the road to failure is paved with good intentions—and bad timing. Often we fail in the attempt to do God's will because we try to do it our own way. We see a need and we rush to meet that need without stopping to ask God for wisdom and discernment. So in our attempt to help we often hurt instead. We have good intentions, but we are not in God's timing.

Whether our failure is a great fiasco or a minor embarrassment, our deepest need is to discover God's perspective on our failure. Few of us have the kind of perspective on failure that J. B. Phillips had when he paraphrased James 1:2—"When all kinds of trials and failures crowd into your lives, my brothers, don't resent them as intruders, but welcome them as friends. Realize that they come to test your faith and produce in you the quality of endurance." As we work to gain this kind of perspective, we should be aware that there are two forms of *pressure* we will almost always feel in those inevitable times when we stumble and fail:

First, in times of failure we will feel *the pressure of our own guilt.* Most of us heap a load of self-reproach onto our honest mistakes—especially those of us with so-called "Type A" personalities. We are programmed with a success mentality, preoccupied with unrealistically high standards. Longfellow once wrote, "Most people would succeed in small things if they were not troubled with lofty ambitions." It's true: when we set unattainable goals for ourselves, we set ourselves up for failure.

I do it myself all the time—writing out such a long "Things to Do" list I can never get it all done in a day. But God is much more compassionate toward us than we are toward ourselves. As the psalmist wrote, "He knows our frame." He never sets unrealistic standards for us. It's taken me a long time to learn this lesson: God doesn't want our activity; He wants our maturity. He wants our *will* more than He wants our *works.*

Secondly, in times of failure we will feel *the pressure of people.* Too often, our favorite indoor sport, even as Christians, is to kick the one who is down. But when you've failed, you already know it; you don't need someone to say, "You blew it." You need someone in your corner, someone to build you up again.

In Lorraine Hansberry's play *A Raisin in the Sun,* there is a poignant depiction of failure. The father of a poor inner-city black family has just died, leaving only a small life-insurance policy. His widow has a dream of using this money to buy a small bungalow in a better part of town. Her son, however, wants to invest the money in a business deal, which he believes can multiply the small legacy. This young man, who has never held a job, sincerely wants to do something to help his family. He pleads with his mother for the money; she refuses at first, but finally relents and gives her son most of the money. He then invests it with a "friend"—and this "friend" skips town with the cash.

When the young man confesses his failure to his mother and sister, the sister flies into a rage, cursing him and condemning him for being so stupid, for gambling away their future. But suddenly the mother steps in, cutting off the sister's tirade. "I thought I taught you to love your brother," she says.

"Love him?" shouts the sister. "There's nothing left to love!"

"There's *always* something left to love—and if you ain't learned that, you ain't learned nothing!" the mother replies. "Have you cried for that boy today? Not for yourself because that money's gone, but for *him,* for what he's been through! Child, when do you think is the time to love somebody the most? When he's done good? That ain't the time at all. It's when he's at his lowest and can't believe in himself 'cause the world done whipped him so!" [2]

That's what God's unconditional love is like in our times of failure. God is always there in your corner, and He wants to get you back into action, not count you out. People may accuse you or write you off after you've failed—but not God.

There's a saying, "You can't knock success." At the same time, I submit that there's something to be said for failure. I don't think I'm being at all glib about this; I honestly believe that some of the greatest growth in my life has come in the aftermath of my biggest mistakes. This is especially true of those times I've failed miserably, and there have been people in my life who have continued to love me and affirm me through it all.

A well-known Christian spokesman made a claim in a recent television commercial that the Bible says, " 'In everything you do, put God first, and He will direct you and crown your efforts with success.' " The passage quoted in this commercial is Proverbs 3:6, as rendered by a popular paraphrased version of the Bible. At first glance, it might seem that God is saying, "I'll make you a deal: Put me first in all you do—and I'll make you successful!"

But is this what the Bible really says? Both the *New International Version* and the *New American Standard Bible* translate this verse, "In all your ways acknowledge him, and he will make your paths straight." Clearly, Proverbs 3:6 is God's promise to guide us in the paths *He* chooses. This is a great promise—but it's not a promise that we will never fail! The path He chooses for us may lead us through the trial of failure. We need to learn that failure is not such an awful tragedy. The *real* tragedy is when we go through failure and learn nothing from it.

As Paul wrote in 1 Corinthians 1:27, "God chose the foolish things of the world to shame the wise; God chose the weak things of the world to shame the strong." And if we are honest, we have to confess that God sometimes chooses the seeming failures of this world to shame the apparent successes of this world. God's guarantee to us is not that He will crown our efforts with success, but that we are permitted to fail.

Your response: your responsibility

One of my favorite places to turn to when I'm experiencing the hurt of failure is Psalm 103. There, in verses 1 and 2, David writes, "Praise the Lord, O my soul; all my inmost being, praise his holy name. Praise the Lord, O my soul, and forget not all his benefits." In this Psalm, David is speaking to his inner self, his soul, as if to say, "Be grateful to God! Even though I'm hurting now, I refuse to focus on my failure. Instead, I choose to focus on gratefully remembering all the blessings God has brought into my life!"

My friend Elton "Gil" Gillam, founder of Church Prayer Ministry International, raises a question that I find helpful, and even crucial, as I try to respond to the hurt of failure in my own life. He asks, "Are you gazing or just glancing at God?" Whenever we find ourselves facing problems, our human tendency is to gaze at our circumstances while merely glancing at God. Our perspective is reversed, as if we were looking through the wrong end of the telescope: our problems loom large while God appears small. We need to learn to keep our gaze on God while glancing at our circumstances.

Even when life has flattened our dreams with a steamroller, we can still make the healing choice to remember God's benefits, to seek His face, to keep our gaze on Him. No matter how bad our circumstances, our response is our responsibility. If we keep our gaze on God, we can get up and keep advancing toward our goal. But if we gaze at our circumstances, we'll lose sight of our goal, and sink into a mire of self-pity.

What are the benefits of God that we are to recall in our trial of failure? David names some of them in Psalm 103:3: "He forgives all [your] sins." *All.* Even the sins that brought us down into failure? Yes, even those. Sin and failure are not the end of the line for us. God calls us to repent and be forgiven, and His grace is always there. God's grace means nothing less than a completely fresh start.

Another benefit is listed for us in Psalm 103:10—"He does not treat us as our sins deserve or repay us according to our iniquities." God's love for us is unconditional. He doesn't say, "If you succeed, then I'll accept you and love you. If you don't fail Me, then you'll win My favor." God accepts us and loves us right where we are.

We should take our cue from God in our relationships with each other. What a tragedy that we put so many pressures on people to think the way we think, to succeed on our terms and never fail us, before we will say, "I love you, I accept you." The distinction between God's love and the love of this world is precisely this: God's love is unconditional.

A surgeon wrote these words shortly after performing surgery on the face of a pretty young woman:

> I stand by the bed where a young woman lies, her face postoperative, her mouth twisted in palsy. A tiny twig of the facial nerve, the one to the muscles of her mouth, has been severed. She will be thus from now on. . . . To remove the tumor in her cheek, I had to cut the little nerve.
>
> Her young husband is in the room. He stands on the opposite side of the bed, and together they seem to dwell in the evening lamplight, isolated from me, private. . . .

"Will my mouth always be like this?" she asks.

"Yes," I say, "it will. It's because the nerve was cut."

"I like it," he says. "It's kind of cute." . . . Unmindful, he bends to kiss her crooked mouth, and I so close I can see how he twists his own lips to accommodate hers, to show her that their kiss still works.[3]

That's what God's love is like. He reaches out to the deformities and failures we have made of our lives, and He gives us a cue as to how we are to relate to one another. God is the One to whom we can turn—even in the worst of our failures—to receive His amazing touch of grace and forgiveness.

David describes this kind of unconditional love in Psalm 103:11–12, "For as high as the heavens are above the earth, so great is his love for those who fear him; as far as the east is from the west, so far has he removed our transgressions from us." He remembers our sins and failures no more; they're buried in the deepest sea. Some of us have carried a weight of guilt and self-reproach for years. God wants to free us from that weight, and give us His freely flowing grace and forgiveness. Our focus when failure comes should be on grace, not guilt.

Failure is *never* the end. It certainly wasn't the end for Peter. This bold, self-confident disciple was so sure, so determined to stand by Jesus no matter what came; but when Jesus was led away to be crucified, Peter's courage and determination *failed*. He not only forsook his friend Jesus, but before the night was over he had actually denied Him, and sealed his denials with a terrible oath.

Peter was a miserable failure, and he knew it. But failure wasn't the end of Peter's story. John 21 records that, following the Resurrection, Jesus met Peter by the Sea of Galilee. There He mercifully forgave and restored Peter, charging him with an awesome responsibility: "Feed my sheep," shepherd the new community which was to become the Church. Writing in *Discipleship Journal,* Stephen D. Shores finds application for our own trial of failure in the story of Peter:

Could God forgive such a colossal failure? Was Peter even worth the try? Are we? Yes! . . . Peter found himself not only forgiven but trusted. He learned that failure is not the ultimate.

> Failure is the unforgivable sin in American culture—
> so much so that it often paralyzes the individual in a
> deep-freeze of depression, self-condemnation, and resigna-
> tion. The Bible, though, is full of the idea that our failures
> are not irreversible in their effects. Peter failed utterly
> but not ultimately, for God used him as an awesome force
> in the early Church. Our Father's ability to forgive and
> restore far outweighs our capacity for failure.[4]

Failure was not the end of the line for Peter. It was a *lesson* —
and a new beginning. So it is with you and me. We can grow
through failure, we can be changed by it so we can face even
greater challenges in the future. Someone once said, "There
is the greatest practical benefit in making a few failures early
in life." Why? Because failure is not the end; it's the beginning
of a new adventure.

A fresh start

An experience of failure often affects our sense of security.
We begin to feel if we're not achieving, then perhaps we're
not fully accepted by God. But God wants us to know that
our true security lies not in our achievements, but in His unconditional love for us. Psalm 103:13–14 assures us, "As a father
has compassion on his children, so the Lord has compassion
on those who fear him; for he knows how we are formed, he
remembers that we are dust." God accepts us as we are.

If God expects achievement from us before He will love
us, then a friend of mine, Peggy, has nothing to look forward
to. She is retarded, paralyzed from the neck down, and her
capacity to achieve is severely limited. But I'm convinced Peggy
receives abundant grace and love from God—not because she
is accomplishing great things for Him, but because He accepts
her unconditionally. He knows her heart.

And He knows your heart. When you fail, even when you
fall flat on your face in full view of the whole world, God
loves you just the same.

I confess I've lived most of my life from this false premise:
"If I only achieve, people will love me more, God will love
me more, and I'll be able to accept myself." Living that way
is an emotional rollercoaster. Succeed at something and you're

riding high—but just one moment of failure is all it takes to send your self-esteem plunging to the depths. God doesn't call us to that kind of life. He loves us even in our failure, and He wants us to see and accept ourselves just as He does.

The hurt of failure often leads us to compare ourselves with other people. We think, "I've worked harder and I'm more qualified than this other person, yet I've lost my job and he's getting a promotion!"

Or, "I've been a Christian longer than this other person in this church, yet his ministry is flourishing and mine is declining!"

Or, "We have a deeper relationship with Christ than those people, yet their children are Christians while our children have rebelled against God!"

Don't look at another person and say, "Compared to him or her, I'm a failure." If you compare your momentary failure with the momentary success of another person, you will probably end up in a prolonged depression. But if you compare your present failure with the everlasting love of God, a love that just goes on forever, you won't stay down for long.

Jesus always saw men and women not for what they *were,* but for what they were to *become.* That's the basis on which He chose the Twelve—seemingly a bunch of illiterates, malcontents, and selfish, petty failures. He knew what they would become, and so He allowed a lot of room for failure in their lives. He knew how they could learn and grow through failure. We need to learn that too.

A major failure is a sign that we need to make a significant change in life. It's time to relinquish the past and look to the future for a *new* challenge. Most of us can't keep from looking back, even when it's clear that the past is dead: "If only I could get my job back." Or, "If only I had my marriage again." Or, "If only I could change the fact of this bankruptcy." But we can't. The past is over; it's time for a fresh start.

Jesus: our example in failure

Isaiah 53:2 gives us a compelling portrait of a failure. His name: Jesus Christ. This messianic passage from the Old Testament says, "He had no beauty or majesty to attract us to him, nothing in his appearance that we should desire him."

In short, He looked like a failure. Where were His achievements and honors? What accomplishments was He recognized for?

He was born in the middle of nowhere to an unwed teenage girl. A mere three years of public ministry was all He could muster before He was hauled off and executed like a criminal. He was surrounded by illiterates and rabblerousers—and when He ended up on a cross, they deserted Him and left Him to die. His cause appeared lost. Men looked at Him and said, "How could this failure save anybody?"

Yet as Jesus offered Himself for our sin, He did nothing less than conquer sin and disarm death. He ascended from that tomb and *exploded* in resurrection power. This same Man who looked like such a failure to the world became the Redeemer of the world. It was Peter Marshall who said, "It is better to fail in a cause that will ultimately succeed than to succeed in a cause that will ultimately fail." Jesus knew that and He proved it.

Jesus is our example in failure. We may suffer setbacks and appear as fools before a scoffing world. But we know that our cause will ultimately succeed because the same Power that raised Jesus from the grave is working out His eternal plan through us.

There is an apocryphal story about a young man named Philo. According to the story, Philo was the only son of Pontius Pilate, the Roman official who ordered Christ's crucifixion. Even before Philo was born, Pilate had great ambitions for him. Pilate wanted a son who would one day be a great military leader, a son who would make him proud. But when Philo was born, Pilate's pride was dashed: Philo was born sick, weak, and permanently crippled. Throughout the years Philo was growing up, he was the object of his father's hatred and bitterness. "You're not the son I wanted," was Pilate's constant reminder to his broken son.

As soon as he was old enough to leave home, Philo left the palace of his father and wandered alone in the countryside. There he heard of a Galilean who went about preaching love, healing the sick and lame, and feeding the hungry. Philo sought out Jesus and Jesus healed him, not only physically but spiritually and emotionally. Philo was even able to forgive his father for making him feel like a failure as a son for all those years.

From then on, Philo followed Jesus wherever He went, and

it is said that on the day God's only Son Jesus was crucified, Pilate's only son Philo was at the foot of the cross, weeping over the death of his Lord and Friend.

Jesus has come to heal us of our deformities, to heal the past and point us toward the future. The sacrifice of Christ covers our sins and reconciles us to God—and He is sovereign over everything, including our failures. As we continue to gain more and more of God's perspective on the sins and mistakes of the past, we will increasingly see that failure is never the end, but a truly new beginning.

6

Healing the Hurt of Inferiority

*To accept yourself positively and live creatively . . .
is the way to joy, but to deny and reject God's gift
of yourself is the way to ruin.*
                                        —John Claypool

*You are a chosen people, a royal priesthood, a holy
nation, a people belonging to God, that you may
declare the praises of him who called you out of
darkness into his wonderful light.*
                                        —1 Peter 2:9

As usual, he closed the front door behind himself and wearily announced, "I'm home!" He set down his briefcase and newspaper by his easy chair and began to loosen his tie, muttering, "What a day. . . ." Pressures, problems, and forty-five minutes' overtime!

"Dinner'll be ready in fifteen minutes, dear!" came a lilting voice from the kitchen.

"Thanks, sweetheart!" he replied. He sank into his easy chair, sighed deeply, and opened the newspaper. He only got as far as the first headline when—

"Daddy! Play football with me!" The four-year-old halfback scampered into his father's lap, fumbled his Nerf football, and sent sections of the *Chronicle* fluttering out of his father's hands.

"Ooof!" said Daddy, snatching at the newspaper which slithered, section by section, onto the floor. "Oh, son, I'm too tired to—" Then something in the newspaper caught his eye: a full-page advertisement featuring a NASA photograph of the earth. Inspired, he started tearing the ad in pieces.

"Son, I'm going to make a puzzle out of this picture of the world. Now I want you to put the world back together, okay?" He handed the pieces to his boy, then settled back for what he thought would be *at least* fifteen minutes of uninterrupted reading.

His boy was gone for just a little less than two minutes. "See!" he announced, proudly holding the picture of the earth, completely reassembled and held together with shiny Scotch tape.

The father blinked. "How did you do that so *fast*?!"

"It was easy!" said the boy. He turned the newspaper puzzle over, which revealed a picture of a man. "I just put the man together. And when I did that, the world came together, too!"

The world is a broken place, filled with broken people. But the gospel of Jesus Christ is the good news of wholeness for a broken world. The world can never be mended until we begin the task of mending our broken selves.

"In my judgment," says John Claypool, "there is no issue of any greater practical significance than the issue of self-image." As I consider all the people with whom I've counseled and prayed, I can think of no more universal human problem than that of broken self-image and feelings of inferiority. I'm convinced that *all* of us, to some degree, know the hurt of feeling inferior, feeling broken in our sense of self-worth. Some of us experience deep, unrelenting pain because the puzzle of our personality lies in pieces, and we feel no hope of *ever* reassembling the picture of ourselves as people of worth and value.

Feelings of inferiority almost always seem to begin in childhood. Self-image problems usually occur as parents compare their children according to a false scale of values which have been determined by the culture. The two most deceptive values on this scale, according to Christian psychologist Dr. James Dobson, are what he calls "Beauty: The Gold Coin of Human Worth," and "Intelligence: The Silver Coin of Human Worth." In his book *Hide or Seek,* Dobson observes that a common tragedy of childhood is that so many parents expect their children to be, first, beautiful, and second, smart—and when they don't quite measure up to these standards, feelings of inferiority usually set in.[1]

Other children sometimes join in the process of breaking down self-esteem with cruel teasing or isolation of a child. Then comes adolescence, with its tentative first contacts between the sexes, its rapid physical transformations, and its Clearasil crises—a time of life when most young people begin to feel too short, too tall, too fat, too skinny, too awkward, too shy, too much something, or not enough something else. Many of us have experienced the brutal assassination of our self-image by our peers when we were at a vulnerable stage in life. The hurt of old wounds can stab as deeply as if it were only yesterday.

In adulthood, we find ourselves barraged by an endless stream of films, songs, magazines, televisions shows, and commercials—all *calculated* to make us feel inferior. This planned assault on our self-esteem is designed to motivate us to buy a range of wonder-products which will magically rid us of our inferiority feelings. So it's no wonder we grow up feeling short-changed in the coinage of human worth, that we see ourselves as unlovely and unloved.

The Red Queen's Race

We act out our inferiority feelings in various ways. Some withdraw into a shell of painful shyness. Others mask their inner hurt, compensating for a sense of inferiority by assuming an air of *superiority.* That conceited, self-important person you find so unbearable is probably trying to prove to himself that he's not really as insignificant and inferior as he unconsciously feels he is.

Others respond to inferiority feelings by desperately seeking the acceptance of others. Some, in fact, become so intent on gaining approval and meeting the expectations of others that they never authentically become *themselves.* I've been down that road, and I found that hiding my true self to avoid being rejected never ended my sense of inadequacy; it only compounded my problems.

Tucked away in a quiet corner of Scripture, there's a phrase that brims with emotion, ancient words from the pen of Job: "The souls of the wounded cry out" (Job 24:12). Maybe your soul is crying out even now; I've felt that way many times. All of us have been wounded in our self-image at one time or another, and whether we tend to respond to these wounds with shyness, or a mask of superiority, or by seeking approval, there is a healing choice we can make for the hurt of inferiority.

How do we begin building a stronger self-image into ourselves and those we love?

We can learn a lot from the example of a man named Fred Rogers. If you have small children, you probably already know the host of Public Broadcasting's *Mister Rogers' Neighborhood.* In 1963, Mr. Rogers was ordained a Presbyterian minister with the special charge to "serve children and their families through the media," and he's been lovingly ministering to children on public TV ever since.

There's no secret to building self-esteem. As Mr. Rogers has demonstrated every weekday for the past twenty years, it's something a child can understand. He sings songs that tell children, "You are my friend, you are special to me," and "I like you just the way you are." He helps children to believe in themselves, to be kind to one another, and to understand that everybody is wonderfully unique.

Mr. Rogers knows the difference between *affirming* someone and *flattering* someone. Flattery doesn't build self-esteem; it only reinforces a pattern of approval-seeking. Flattery says, "I love you *because* you do the things that win my acceptance." Embedded in such statements is the tacit (and frightening) condition: "And I will love you *only* so long as you continue to please me."

Authentic affirmation, however, builds security and healthy self-worth. Affirmation says, "You don't have to earn my acceptance. I love you just the way you are. I'll never pressure you to be anyone but who you are. I'll always love you, and nothing you will ever do can change that."

In the classic children's fantasy *Through the Looking Glass,* Lewis Carroll pictures a scene in which little Alice is running hand-in-hand with a chess-piece, the Red Queen. Though Alice runs as fast as she can, trying to keep up, the Queen repeatedly shouts, "Faster! Faster!" But as fast as they run, the scenery never changes.

Finally, Alice and the Queen collapse under a tree—the same tree from which they started. "Why, we've gotten absolutely nowhere!" gasps Alice. "Everything's just as it was!"

"Of course!" sniffs the Queen. "In the Red Queen's Race, it takes all the running you can do just to keep in the same place! If you want to get somewhere else, you must run twice as fast as that!"

The Red Queen's Race is a dead-heat on a treadmill, with the finish line forever beyond reach. The race for acceptance so many of us run is the Red Queen's Race of the Soul: our goal—secure self-worth—is always in sight, but never in reach. The finish line is a mirage. There's no way to win, no way to get off. In the Red Queen's Race, self-esteem rises and falls on the see-saw of achievement and failure.

Lauren Tewes was sprinting in the fast lane of the Red Queen's Race. A recent *TV Guide* cover story relates that she was making more than a million dollars a year as the co-star of a top-rated television series.[2] Talent, beauty, and personality combined to make her one of the most recognized people in the world. But despite the glamor that surrounded her public image, her private life became a struggle for self-worth from her first days on the set. Studio executives criticized her mercilessly. "I felt so insecure," she said. "I spent a lot of time trying to please people who demanded I change myself. They told me I was a star, but I felt like nothing."

In the attempt to escape her prison of insecurity, she sought refuge in the euphoria of cocaine. But this drug eventually stole everything from her, including the last remaining tatters of her self-esteem. She was fired from the series and forced to begin a long, slow struggle to rebuild her career from scratch. Only seven years after she attained television stardom, her career, her money, and her home were gone—traded for cocaine.

One morning after a sleepless night, feeling worthless and totally alone, she turned on the television and fell into bed. The screen flickered to life, and a kindly man in a red cardigan sweater smiled and said, "I'll be your friend. Will you be mine?"

The young actress broke down in tears and answered him aloud, "Yes."

"I resolved at that point to get my life together," she later said. "I was totally collapsed, and Mr. Rogers saved my life." On that day, she began the long process of withdrawing from cocaine and rebuilding her career—and the one who gave her the courage to believe in herself was Fred Rogers. With just a few simple words of friendship in a children's television show, he had helped to change the direction of this young woman's life. Rumor has it that Lauren will be reinstated as cruise director of the "Love Boat" this fall. You never know when

a quiet, simple act—a hug, a smile, or a word of friendship—
might rescue someone from despair.

Worm theology

Jesus taught, "Blessed are the poor in spirit." The apostle
Paul wrote, "I know that nothing good lives in me." Martin
Luther said, "God creates out of nothing, and until a man
becomes nothing, God can make nothing out of him." And
Christianity has long been misunderstood on this point. Many
people have historically seen Christianity as teaching the *aboli-
tion* of human self-worth.

In response, a secular movement has arisen, saying, "Look
out for Number One! Be your own best friend! Be good to
yourself! You're *worth* it!" Best-selling books, TV talk shows,
and advertising have joined forces to proclaim, "You can have
self-esteem—and we'll sell it to you!" So the church, afraid
of losing its audience, has chimed in, "Oh, yes! We believe
that too!" and desperately tried to tack the name of Jesus
onto the secular self-fulfillment fad.

The problem is that society's approach to realizing self-
worth stands opposed to the authentic sense of worth found
in Scripture. These two approaches cannot be synthesized.
Whereas the self-fulfillment movement says, "Find self-worth
through achievement and self-sufficiency," the Bible says, in
effect, "Self-esteem lies in how we are unconditionally loved
and valued by God."

Isaac Watts wrote over six hundred hymns, and probably
the best-loved of all those hymns is the one which contains
the words:

> Alas! and did my Savior bleed,
>   And did my Sovereign die?
> Would He devote that sacred Head
>   For such a worm as I?

As much as I love that hymn, I'm troubled by that last phrase.
I wonder what it does to our image of ourselves to ask, "Why
should Christ have gone to the Cross for a *worm* like me?"
Certainly, as we look back on our lives, we can't escape the
conclusion that we stand flawed and sinful before God. Clearly,

this is the truth Watts intended to portray in this hymn. The trouble is many of us grew up in homes and churches where "worm theology" is all we ever heard.

If Jesus Christ is the Savior and Lord of your life, then it's time to shed your "worm theology" and begin seeing yourself as God sees you. The Bible says that you are fearfully and wonderfully made, created in the image of God. As a follower of Christ, you have been chosen and endowed with special gifts to fill a unique place in the church. You are a child of His handiwork, a saint, part of a royal priesthood, a joint-heir with Christ.

Chuck Swindoll once said, "No one who actually hates himself can adequately share the love of Christ." Why? Because Jesus taught us to love others *as we love ourselves*. When we are hindered in our ability to unconditionally accept ourselves, we are crippled in our capacity to effectively love others.

Not long ago, I was talking to a young man whose life is beginning to reflect a healthy sense of self-esteem and Christian dignity. That was not always the case. He had grown up in a number of churches, beginning with a Roman Catholic church until he was nine years old, followed by two mainline Protestant churches, a fundamentalist church, and a charismatic fellowship. "In every one of those churches," he told me, "I heard dignity and self-esteem condemned. I was made to feel doomed as a sinner unless I condemned myself—so I did. I actually began to *hate* myself."

But he brightened as he said, "Then I had a new encounter with Christ. And He didn't tell me how bad I was—I already knew that. He just told me how great I was going to become as we walked on through life together!" This young man had discovered the liberating truth of the gospel: Jesus has come to set us free from our feelings of inferiority. He didn't die for worms, but for men and women made in the image of God.

A grand performance—or an act of love?

The composer Verdi stood in the shadows of the concert hall in Florence during the performance of his very first opera. Though he would later garner the acclaim of the music world, at this point in his career he was unknown. Throughout the performance Verdi waited in the darkness with his eye on one person in the audience: the master composer Rossini. Verdi did not care whether the crowd would cheer him or jeer him. All he wanted was the smile of approval from the master.

Most of us tend to be very fragile, sensitive to the least slight or slur. That's because we seek approval from the world; we let others determine our opinion of ourselves. But when our object is to please the Master alone, then even the most cruel slap of rejection cannot harm our inner being; we become invincible. As a wise friend once told me, "I'm gradually learning to play out my life before a grand audience of One." It's a lesson I'm gradually learning, too.

I have to confess that I'm crippled. I don't wear braces on my arms or legs, but I'm crippled spiritually and emotionally. The Great Physician is bringing healing to my crippled self-image, but even as I write these words, I'm still inching my way toward wholeness.

For much of my life I sought the recognition of my peers. I can see clearly now that I really wanted that approval more than I wanted God. My sense of inadequacy grew worse as I entered high school and college. I was sprinting full-tilt on that treadmill race for self-acceptance, and the finish line was always beyond my reach.

Then, as a freshman in college, I met Jesus Christ in a dramatic way. I had been raised in a Christian home, and had grown up with a faith in Christ as Savior, but on this particular occasion I met Him as *Lord.* That's when a great *tension* moved into my life—tension between my desire to serve Jesus Christ and that deeply ingrained drive to be accepted for my achievements.

In my new commitment to Christ, I felt like a reborn person, with a newfound enthusiasm for boldly sharing Christ with others. Yet around my closest friends—whose approval I desperately wanted—I remained silent about my new relationship with Christ, afraid to be labeled a "religious fanatic." There was a tension between pleasing Christ and pleasing others.

Soon after giving my life to Christ, I felt the call of God to preach the gospel. At the age of eighteen, I began preaching in small churches, youth rallies, and meetings. But even as I preached, I knew there was a duality in my personality—the tension between wanting to preach Christ and wanting to gain some recognition and praise for myself.

Then, about ten years ago, I accepted an invitation to give the commencement address at the seminary from which I had graduated some years earlier. As I went, I knew I was going with tainted motives. I wanted to preach Christ—but I also hungered for recognition. I got no sleep at all the night before I was to speak.

The next day on the platform, as I awaited my turn to speak, I was filled with anxiety. My hands shook so badly I could hardly read my notes. I prayed that God would give me His peace, but no peace came. Then some words came to me through my conscience, just as though God were saying, "Ron, the reason you're so nervous is that you want to impress people. I don't need you to impress these people. I need you to love them. Ron, I don't need a Grand Performance. I want your life to be an Act of Love."

That was a transforming moment for me. My inner obsession with obtaining praise and honor fell away like a weight. The message I shared that day was not much different from what I had planned to say, but the heart from which it flowed was beginning to be changed.

Yet my struggle is not ended. The apostle Paul, writing in Galatians 1:10, delves unerringly into my own crisis of self-acceptance with this question: "Am I now trying to win the approval of men, or of God? Am I trying to please men? If I were still trying to please men, I would not be a servant of Christ." This is probably the most convicting portion of Scripture in all my life and ministry. I wrestle with the truth of Galatians 1:10 literally every day.

Today, virtually every time I get up to speak, I hear the words come back to my mind, "Not a Grand Performance, but an Act of Love." I've lived most of my life for the sake of impressing others, and a lifelong pattern does not change overnight. I'm still involved in a process of becoming healed of the hurt of inferiority.

We're all crippled. We all have feelings of inadequacy in our lives, and these feelings hold us back from being everything God wants us to be. God never intended us to feel beaten down by the past or paralyzed by a sense of inferiority. Rather, He calls us to make the healing choice for the hurt of inferiority—the choice to dwell on His *truth* about ourselves:

We are made in God's image, chosen to be His children. He bought us with the blood of His Son Jesus because we are incalculably precious in His eyes. We are men and women of value and importance, children of light in a dying age. *These* are the truths that heal us of the hurt of inferiority—truths which give our lives meaning in the eternal plan of God.

7

Healing the Hurt of Doubt

In order to believe greatly, one must doubt greatly.
— Malcolm Muggeridge

Now we see but a poor reflection; then we shall see face to face. Now I know in part; then I shall know fully, even as I am fully known.
—1 Corinthians 13:12

Not long ago, I received a letter from my friend Tom. The last time I had seen him, he was an active lay leader in a church in the Midwest. "The process of the erosion of my faith has taken years," he now wrote, "but now it's entirely gone. I feel like my life is ended. A few years ago, I was a strong Christian with what I thought was an invincible faith. Now I'm just a hollow shell. I feel so unworthy in my church because of my doubts."

To many of us, doubt is the deep, dark secret of the Christian life, a skeleton in the closet of almost every Christian's soul. Most of us are afraid to confess our doubts and questions because we're afraid others will judge us for our doubts, or perhaps because we're afraid our doubts might "rub off" on others and hinder their faith. And since everyone else is just like us, afraid to be honest about their doubts, we usually feel very much alone with our most troubling questions.

Perhaps you've had an experience like this: A question about your faith has been gnawing at you. You try to put it out of your mind, but it keeps coming back to haunt you. You feel you're the only person in the world who has been plagued with this particular doubt. One evening, you're in a Bible study, or having coffee with some Christian friends, and you venture to open up a little and confess your doubt to those friends—

Usually one of two things will happen. Your friends may gasp and begin to reprimand you. They may tell you it's a sin to doubt. In short, they may cause you to feel *unworthy* because of your doubts. That's what happened to my friend Tom. "I feel so unworthy in my church," he wrote, "because of my doubts." Sometimes our Christian friends have a hard time accepting the honest struggle of faith we go through.

However, you may get a different response when you confess your doubts. You may hear one of your friends say, "I know what you mean. I've felt that way, too." And another friend may say, "You have doubts like that too? I thought I was the only one!" And another, "I really appreciate your openness. It really helps me to hear that the doubts I've been feeling aren't so unusual."

We need to see doubting not as the enemy, but as a necessary component of faith. I can affirm the words of Alfred Lord Tennyson, "There lives more faith in honest doubt, believe me, than in half the creeds." This doesn't mean that doctrines are unimportant, but rather that courageously testing the reality of our faith has more meaning than the rote-reciting of some doctrinal statement. Doubts are an inevitable part of life and faith. When times of doubt come we should face our questions, not run from them.

I've seen it again and again: broken faith, like broken bones, almost always mends stronger than before.

Jesus and the doubter

The Bible affirms that there is room for questioning in our pilgrimage toward mature Christian faith. We need to have the same reverent skepticism we see in the Bereans of Acts 17:11, who "examined the Scriptures every day to see if what Paul said was true." As A. W. Tozer wrote, "We would do well to cultivate a reverent skepticism. . . . It is no sin to doubt some things, but it may be fatal to believe everything." [1] Tozer's words are prophetic indeed: if only there had been more doubters in Jonestown, Guyana! Indeed, the many cults that proliferate today could not long exist if they permitted this kind of reverent doubting.

Jesus gave us the right to inquire into truth when He proclaimed Himself to be the Way, the Truth, and the Life. In John 8:31-32, He told those who had chosen to believe Him, "If you hold to my teaching, you are really my disciples. Then you will know the truth, and the truth will set you free." Certainly, it takes belief, it takes *holding* to Jesus' teaching to really be His disciple. But Jesus also promised that we will know the truth, and the truth will set us free. Thus Jesus sanctifies the human process of rational inquiry, and He honors the human intellect, which was fashioned by the intellect of God.

Many of us have never noticed in the Scriptures how tenderly Jesus dealt with the doubters whose lives He touched. Remember John the Baptist, languishing alone in prison, awaiting his death? He had once proclaimed Jesus to crowds of people, but now he had begun to doubt. So he sent messengers to Jesus, asking, "Are you the One who was to come—or should we expect someone else?" Jesus sent those messengers back to John with His assurances, then turned to those around Him and affirmed John, even in the midst of his doubts: "I tell you, among those born of women, there is no one greater than John."

Remember Peter, who despaired so deeply in his faith that he actually denied Christ three times? Jesus' gentle response to Peter was to affirm him, to reinstate him in his faith, to tell him, "Go, Peter, and feed my sheep."

And remember Thomas, that classic I'm-from-Missouri skeptic who adamantly refused to believe the report of his friends that Jesus had been raised from the dead? "Unless I see the nail marks in his hands and put my finger where the nails were, and put my hand into his side," he declared, "I will not believe it!" You can almost feel the warmth of Jesus' smile and the tenderness in His voice when He appeared to Thomas and said, "Put your fingers here, Thomas. See my hands. Reach out your hand and put it into my side." Jesus did not rebuke Thomas for his doubts; rather, He invited Thomas's inquiry into the truth of the Resurrection.

Doubt is a valid part of our pilgrimage of faith, too. As we ponder our honest questions about our faith, Jesus would deal just as gently and affirmingly with us as He did with John the Baptist, Peter, and Thomas. God has given us the ability to reason, to wonder, to question—and He wants to use our intellect to bring us to an authentic faith in Him. T. M. Kitwood writes that the denial of honest questioning in our faith amounts to "the crucifixion of the intellect." He explains,

> This means that the believer, never being convinced in his mind, cannot give the full assent of his personality to God. He cannot believe with integrity. This is a serious departure from the Christianity of Christ who, though proclaiming . . . a revelation of God's truth, constantly appealed to the mind and the critical faculty.[2]

God calls us to a truly realistic and biblical kind of faith which touches us in our totality. Our faith will be a sound and reliable anchor for our lives only when it deeply involves *all* parts of our humanity, including our intellect.

Faith doesn't have to be blind

All around us, our fellow Christians are struggling with deep and troubling questions of their faith. Are we helping them work through their doubts? Jude verse 22 tells us, "Be merciful to those who doubt." Not critical, not easily shocked, not judgmental, but *merciful.*

The evangelical church has been slow to acknowledge the role of doubt in faith. In some ways, the church has been buying into the growing antirational, anti-intellectual mood of the dying culture in which we live—the mood that says there is no certainty, no objective truth in life; there is only a choice between "blind faith" or despair. It's time we affirm that blindness in one's faith is a handicap, just as physical blindness is a handicap in the physical world.

Many parents today are blindfolding their children intellectually, and thereby handicapping their faith even as they seek to protect them from error. I have two children, and I love them so much that I would spare them the hurt of doubt in any way I could. Yet to do so would actually hurt them in the long run because they *need* these growing pains of faith to become strong mentally, emotionally, and spiritually.

Those parents who desperately try to shield their children

from doubts are leaving them defenseless. It won't be long before an agnostic friend or teacher poses some hard questions to them—questions they can't answer, questions they were never allowed to think about before. Francis Schaeffer once said that of all the troubled young people who journeyed to his L'Abri retreat in Switzerland—bringing their deep confusion and anxiety about their faith—the vast majority came not from nonbelieving homes, but from evangelical or fundamentalist homes which communicated to them, "Don't question, just believe!"

It's normal and healthy for children, as they go through adolescence, to begin to question the values they've received from their parents. As children begin to approach adulthood, they naturally begin to establish their own separate identity. They need to come to a place where the Christian faith is authentically *their* faith, not just something handed down to them. When our young people doubt, it doesn't mean they're going to reject the Christian faith. It simply means they will ask questions—and we need to help them find the answers. We will never strengthen their faith by denying their questions.

Tragically, many parents feel threatened by the doubts and questions of their children. They react strongly—and their children are repelled rather than convinced. When our children come to us with their honest doubts, we have an opportunity to welcome and affirm their hunger for knowledge. We can respect their God-given intellect and say, "I'm glad you asked. That's a hard question, and I've wondered about it myself. Maybe we could try to find the answer together." And then we can seek out a relevant book or Scripture passage or a knowledgeable person for help and insight.

When our children have learned not to be afraid of the truth, but to *embrace* the truth, they will have a strong foundation for a living, growing faith. If the gospel doesn't make sense amid doubts and intellectual questioning, then it doesn't make sense at all. But thank God, the gospel does make sense. Our faith doesn't have to be "blind faith."

Doubting in the darkness

Our hardest trials of doubt come as an accompaniment to pain and loss. When we suffer, we often find ourselves sinking in a sea of darkness. God becomes hard to find in that darkness, and our trial of pain becomes a crisis of faith. Don Baker shares these insights about the link between suffering and doubt:

> Pain speaks a strange language—it plays funny tricks on us. It makes us think things and say things and even believe things that are not true. When pain begins to bore its way through human flesh and on into human spirit and then just sit there and hurt and hurt and hurt, the mind becomes clouded and the brain begins to think strange things like—*God is dead* or *He's gone fishing* or *He's just plain not interested.* [3]

I have to confess that there are times when I wrestle with the deep mysteries of God. It's not that I any longer question His existence; that fact has been settled in my heart. Nor do I any longer question the reality of the Resurrected Christ in my life; He is my Friend, and the greatest reality and truth in my life. I no longer question whether God loves me unconditionally; I'm secure in the knowledge that love and forgiveness are inextricably part of His nature. There have been times early in my pilgrimage of faith when I struggled with these issues, but no longer; they are settled for me.

Yet there's one area of faith where I confess I still struggle: the area of God's omnipotence. It's a struggle I've faced many times, such as when I've officiated a funeral for a little child or when I've stood in a famine-ravaged village in Africa. I felt it keenly when my brother died at the age of forty-one. During my time of grieving for Paul, I've had a genuine and continual experience of the presence and grace of God—yet at the same time there is a deep disappointment that God would allow him to get cancer and die. In these days, I've had to honestly ask God, "Are You really all-powerful? If You're really all-loving and all-powerful, then why have You allowed Paul to suffer and die?"

Doubts such as these can have a paralyzing effect on our faith. We can begin to focus on our doubts so completely that we can become incapable of functioning. It was Shakespeare who wrote in *Measure for Measure,* "Our doubts are traitors, and make us lose the good we oft might win by fearing to attempt." This is an accurate assessment of the power of intense doubting to immobilize us. How can we be healed of the paralysis that doubt so often causes?

We need to understand that God calls us to a kind of faith that leaves no part of our lives untouched. Biblical faith must touch the mind, the heart, and the will. If our faith is only an intellectual kind, then we'll probably never move beyond our doubts and questions.

The proof that our faith has touched our *hearts* is in the way we love and care for people in the name of Jesus Christ. At the end of Matthew 25, Jesus describes a time of judgment that awaits us, and in this great final exam of the Christian life, we won't be asked any questions about doctrinal knowledge or our orthodoxy. The quiz we will have to answer is this: "When people were starving, did you feed them in My name? When they were thirsty, did you give them drink? When they were alone and friendless, did you befriend them? When they were ill-clad or sick or in prison, did you go to them and meet their needs in My name?" That, says Jesus, is the test of whether our hearts have been touched by our faith.

The proof that our faith has touched our *will* is in the way we live increasingly more obedient and courageous lives for Christ, willing to step out and risk for Him, willing to *act*. C. S. Lewis illustrates this truth for us in *The Screwtape Letters* as he depicts the senior devil Screwtape advising the junior devil Wormwood to lure his human "patient" (a Christian whose faith Wormwood is seeking to subvert) into inaction. "No amount of piety in his imagination and affections will harm us," says Screwtape, "if we can keep it out of his will." [4]

Not long ago, I stood in the dusty streets of a little African village called Goram Goram in the country of Burkina Faso (formerly Upper Volta). This village had suffered for years from ground-cracking drought and famine, followed by sudden rains and flooding. All the mud huts of the village had been destroyed. Now cholera plagued these homeless, devastated people.

During my time in Goram Goram, I held little children in my arms who were dying of malnutrition and childhood diseases that would have been easily treatable in the United States. And at the end of the day, I would just go to my knees and ask, "Why, Lord? How can there be so much needless suffering in this place? If You are all-loving and all-power-ful, Lord, why does this happen?" And in my helplessness before all the tragedy I had witnessed, I often felt totally over-whelmed, and tempted to immobility and despair.

I finally had to pray, "Lord, I'm going to have to yield this tragedy to You. I don't understand why You've allowed all this suffering, but I can't take it all onto myself. Lest I become immobilized by my depression and my questioning, I'm going to have to yield the Why of this situation to You. I refuse to give in to the paralysis of doubt. I'll do all I can to help while I'm here, and then I'll tell this story to my friends back home. But the incomprehensible Why I surrender to You."

The questions I asked God on my knees in Goram Goram are the oldest and hardest questions human beings have ever asked. They're the same questions Job asked in his crisis of suffering. Throughout the book of Job, he probes God deeply with such questions as, *Are You all-powerful, and are You in control? Are You just? Are You loving? If You are, then why do You allow the innocent to suffer?* By the end of the book, Job finally comes to a place of acceptance and peace with his doubts.

But it's important to understand that God *never* answers Job's questions. God never tells Job *why* he suffered. We won-der why, don't we? And we identify with Job. When we face illness or loss or the end of life itself, we want to know why. We implore God with our questions, but the sky is silent.

We think, "Well, God *owes* me an explanation!" And then we immediately realize, "And yet, if He is really the sovereign God of the Universe, He really doesn't owe me anything." But then we think, "Well, if He's a God of love, then doesn't He *want* me to understand the reason for my suffering?" And to these questions, I have to answer, *Yes,* I believe God does want us to understand—at least to the extent we *can* under-stand.

Yet we are finite beings seeking to understand the ways of an Infinite God. It may well be that if God gave us the answers to all our questions, we wouldn't be able to comprehend them. The problem of suffering is one of the deep mysteries of the universe, as impenetrable to our minds as quantum physics. We have to acknowledge with Paul that all we can grasp is a poor reflection in a dark and imperfect glass. One day we shall see face to face, and we shall know fully—but for now we know only in part.

In the end, our hardest questions will remain unanswered. Our reasoning and questioning of God can take us, perhaps, 90 percent of the way toward a settled assurance and trust. But we're going to have to take that other 10 percent *by faith.* Not "blind faith," but a faith that proceeds from an honest quest for truth. I affirm these words of Ralph Waldo Emerson: "All I have seen teaches me to trust the Creator for all I have not seen."

Will it ever end?

I think most of us, in the back of our minds, are vaguely hoping for that day in our walk with God when our faith has solidified like concrete, when we have no more doubts to trouble us. I don't believe that day will ever come, because I don't believe God intends for any of us ever to stop growing and learning.

But I am convinced we can come through our times of doubt and emerge into a faith that stands firmly, resolutely, and confidently. It was Francis Bacon who once wrote, "If a man will begin with certainties, he shall end in doubts. But if he will be content to begin with doubts, he will end with certainties." We can come to a haven of settled and secure faith. In fact, that is the goal of doubt: to strengthen our faith. For while it is no sin to struggle with doubt, it is certainly no virtue to prolong our doubting endlessly.

I've encountered some people who appear to take masochistic pleasure in endlessly questioning everything about their faith. They seem perversely proud of their continual doubting—and they never seem to arrive at a point of conviction and liberating assurance. God never intended this kind of perpetual turmoil to be the norm in the Christian life.

What can we do to come safely through a time of crisis in our faith? First, we need to *spend time in the Word of God.* Often, we respond to doubt by laying aside our Bibles and turning elsewhere for the answers to our questions. Yet, it is precisely at such times that we most need the companionship and wisdom of God's Word. J. I. Packer calls faith "the subjecting of mind and conscience to the Word of God." In *God Has Spoken,* he writes, "In the absence of certainty as to just what the Word of God is, superstition prevails, and instead of faith there is fog. . . . Doubts and uncertainties about God and our standing with Him are poor companions to live and die with; but many today are never out of their company, because they know of no assurances from God on which their faith may rest." [5]

Second, we need to *spend time in prayer.* You may be thinking, "Prayer! How can I pray when I am doubting so deeply?" But now is when you need prayer the most! James 1:5 tells us, "If any of you lacks wisdom, he should ask God, who gives generously to all without finding fault, and it will be given to him."

Yet as we look further in that passage we may become confused about the role of prayer in a time of doubt. James 1:6–8 tells us, "But when he asks, he must believe and not doubt, because he who doubts is like a wave of the sea, blown and tossed by the wind. That man should not think he will receive anything from the Lord; he is a double-minded man, unstable in all he does." Doesn't this verse say that any doubt at all is fatal to one's prayers? No, there's an enormous difference between people who struggle with questions about their faith and those who are "double-minded," "unstable," who allow themselves to be blown and tossed on a sea of perpetual doubting.

What God is saying to us through James is precisely what Jesus said in Mark 9, as He answered the plea of a father to heal his son. "Everything is possible," said Jesus, "for him who believes." And our prayer to God must echo that anxious father's reply: "I do believe; help me overcome my unbelief!" As we come to God in prayer, offering our doubts and asking for wisdom, we have to honestly confess to God, "I believe you, Lord—at least I believe you enough to come to you in prayer. But I also have to honestly confess my doubts. In fact, there are times when I'm not sure I really believe in you. But I'm asking you to help me overcome my doubts. Help me to have a deeper faith in you."

Third, we need to *act in obedience.* We need to commit our *will* to God even though our minds and emotions are in turmoil. You see, doubt is not the opposite of faith. The opposite of faith is *disobedience.* When we choose to be obedient to God, even as we are raising our questions and doubts, we are able to see more clearly that the process of doubting is really woven into the process of faith.

Matthew 14 tells of a time when Peter and his friends were out fishing on a lake, and a storm rose up and began to swamp their boat. Suddenly Peter saw Jesus walking toward them across the water. Peter was terrified; he couldn't believe it was really Jesus. "Lord," he called, "if it's really you, tell me to come to you on the water." Jesus' reply? "Come."

So Peter acted against the counsel of his doubts; he left the safety of his boat and stepped out in faith upon the water—and he began to *walk!* After a few steps, he paused to check out his circumstances. Seeing the wind and the waves, he suddenly realized that what he was doing was plainly impossible—and this realization began to *sink* him. As he started to go under, the Lord reached out to him and saved him.

We could all be a little more like Peter, stepping out in risky obedience, disregarding our doubts and circumstances. We may, like Peter, begin to doubt and get ourselves in deep water—but Jesus is always there to pull us up again.

Josh McDowell tells the story of a tightrope walker who came to town with the circus. Before an awed crowd of onlookers, he performed many daring feats—riding a bicycle, carrying chairs, walking on his hands, pushing a wheelbarrow—all on a tenuous span of rope hundreds of feet above a river. Finally, he came to his last feat. "I will now push this wheelbarrow across that rope with another person in it! Do you think I can do it?"

"Yes!" answered the confident crowd. "You can do it!"

"That's wonderful!" said the tightrope walker. "Then who among you wants to be first to volunteer as my passenger?"

Total silence.

"I'll volunteer," said a young woman, stepping confidently to the front. The crowd was amazed at her courage. The stuntman took her across the river in the wheelbarrow, then back again, all without a hitch.

Afterwards, someone ran to the young woman and asked, "Where on earth did you get the courage to do that? Weren't you scared to death?"

"Not at all," she smiled. "You see, the tightrope walker

is my *father*—and I've been performing that feat with him all my life."

And so it is with us. As we live according to our faith instead of according to our doubts, our faith and assurance grow. We come to know the Father *personally,* not just intellectually. Through our active daily reliance upon Him, we can finally reach a place where we can say, "I'm not afraid to trust my heavenly Father. I've been performing the feat of faith with Him all my life."

Accepting the mystery of God

Trembling and feeling very small, we come to God with our little portion of faith in our hands, and we lift it up to Him. And He smiles upon us, and we warm ourselves in His love. He takes that little portion of faith that we offer Him, and He blesses it—

And He *breaks* it. And He breaks it again. And again. And each time He breaks it, it multiplies before our wondering eyes. And He gives us back our enlarged and multiplied faith, and we feed on it, and we *grow.* As we grow, our vision of God becomes clearer and greater and more assured.

In *Prince Caspian,* the second volume of The Chronicles of Narnia, C. S. Lewis portrays a reunion between Aslan—the great golden lion who in many ways represents Christ—and a young girl named Lucy:

> A circle of grass, smooth as a lawn, met Lucy's eyes, with dark trees dancing all round it. And then—oh joy! For *He* was there: the huge Lion, shining white in the moonlight, with his huge black shadow underneath him. . . .
> She rushed to him. She felt her heart would burst if she lost a moment. And the next thing she knew was that she was kissing him and putting her arms as far round his neck as she could and burying her face in the beautiful rich silkiness of his mane.
> "Aslan, Aslan. Dear Aslan," sobbed Lucy. "At last.". . .
> "Welcome, child," he said.
> "Aslan," said Lucy, "you're bigger."
> "That is because you are older, little one," answered he.
> "Not because you are?"

"I am not. But every year you grow, you will find me bigger." [5]

I really identify with those words. Every year I grow, I seem to find that God is bigger in His goodness and love than I ever thought possible. The more we grow, the bigger God will seem. Our doubts, though they will continue to come, will seem less important, less of a hindrance. As we begin to see faith more as a commitment to a relationship than an assent to a creed, we will experience increasingly more of the reality of God. Even more, we'll discover that we don't need to understand everything about God in order to love Him.

We believe in the Almighty God of the Universe, the One who created heaven and earth, who spoke the billions of stars into existence, who so amazingly and wonderfully made us as human beings. Such a God could never be enclosed within the boundaries of our finite understanding. We can understand a great deal about Him, especially as He discloses Himself to us in His Word. But ultimately there must be aspects of His nature that we can only accept as Mystery for now. Our understanding can penetrate so far into that Mystery, and no further. Only a God who is great enough to inspire our doubts and questions could be great enough to inspire our faith.

8

Healing the Hurt of Conflict

Conflict isn't necessarily good or bad. Conflict just is.

—David Augsburger

Blessed are the peacemakers,
for they will be called sons of God.

—Matthew 5:9

The gray chill of winter clung to him as he trudged up the snow-covered walk. His mood was as bleak as the word *divorce*. He mounted the steps to the front door and rang the doorbell of the house that used to be his home. A few moments later the door opened just a crack. "What do you want?" said the woman behind the door.

"I just came to pack my things. I won't be long."

The door opened wider and the woman stepped aside. The man entered, noting the lonely seeming Christmas tree in its usual corner of the living room. The ornamentation seemed half-hearted.

She eyed him coldly. "What are you going to pack your things in? Didn't you even bring a suitcase?"

"*You* got all the luggage," he replied bitterly, "along with the house, the refrigerator—"

"All right."

"—the stereo—"

"*All right!* Just take what you came for and get out! There are trash bags under the kitchen sink! I'll be in the bedroom, dumping your clothes out on the floor!"

He went to the kitchen. Muttering, he flung the cabinet

doors wide and began rummaging about for the trash bags. He spilled cleanser and sent a lightbulb wobbling across the floor. "I can't find them! Where did you—Oh, here they are."

As he strode down the hallway toward the bedroom, he turned over various phrases in his mind, searching for just the right words to hurt her as deeply as possible. When he was sure he was in earshot, he began, "Soon as I get out of here, I won't have to take any more of your—" He fell silent at the doorway.

She was kneeling on the floor in front of the dresser, surrounded by piles of underwear and socks. All the anger was gone from her face. She reached into the bottom of the open drawer before her and pulled out a little pair of blue jeans, and a small T-shirt with teddy bears on the front. Tears spilled down her cheeks as she clutched these reminders to herself—reminders of the little child who had passed through their lives a few short years before.

The man knelt beside his wife and pulled her close. Her head fell onto his shoulder and she began to sob. Then his tears began to fall, mingling with hers. "What are we doing?" he said at last. "God held us together when Timmy got sick—and even when he died. Can't He hold us together now?"

This moment of warmth in a cold, gray day was just the beginning, the first tentative step for two people on a long, uphill road to reconciliation. There were many painful memories to be healed, many hurtful words and acts to be forgiven. There were still many tears, recriminations and angry silences ahead for these two people—but there were also many embraces and words of love and repentance. The conflict of the past could never be undone—but it could be healed. It's never too late for faith, hard work, and love to bring a new beginning out of the deepest trial of conflict.

Surrender

Conflict can break relationships—but it can also *strengthen* them. It all depends on the choices we make in our trial of conflict. Whatever your conflict right now, God is calling you to learn to surrender—not necessarily surrender to the person who opposes you but surrender to God, and to His healing solution for your struggle. It takes two to make an argument, but it only takes *one* to make the healing choice, the positive response which results in healing for *both* people involved, the response that brings strength instead of destruction to a relationship.

You may have grown up in a home where continual conflict was the norm; you may believe "fighting it out" is the only way to face any conflict. Or you may come from a home where anger was suppressed, not expressed; conflict was avoided to such an extent that there was very little truth and openness in your relationships. When these are the only two options, there will inevitably emerge a winner and a loser—and the relationship between these two people will be damaged or broken. A choice between "fight" or "flight" is a choice between two forms of calamity: For whether we win our conflict through intimidation or lose through retreat and withdrawal, we have allowed an *opportunity* to turn into *tragedy.*

The good news the Bible offers us is that there is a *third* option for our trials of conflict: not winning, not losing, but *healing* the conflict. When we choose neither to fight nor to fold in a confrontation, then we can *grow* in our relationships with others. As we listen carefully and actively to the other person's views, we gain new insights and we learn to *act* on his concerns rather than simply *react* to his anger. We find validity in his arguments, and we test and strengthen our own views in the crucible of conflict.

The only true solution to the dilemma of conflict is the realization that conflict must not be won or lost, but *healed*—and the ultimate source of healing power for all our trials, including the trial of conflict, is God. Conflict that has been either won or lost is conflict that has been resolved by natural, human means. But a *healed* conflict has been resolved by *super*-natural, *super*human means. The same Holy Spirit who comes into the Christian at the moment of conversion is there as a counselor, a confidant, a power source in times of conflict. He is there for us to draw upon in times of conflict, helping us reweave the fabric of our torn relationship.

But how do we draw upon the Holy Spirit during the heat of conflict? Conflict comes in so many ways. We may pick up the phone or answer the door to be surprised by a hostile confrontation. Or conflict may creep up on us imperceptibly, as a discussion with a friend gradually degenerates into a heated argument. Whether we fall into conflict suddenly or subtly, it's my experience that there's always time for a moment of silent prayer.

I confess that it's not always my first instinct to respond to conflict with prayer. But whenever I do, the outcome of the conflict is invariably far different than when I simply meet that confrontation in my own strength and wisdom. My prayer usually goes something like, "Lord, please fill me with the power and insight of the Holy Spirit. Give me Your words of peace and forgiveness to speak." I may have to pray this prayer repeatedly during the crisis as the temptation to respond in anger arises again and again. Prayer is surrender to God, and that surrender must be continuous.

Through prayer, God can empty us of our defensiveness, while filling us with Christlike qualities of humility and forgiveness. In reliance upon God, we can listen with sensitivity and speak the truth in love. Surrender to God is the true basis for a healing, loving resolution of our trial of conflict.

Glorious slavery

Mike and Susan were at odds, embittered and hostile toward each other. Their ten-year-old marriage was slowly being destroyed by continual conflict. Whenever Mike began to speak, Susan would interrupt with the words "Yes, but—" and go on to assert her defense. And Mike, not to be outdone, would soon interrupt in his own defense with the same words, "Yes, but—"

Susan: "Yes, but what about you? You're never home on weekends! You're always out rafting or skiing or—"

Mike: "Yes, but I've invited you to come along! You just never want to do the things I want to do—"

Susan: "Yes, but do you ever consider *my* feelings? Do you ever think of spending just one day a week doing something *I* like to do?"

Mike: "Yes, but the *only* things you like to do are going shopping or visiting your mother or—"

Susan: "Yes, but the only thing *you* ever want to do with me is—"

Mike: "Yes, but what do you do as soon as I want to show you a little affection? You pull back and—"

And on and on.

After a couple weeks of refereeing this kind of dialogue in my counseling office, I stepped in and said, "Mike, there are two things you need to begin doing, as I perceive it: First, you need to begin affirming Susan's self-worth and her value as your wife and the mother of your children. Second, you need to love her as Christ commanded you, to give her more of your evenings and weekends, and more of yourself."

"Yes, but—" came the predictable reply, "what about Susan?"

Then I said to Susan, "You know, Susan, you're not giving Mike any encouragement or sense of significance in his role as the husband-father in the home. You're also withdrawing all your affection and sexual interaction with him because you want to punish him until he becomes all you want him to be."

And, predictably, she replied, "Yes, but—"

And it continued that way for several more weeks. But finally, as the love of Christ began to seep deeper into their lives, it began to be not "Yes, but!" but *Yes:* "Yes! I see that now. Regardless of how my spouse responds, *my* response is my responsibility, and—Yes!—I want our marriage to be healed." And healing began to take place in this marriage.

In his book *Caring Enough to Confront,* David Augsburger writes,

> Nothing ends blaming games like the recognition that the blame must be scored 50–50. . . . If there is blame to be fixed, it includes both persons involved.
>
> It takes two people to have a problem. In a marriage, for example, neither I nor you is the whole problem. "We" are our problems. The trouble is with "us." Both people are involved in the hurt, the problem, the tragedy of a marriage in pain.[1]

The healing of our relationships and our conflicts begins when we stop saying, "Yes, but—" and start simply saying *Yes;* when we stop defending ourselves and blaming others, and begin taking ownership of our own failures and sins; when we recognize that our attitude is always ours to choose. The healing choice in a time of conflict is the decision to stop saying, "*You* make me angry," and to start saying, "*I'm* feeling angry about the problem between us. Let's focus our energy on solving the problem, not on hurting each other."

The healing choice doesn't come easily to us in times of conflict. As human beings we are fighters by nature. "What causes fights and quarrels among you?" asks James 4:1-2. "Don't they come from your desires that battle within you? You want something but don't get it. You kill and covet, but you cannot have what you want. You quarrel and fight. You do not have, because you do not ask God." Here, James addresses Christians—you and me—and he confronts the choice we so often make to create tension and conflict between ourselves and others. Our own sinful desires are at the root of much of the conflict we experience in life. We kill and covet, says James; we kill with our words, we kill with our thoughts, we kill with cruelty and accusation and sarcasm.

The Word of God confronts us head-on in our sin. We are to love unconditionally, even in the midst of conflict. The gospel, in the final analysis, is *slavery*—a glorious kind of slavery that ultimately leads to true freedom. The gospel binds us against our natural will to do what is *un*natural—and even what is *super*natural. The gospel constrains us to love.

In his New Testament letters, the apostle Paul continually calls himself a "slave" to Jesus Christ, and this is no mere figure of speech. To Paul, Jesus is Lord and Master, and that means Paul surrenders to Him all rights, including the right to defend himself, the right to resentment, the right to revenge. At the heart of our slavery to the gospel is unconditional, volitional love.

In marriage, unconditional love is expressed in *commitment.* Often when a Christian husband and wife come to me for counsel, they tell me their romantic love is fading and they are falling deeper and deeper into conflict. At such times I encourage them as two people who have placed themselves under the lordship of Christ to see themselves as *slaves.* I show them in the Scriptures that the command of their Lord and Master is to *love one another.* It's amazing how much harder we work at our marriages once we have accepted this fact.

To love unconditionally means to love *even when we don't feel like loving.* And you may wonder, "Well, isn't it really

hypocritical to love when I don't feel like loving?" No, there's
nothing hypocritical in acting in ways you don't *feel;* hypocrisy
is the sin of acting in ways you don't *believe.* When we truly
commit ourselves to loving others as Christ commanded,
then we will be sincerely and obediently living out our
Christian beliefs—whether we *feel* like it or not. God calls us
to love in unlovely situations, to show kindness to enemies,
to bless those who curse us. The amazing thing is that as
we love when we don't feel like loving, often the feelings
return as well.

"Ungraceful people"

Who is the most "ungraceful" person in your life right now?
Who is that one person who seems to communicate to you a
total lack of understanding of the grace of God? Someone
probably comes very readily to mind.

Your "ungraceful person" may in fact be a fellow Christian.
In *Of God and Men,* A. W. Tozer describes these "ungraceful"
Christians: "Unsaintly saints are the tragedy of Christianity.
People of the world usually pass through the circle of disciples
to reach Christ, and if they find those disciples severe and
sharp-tongued they can hardly be blamed if they sigh and
turn away from Him." [2] You've probably encountered some
of these "unsaintly saints." They are genuine Christians, people
who have received the grace of God—yet they seem to have
no understanding of the fact that they have been called by
God to *show* that same forgiving grace to others.

Then again, your "ungraceful person" may be someone who
is indifferent or even hostile to God. You may actually be
experiencing conflict with this person *because* you are a Christian, and your "ungraceful person" feels confronted by the
evidence of God's grace in your life.

Your "ungraceful person" is the one who always takes the
opposite point of view; the one who tends to be cynical and
sarcastic; the one who continually rubs you the wrong way;
the one who never says, "I'm sorry" or "I was wrong" or
"please forgive me"; the one who is insensitive to your feelings,
your beliefs, and your needs. Your "ungraceful person" may
even be a member of your own family.

Josh McDowell's "ungraceful person" was his own father.

In *Evidence That Demands a Verdict,* he writes that his father "epitomized everything I hated. . . . He was the town drunk. My high school friends would make jokes about him making a fool of himself around town. . . . Sometimes when we had company I would tie Dad up in the barn and tell them he had to go on an important call." [3]

But when McDowell became a Christian, God's grace was able to transform his hatred for his father into *love.* A few months after his conversion to Christ, McDowell was injured in an automobile accident. His father came to visit him in his hospital room. At one point as they were talking together, he broke down and said, "Josh, I've been the worst kind of father to you. How can you love a man like me?"

"Dad," said McDowell, "six months ago I couldn't. But now, through Jesus Christ, I *can* love you." And he explained to his father the meaning of God's grace in his life. Before leaving that hospital room, Josh McDowell's father had committed his life to Jesus Christ. From then on he was a changed man. He put alcohol out of his life, and scores of people who saw the change in his life also came to know Jesus Christ. About a year later this changed man died at peace with God and at peace with his son.

That's what God's grace is all about: When you don't deserve love, you're loved. When you don't deserve forgiveness, you're forgiven. When your life seems no longer worth living, you're given a second chance—you're even given *new* life, *eternal* life. That's the grace of God, and everyone who has committed himself to Christ has received this undeserved kindness from God. God in His grace loved us while we were still His enemies, locked in rebellious conflict against His will. He loved us patiently, aggressively, continuously, even while we fought Him, until at last we surrendered and confessed to Him, "My Lord and my God!"

The ultimate test of the reality of God's grace in our hearts is our willingness to love the "ungraceful people" who come into our lives. Grace pursued us while we were still in rebellion against God, and grace calls us to reach out in love, acceptance, and forgiveness to our "ungraceful person." Grace calls us to respond to abuse and anger with patience and understanding. Grace calls us to be sensitive to the hurts and insecurities that so often underlie the abrasiveness of our "ungraceful persons," to look beyond the irritation to the *need* of that person.

In our own lives there will be times when our "ungraceful persons" will be changed and won over as we patiently model the grace of God toward them. But there will be other times when there will be no change, no reconciliation, no happy ending. If that is your trial right now, I know there is great pain in that. I've known that pain in some of my own relationships.

But you *do* have one promise for your trial of conflict, even when it seems your "ungraceful person" has hardened his heart against you and will *never* change—the promise that God's grace is sufficient in your life, even for the hurt of conflict that won't go away. It's the same promise God made to Paul in his trials: "My grace is sufficient for you, for my power is made perfect in weakness" (2 Cor. 12:9). God has promised to supply His strength for your weakness, and His grace for your "ungraceful person."

An allegiance to relationships

Jesus said, "Blessed are the peacemakers"—but He didn't mean we are to seek peace at any price. There are some issues that *demand* we take a stand, for to do any less would be disobedience to God: the centrality of Christ, and His sacrifice for our sin; His bodily Resurrection; the absolute authority of Scripture; salvation by grace through faith, apart from works; the reality of eternal life with Christ for all who believe in His name; the Great Commission of the church to claim, train, and send people into the world for Christ; the absolute demand of God on our lives that we love Him with all our heart and strength, and that we unconditionally love one another. These are unbendable truths, and we must stand firm on them.

We are to stand for the truth, but as Ephesians 4:15 tells us, we must speak the truth *in love*. Christian peacemaking is a truthful, positive, aggressive ministry of bringing divided people together into a healed relationship. Christian reconciliation takes place only as we face our conflicts and work through them to a point of true understanding and acceptance. We may not always reach total agreement with our opponents, but we can weather our conflicts with our capacity to love one another intact—and even strengthened.

I've found that in time people will either develop an allegiance to issues or an allegiance to relationships. So if we don't make the healing choice to make relationships our priority, then we will gradually become more and more exclusively committed to issues, and the unconditional love of Christ will be choked out of our lives. A true Christian peacemaker genuinely cares about issues—but he cares even *more* about relationships.

Once when I was in high school, three of my friends and I were going to the drive-in at the edge of town, and each of us had a date for the evening. So there were eight of us in our family car, an old Ford Fairlane. My friend Pedro Garcia was one of the eight people in the car that night. In fact, his presence was *keenly* felt that evening because Pedro is 6′ 5″ and weighs about 220 pounds.

About a half-hour into the movie, Pedro said, "It's too crowded in here. My date and I are going to get out and sit somewhere else." So he and his date got out and walked around for a while, and they finally decided that the best seat in the place was atop the roof of our Ford Fairlane. So Pedro and his date (who was not particularly petite either) got on top of our car. About half-way through the movie, the rest of us in the car felt something coming down on our heads: the roof of the car, sinking under the combined weight of Pedro and his girlfriend. The rest of us sat through the remainder of the movie hunched down in our seats.

Driving home, I knew I had some explaining to do. So I pulled in the drive, went in the house and told my Dad what happened. He looked out the window at the car in the drive and saw that the roof was caved in exactly as I had described it. I'll never forget the first words he said to me at that point: "Ron, you know I love you—"

Naturally, he had a good deal more to say—in fact, it was a fairly comprehensive discourse on the subject of the economic implications of auto body repair. But the *first* thing he said was, "Ron, you know I love you." In other words, he was telling me, "Ron, our relationship is more important than this issue. I love you more than that bashed-in Ford out there."

How are you doing at communicating that *people* are more important than the issues you confront? How are you doing at maintaining a priority of *relationship* with others in your family, your friendships, and your church?

The best place to work through conflict is not on our feet, with our jaws set and our fists doubled up, but on our knees— pleading for understanding, weeping over our sins, praying for the wisdom and unity of the Holy Spirit. "Blessed are the peacemakers," says the Lord, "for they will be called the children of God." The approval and blessing of God rests upon those who gently, humbly, lovingly speak the truth in love.

Unity in diversity

Some time ago, I received a call from a friend, an elder in another church. He was weary, exasperated, and there was a note of defeat in his voice. He told me he had been up until 2:30 in the morning in a long, hard meeting with the church board. This respected and influential evangelical church had now broken into bitterly divided factions.

How had this happened?

In talking further with my friend, I found that his church had fallen into an all-too-familiar pattern: Personalities had grown into parties. Convictions had degenerated into contentions. Rich diversity had been perverted into ugly division by an unloving, unyielding spirit. People had ceased to think of themselves as "one people" and instead aligned themselves into manipulative factions—"our people" versus "those people."

Ephesians 4:1–16 tells us that all Christians are called to unity and peace in the Holy Spirit. We have *one* hope, *one* faith, *one* Lord—and yet God has deliberately created the church to be richly *diverse* so that the greatest good can flow to the most people. Tragically, we often take the very diversity that God gave us for the sake of building the church and we set one part of the church against another, destroying each other and the work of God.

Where there is diversity there will be conflict. That is only natural, and conflict should not be avoided or papered over. We need to learn to *use* conflict in a way that brings about healthy growth and change, and an appreciation of other points of view.

Diversity can be our greatest strength in the church, as we move out in power and bold witness, changing lives and impacting the world for Jesus Christ by every possible means. But our diversity can *destroy* us if we begin to see one another as rivals instead of partners; if we begin living out a spirit of suspicion and competition rather than humility and gentleness; if our allegiance to *issues* becomes stronger than our allegiance to *relationships*.

John and I graduated from seminary together. Shortly after our graduation, John took his first pastorate in a small church in the Midwest. He had only been in that church a short time before a series of major conflicts developed, principally between himself and an elderly gentleman in the church. John wanted to bring in some newer kinds of music; the older man opposed it. John wanted to start some new forms of outreach and ministry to youth and adults; the older man opposed it. There was conflict in this church—conflict born of a diversity of opinions and gifts and approaches to ministry.

And yet there was a special dimension to the conflict in this church. These two men who were in such frequent and sharp conflict together were also best friends. They played golf together. They had fellowship together in each others' homes, sharing dinner and conversation and prayer together. This puzzled many people within and outside the church: How could these two men, divided as they were over so many issues, be such close friends?

One of the members of the church was talking with this elderly gentleman one time and asked, "I don't understand. You and John differ on just about every major issue in the church, and yet you seem to be such close friends. How can that be?"

"Oh, that's not so hard to understand," the old man replied. "Remember when John first came to our church? My wife was dying and this young pastor, whom we just barely knew at the time, came over to our house and sat by her bedside for twenty-four hours straight. He just held each of our hands in both of his and waited with us and prayed with us until morning came and my wife passed on into eternity. And then John just put his arm around me and wept with me. So, you see, we can differ over a lot of things, but the love of Jesus covers all those differences."

Issues are not our center. We have one center, one focus, one Lord: Jesus Christ alone. Our allegiance must not be to issues, but to *relationships*—first our relationship to Christ, and then our relationship to one another. When we are centered in Christ, then there is *unity* at the center of all our diversity, and over all our conflicts there is love.

Iron sharpens iron

God is not merely building individuals; He is building His church, the body of Christ, as an integrated whole. Each part must relate to all the other parts in order for the body to function properly. We cannot be all God intends us to be if we are isolated from other Christians, nor can we be whole in Christ if we are broken in relationship to other Christians—for together we *are* the body of Christ.

Proverbs 27:17 tells us that in the same way that iron sharpens iron, so do two friends sharpen each other. The image here is of a sword being honed and tempered for keen-edged strength. The sharpening process means *friction;* it means grinding off whatever impedes the efficiency and usefulness of the sword, whatever keeps the sword from being keen and sharp. Christian friends "sharpen" one another by telling each other the truth. The truth, expressed in love, makes us keen, sharp, useful tools in God's hands.

But truth often brings with it *conflict*—and that is why truth must always be accompanied by unconditional love, the kind of love that says, "No matter what you do or say, I will always accept you. I will always uphold you, and I will always try to build you up." Unconditional love gives unconditional affirmation.

A sword-edge that is mercilessly ground down or beaten with a sledge-hammer will not be sharpened; it will be *destroyed.* So it is with people and relationships. Unsparing truthfulness without love only serves to beat people down. But if we spend most of our time in our relationships giving encouragement and affirmation to others then we will have earned the right to be truthful at those times when the truth has to hurt in order to help.

In Galatians 6:1 Paul tells us, "Brothers, if someone is caught in a sin, you who are spiritual should restore him gently. But watch yourself, or you also may be tempted." There will probably be times in your life when you observe a fellow Christian slipping into a pattern of living which is harmful to himself or others. At such times, says Paul, it is our Christian duty to go to that person and gently confront him in love. Our goal in such situations is not merely to rebuke but to *restore*— and the restoration process can often be hard. Sometimes love calls us to confront. Caring often draws us into conflict. In *Caring Enough to Confront,* David Augsburger observes:

> Wholesale approval of another suggests that one is either totally unconcerned or radically uninvolved with the other. Cheap approval can be lavished on anyone at any time to any extent. But caring requires that one get interested in the direction the other's life is taking and offer real immediate involvement.
> If you love, you level. If you value another, you volunteer the truth.[4]

God's Word calls us to humility in our relationships with others, and warns "watch yourself, or you also may be tempted." Aware of our own fallibility, we can easily overlook the small slights and errors of others; we can confront with tears and sorrow instead of accusations; we can *accept* and *embrace* the erring brother or sister, knowing we too can fall into equally serious sin.

In all our relationships, there will be some honest differences, there will be misunderstandings, there may even be feelings of distrust and anger. Through it all, God in Romans 14:19 calls us to "make every effort to do what leads to peace and to mutual edification." And that word "peace" in the original New Testament Greek doesn't mean a cease-fire or an absence of conflict; rather it suggests a quality of being bonded and fused together in relationship with one another. That's the only truly healing choice for the hurt of conflict: to aggressively pursue real peace, reconciliation, and mutual upbuilding in all our relationships.

It takes a great deal of courage to make the healing choice in times of conflict—and all the more so since there is no guaranteeing the response of the other person in our conflict. "If it is possible, *as far as it depends on you,*" says Romans 12:18 (italics added), "live at peace with everyone." Our response is our responsibility; the other person's response is between him and God. But by the grace of God, we will seek

His approval and be His peacemakers in times of conflict.

A few years ago at a conference sponsored by the Fellowship of Christian Athletes, I met three young athletes who had come from the same small town in the Midwest. They had given their lives to Jesus Christ as Savior and Lord at this conference, and then they went back to their hometown with a burden to begin an evangelistic Bible study among their fellow athletes.

After the first meeting of this Bible study, these three young men went out for pizza, each wearing his F.C.A. T-shirt with a large cross on the front. They were sitting at a table eating pizza and drinking Cokes when a number of black-jacketed members of a motorcycle gang swaggered loudly through the front door.

Seeing the young athletes with their Bibles and the Christian insignia on their T-shirts, these bikers decided to have some fun. Laughing, pointing fingers, and swearing obscenely, the gang members circled the table of the three young athletes, who found themselves outnumbered more than three-to-one. One of the gang members began to bow mockingly, and said, "Hail to you, lovers of Jesus! Hail to you, Jesus-lovers!" His comrades began taking up the chant.

One of the Christian young men stood and leveled his gaze at the pack-leader. Nothing was said for a few moments, and the tension in the place was electric. The owner of the restaurant began to mentally calculate the damages from the fight that now appeared inevitable. Then the young athlete said with utter sincerity, "I want to thank you men for paying me the greatest compliment I've ever received. Thank you for calling me a lover of Jesus Christ."

The biker was dumbstruck. A tense confrontation had been turned into a bold but peaceful witness for Jesus Christ.

Has anyone ever paid you the compliment of *accusing* you of being a lover of Jesus Christ? When Jesus is the focus of all our desires, when He is the model for our character, when people are more important to us than issues, then God can take our trials of conflict and *transform* them into something beautiful and holy. That's the healing choice you can always make, no matter who opposes you, no matter how tough your struggle: the courageous *decision* to become a channel of God's unconditional love and grace to others, even in the crisis of conflict.

9

Healing the Hurt of Mistreatment

Jesus knew that the old eye-for-an-eye philosophy would leave everyone blind. He did not seek to overcome evil with evil. He overcame evil with good. Although crucified by hate, he responded with aggressive love.

—Martin Luther King, Jr.

Bless those who persecute you; bless and do not curse.

—Romans 12:14

Karl and Edith Taylor [1] had been married for twenty-three years. Edith considered herself "the luckiest woman on the block" to be married to such a loving, thoughtful man. In his job with the government Karl often had to go out of town, but he always wrote her faithfully and sent her a gift from every place he visited.

When Karl learned he was being assigned to Okinawa for a few months, the Taylors were saddened. It would be a long separation, but to keep their spirits up they made plans to put a down payment on a cozy little cottage-with-a-view just as soon as Karl returned.

So Karl went to Okinawa, and Edith was thrilled when his thoughtful cards and letters began to arrive. There were no gifts this time, but Edith knew her husband was putting every spare cent into savings for their dream house. Within a few weeks, however, the letters became fewer and briefer. Then, just as she was beginning to prepare for his return, Edith received word from Karl that he would have to stay three more weeks. Later, he wrote "just one more month." Then, "a couple months longer."

Finally, after Karl had been gone over a year, Edith received the letter that shattered her heart. It began, "Dear Edith, I wish there were a kinder way to tell you we are no longer married. . . ." Karl had obtained a mail-order divorce from Mexico, and he was now married to a nineteen-year-old Japanese girl named Aiko.

Edith was devastated. The world ceased to make sense to her. There was no sound, no color, no taste anymore—only unrelieved pain. Finally, Edith took all her anguished feelings and honestly spread them out before God in prayer. As she wrestled with God, she realized she had a choice to make: she could become bitter and resentful, hating Karl for his betrayal and mistreatment of her—or she could choose to continue loving her husband. After a deep inner struggle, Edith made the healing choice for her trial of mistreatment: she wrote to Karl, told him she forgave him, and asked that they continue to keep in touch.

So for the next few years Karl and Edith exchanged cards and letters frequently. As time went by, Karl wrote Edith to tell her of his and Aiko's first child, a girl named Marie, then two years later another little girl named Helen.

A couple more years went by and Edith received another letter that broke her heart: Karl was dying of lung cancer. The medical bills were mounting, taking all the money Karl had saved to send his two little girls to school in America. Aiko and the girls would soon be left without anyone to provide for them. "What's going to happen to them now?" was the closing, despairing question of one of his letters.

Edith wrote back that she would like to pay the airfare to bring Marie and Helen to the States to live with her, if Karl and Aiko agreed. So a short time after Karl's death, fifty-four-year-old Edith Taylor became "the other mother" to a three-year-old and a five-year-old. A few months later, Edith arranged for Aiko to join her and the girls in America.

At the airport, Edith waited until the last person came off the plane—a thin, frail Japanese woman who seemed totally alone and afraid. Edith called Aiko's name, and they rushed into each other's arms. There they promised that together they would raise the girls for Jesus Christ. Edith Taylor later wrote, "Though Karl was taken from me, God has given me three others to love." She offered her trial of mistreatment to God, and God *transformed* her trial into healing for Aiko, Marie, and Helen—and for Edith herself. That's what God wants to do in our lives when we are victims of mistreatment.

The scales of justice

The normal human response to mistreatment is summed up by that bumper sticker we've all seen: "Don't Get Mad—Get Even!" Revenge is one of the oldest of human impulses. The stern existential philosopher Friedrich Nietzsche called revenge "the greatest instinct of the human race." Lord Byron wrote of "the sweetness of revenge." Francis Bacon called revenge "a wild justice."

When mistreated, our *natural* instinct is to choose the most hurtful words, to bring up old wounds, to do whatever we have to in order to balance the scales of that "wild justice" called revenge. But God has a better idea. It's not a *natural* solution to the hurt of mistreatment; it's a *supernatural* solution.

First Peter 2:19–20 tells us, "It is commendable if a man bears up under the pain of unjust suffering because he is conscious of God. . . . If you suffer for doing good and you endure it, this is commendable before God." Why do we receive God's approval when we endure mistreatment? The answer is in verse 21: "To this you were called, because Christ suffered for you, leaving you an example, that you should follow in his steps." Jesus committed no sin, yet He was insulted, tortured, and killed. He did not retaliate, He didn't threaten, He didn't get even. On the cross He modeled for us a kind of response to mistreatment that the world does not understand: "Father, forgive them." When we suffer mistreatment with patience and forgiveness, we are living after the example of Christ, following in His steps.

The attitude of the world is, "Why should I let someone insult me or hurt me—and then *forgive* him as if nothing ever happened?" But the attitude of the biblical Christian is, "I *must* forgive, even as I've been freely forgiven by God." Forgiveness is the grace that balances out the injustice of an unfair world. When another person acts unjustly toward us, the healing choice is to aggressively *forgive* that unjust treatment. We didn't deserve to be mistreated, nor does that person deserve to be forgiven—but when we choose to forgive, we counterbalance the other person's sin with the grace of God.

Yet it's so hard to let go of our resentment until we know that the score has been settled. Even when the one who hurt us has repented of his sin and asked forgiveness, it's still not always over for us. We've got the offender in the corner now, right where we want him. He's sinned and he knows it—and that gives us an edge. So we pile on a little guilt, a little blame, maybe do a little manipulating. If we're subtle, we'll use a few deftly chosen words here and there, carefully keeping the guilt feelings alive in the other person. And some of us aren't so subtle.

A few years ago, I was counseling a Christian husband and wife who were experiencing tremendous conflict in their marriage. Several years earlier, the wife had committed some very grievous sins against her husband. She had since repented of her sins, and some years had passed. Now, as their marriage was sinking toward dissolution, she said to me, "You know, it doesn't matter what we are arguing about—finances or our schedule or things that need to be done around the house—there isn't an argument we have on *any* subject that my husband doesn't bring up that one sin I committed years ago." The husband, sitting right next to her, just looked the other way. He couldn't deny it.

This is a marriage that will never truly *be* a marriage until the husband learns to forgive, finally and fully. So it is with you and me.

We're to forgive as we've been forgiven by God, love as we have been loved by God, give grace to others as we've received God's grace in our lives. As Christians, we're not only *saved* by grace but we're also called to *live* by grace. We are to impart God's grace to others—and especially to those who have mistreated us.

The power of forgiveness

I recently participated in a pastors' conference in Seoul, Korea. There I met a remarkable man, Dr. Kim Joon-Gon, National Director of Korea Campus Crusade for Christ. Dr. Kim survived the Communist persecution of the church during the Korean War, and today is one of the leading spokesmen for the amazing revival sweeping Korea. As we were having breakfast together one morning, he told me his story.

During the Korean War, Dr. Kim was in a Communist-controlled area for three months. One night, he was held by soldiers and forced to watch while his wife and parents were tortured and murdered by one Communist official. He himself was then beaten and left unconscious. He revived during the night, located his baby daughter—the only remaining member of his family—and escaped.

He was recaptured by the Communists and beaten again. Starving and suffering from massive injuries, Dr. Kim again faced the cruelty of the same Communist official who had murdered his family. During that time he went in and out of consciousness. He was so exhausted and defeated that he had ceased praying; he had lost all hope that God would answer. He was in total despair, a spiritual condition which he described to me as "the darkness of spiritual death, complete separation from God."

But even in his darkness, God was working in Dr. Kim's life. There came a moment in his suffering and hopelessness when he suddenly awoke to the realization that his lips were moving—and the words he spoke were words of *prayer*. "The Holy Spirit was speaking to me and through me," Dr. Kim said. "In that moment I had gone from death to life. I felt joy and peace spring up in my heart. The Lord had brought me through the valley of the shadow of death—and He was calling me to go and talk to the hated man who had murdered my family."

So Dr. Kim began to pray for his Communist persecutor—and as he prayed, he found new strength, new freedom, new life. Then he rose and went to this man and told him that he loved him, and that God loved him too. This Communist was startled at first to see that Dr. Kim was even alive—but he was absolutely thunderstruck when he heard this ragged, battered, half-dead prisoner begin to talk about the forgiveness of sin through Jesus Christ.

"This Communist leader could not believe I would come to him in love," Dr. Kim concluded. "He began to weep over his sins, and over the killing of my family. He committed himself to Jesus Christ and became a completely changed man from that day forward. Today that man is an elder in a church here in Korea, and he and I pray for each other every day."

Forgiveness is not just an idealistic notion for making people "nice." It's the hard-headed, realistic *demand* of God upon our lives. It's the power to change lives—and it's the only pathway to true inner healing when we have been severely, even brutally mistreated.

Our trial of mistreatment can be a destructive force in our lives—or it can be an *opportunity.* The choice is ours to make. When we are mistreated, we can seize the opportunity to demonstrate to others that Christ is *alive* in us, even in times of trial. Our lives can become a shining witness for Christ when we choose to respond in a supernatural, Christ-controlled way to the unfair treatment of others. We advance the kingdom of God whenever we endure persecution with *patience.*

Patience, remember, is the very first quality Paul attributes to Christian love in the famous "Love Chapter," 1 Corinthians 13. "Love is patient," he writes (or in your King James Bible, "Charity suffereth long"). Christian love, unconditional love, has a long fuse—and the first mark of a person who is growing in Christian maturity is that he is demonstrating more and more *patience* in his life, even when treated unfairly.

Displaying patience and love toward those who mistreat us doesn't mean we will let others walk all over us. There may be times when we will have to actively *respond* to those who unfairly treat us—but we will respond in an attitude of acceptance, gentleness, and love, not resentment or revenge. God may be calling us to firmly, patiently *confront* the offender about his sin for his own benefit, for the benefit of others whom he has hurt, or for the sake of a healed relationship between ourselves and the offender.

Self-defense

Everyone likes to get mail, and I'm no exception. I receive a lot of mail, and I enjoy reading every letter—well, almost every letter. Every few weeks I receive an anonymous letter harshly condemning something I've said or written, or judging my motives for something I've done. When I was younger, these anonymous critics could seriously wound me and even immobilize me.

One time a number of years ago I received a particularly

hurtful unsigned letter, and it made me stop and question *why* these cowardly attacks by unknown people could hurt me so deeply. Then it came to me: I wanted to *defend* myself— but I couldn't. I couldn't even find the person who wrote the letter.

Self-defense is our first instinct when we are mistreated. We want to be vindicated—but how can we ever defend ourselves against an anonymous critic or a false rumor or someone who shuns us and hurts us and refuses to tell us why? Against such trials of mistreatment, there just is no means of defense— but there is still a healing choice open to us: the choice to *stop* defending ourselves.

"We're all born with the desire to defend ourselves," A. W. Tozer once said, "and if you insist upon defending yourself, God will let you do it. But if you turn the defense of yourself over to God, He will defend you." There have been few things as helpful to me in my trials of mistreatment as this realization: *I don't have to defend myself.* Why? Because God has promised to be my Defender. In Exodus 23:22, He says, "I will be an enemy to your enemies and will oppose those who oppose you." And Psalm 72:4 says, "He will defend the afflicted. . . . He will crush the oppressor."

If defensive anger is our first instinctive response to mistreatment, then our next tendency is to nurture our initial anger into feelings of resentment and self-pity. Psychologists tell us anger that is not resolved turns into depression. If you have a tendency to become resentful and depressed when unfairly treated, James 5:8 (NASB) encourages you to "be patient; strengthen your hearts." That word "strengthen" in the original Greek conveys a sense of propping up or supporting something that is heavy. So if your heart is heavy when you have been treated unfairly, James says to let God support your heavy heart. Give your trial of mistreatment over to God, your Defender.

A slow-acting poison

He was an old man, approaching the end of his life. Tragically, he had chosen to grow old full of bitterness. He had become so eaten up by resentment over past injuries and injustices that it could be truly said that *bitterness* was the central pillar of his personality. His life was focused on complaining and rehearsing all the hurts of the past. He was soured on life, soured on people, and bitter toward God. His constant complaining was accompanied by insult and profanity. People hated to be around him.

This is not a description of one particular person, but a number of people I've known. You've probably known people like this too. How did they become so bitter? They didn't begin life with an attitude of resentment. In fact, the family and acquaintances of such people often talk with sadness about the *change* that took place in them over the years as they gradually became more sullen and closed.

Resentment is a slow-acting poison. It begins as we nurture those minor grudges, as we are slow to forgive, as we extract guilty apologies from others before we release them from our judgment. Bitterness takes root in our lives as we see someone who has mistreated us fall into misfortune—and we feel *good* about it. I know that feeling, and you probably do as well: that sinister joy we feel as we think, "He's getting just what he deserves!"

This grudge-bearing spirit is within each of us. If we give it the opportunity, this bitter, resentful spirit will wrap itself around our hearts and choke out all of our life and joy. It will eat us up inside, leaving us hollow and empty, capable only of hating and complaining and cursing the past.

A resentful, grudge-bearing spirit can drive us to do strange things. Not long ago a man was divorced by his wife and the court ordered him to pay a certain amount of alimony and child-support every month—and he grudgingly paid it in *nickels.* Every time his alimony and child-support payment came due, 160 pounds of nickels landed at his wife's door.

Another divorced man was ordered by the court to equally divide all the joint-property of his broken marriage with his ex-wife. He chose to do so with a chain-saw. As his neighbors looked on, he carefully measured the $100,000 suburban home that he and his wife had lived in for several years. When he found the precise mid-point of the home, he revved up his chain-saw and proceeded to cut his own home—floor, walls, ceiling, and roof—precisely in half.

These two men were driven to spectacularly strange forms of behavior because they allowed themselves to be eaten alive by resentment. But before we judge these men too harshly, we need to recognize that we too have that same spirit within us at times. We're usually just more subtle about it.

Resentment can come out at the most unlikely times—even in our prayer times together with other Christians. Others are sharing needs and concerns for intercession, and all the while we're mulling over some unfair treatment we've received. Finally it's our turn to share—and our "prayer request" is really a damaging word of gossip: "We really need to pray for Mary. She has such a problem with the way she treats people and really needs our prayers."

If you've begun to feed on past trials of mistreatment, then beware the tyranny of bitterness: if you're not careful, you'll grow old like that, and you'll die like that. If you don't begin *right now* to make the healing choice in your relationships, even when you are mistreated, then you'll leave a tragic legacy behind—the memory of a bitter, resentful person who just couldn't let go of the past and all that unfair treatment. The healing choice for the trial of mistreatment is the choice to forgive, and to let go of the past. Don't postpone that choice. Do your forgiving *now* so you can live a full, free, joyful life.

The 50:20 Principle

Ultimately we have to acknowledge that it's part of our Christian heritage to be mistreated and misunderstood. The Old Testament prophets were mistreated and killed. Jesus was rejected and crucified. The apostles and the Christians of the early church were martyred. Persecution of the church has taken place throughout the world from the first century to this very day—and it is growing worse, not better. As Paul tells us in 2 Timothy 3:12, "Everyone who wants to live a godly life in Christ Jesus will be persecuted."

You know what it means to be mistreated and misunderstood and so do I. In those times—in all the deep valleys and blue Mondays of my life—I've found encouragement in the biblical truth I call "The 50:20 Principle."

"The 50:20 Principle" comes from the last half of the book of Genesis, which tells the story of Joseph, the dreamer with the elaborate coat who was seized by his jealous brothers and sold into slavery in Egypt; Joseph was mistreated by his own family. The wife of Joseph's Egyptian master attempted to seduce him, slandered him, and had him thrown into prison; Joseph was mistreated by his employer. In prison, Joseph helped a friend, a fellow inmate, who later forgot Joseph and left him to languish in prison for two years; Joseph was mistreated by his friend.

There is probably no biblical figure more symbolic of the trial of mistreatment than Joseph. Yet as I have studied the account of his life from Genesis 37 to 50, I cannot find a single reference to any response of bitterness or resentment in Joseph's life.

By the end of Genesis, God has enabled Joseph to surmount all the episodes of mistreatment and betrayal in his life and he has become the governor of all Egypt. With the power of life and death in his hands, Joseph is now reunited with the brothers who years earlier had sold him into slavery. He has a golden opportunity to get even—and the brothers *know* it. With good reason, they now deeply fear the brother they had once cruelly mistreated. They plead for their lives and the lives of their families. They offer themselves as *slaves* to Joseph.

But Joseph doesn't take revenge. Rather, he *weeps*—then he says, "Don't be afraid . . . You intended it for evil, but God has used it for good." And there, in Genesis 50:20, we find "The 50:20 Principle," God's principle for responding to mistreatment: "You intended it for evil, but God has used it for good" (Genesis chapter 50, verse 20). God had taken the evil and mistreatment that Joseph's brothers intended for him and transformed it into good. Genesis 50:20 is an Old Testament portrayal of the New Testament truth of Romans 8:28, the truth that God weaves together all the circumstances of our lives—even our trials of unfair treatment—into His good plan for our lives.

That's the principle I claim for my life whenever I have been treated unfairly. "You meant this mistreatment for evil, but I believe God is going to use even this for His ultimate good." In our trials of mistreatment, we don't need 20–20 vision, we need 50:20 vision—a vision which enables us to say, with peace in our hearts, "You meant it for evil, but God is going to use it for His good."

Such a response to the hurt of mistreatment goes against

our instincts. It's not going to come naturally. It's only going to come *supernaturally,* as we rely upon God and give our feelings of anger and resentment up to Him day by day, hour by hour, moment by moment.

The hurt of mistreatment puts the promises of God to the acid test. Unjust treatment is the crucible of our faith, testing just how serious we are about following Jesus Christ and living the life He led. The choice is ours: Are we going to insist on defending ourselves—or let God defend us? Are we going to let the past consume us—or are we going to let go of the past? We'll know we've made the healing choice for our trial of mistreatment when we can say, "I know you've meant it for evil, but God is going to use this—*even this!*—for His good."

10

Healing the Hurt of Fear

People of courage are also full of faith.

—Cicero

Even though I walk through the valley of the shadow of death, I will fear no evil, for you are with me.

—Psalm 23:4

The year was 1939. Dietrich Bonhoeffer, a thirty-three-year-old theologian from Breslau, Germany, paced the floor of his New York City apartment. A life-and-death decision loomed before him: Should he stay in the safety and security of America, or rejoin the persecuted Confessional Church in Nazi Germany, risking imprisonment and martyrdom? He fasted and prayed for wisdom.

A short time later, Bonhoeffer was on his way back to Germany. Against the pleading of his friends, he was determined to return home and take a bold stand for Christ against Hitler's tyranny. In 1943, he was imprisoned by the Gestapo, and later transferred to a succession of prisons and concentration camps. While in prison, he conducted worship services and encouraged his fellow prisoners. His ministry even extended to the prison guards, who were often heard to apologize to Bonhoeffer before carrying out some officially ordered act of cruelty.

One day in April 1945, as he was praying with the relatives of some men who had been executed, his captors took him away to be hanged. Just a few days before Allied forces liberated the death camp where he had been held, Dietrich Bonhoeffer died calmly, with a prayer of praise on his lips.

Why did he go back to Germany, knowing he risked persecution and martyrdom at the hands of the Nazis? Wasn't he afraid?

Bonhoeffer loved life, and he treasured its blessings: nature, music, art, books, and especially people. He had family, deep friendships, and a fiancée whom he loved dearly. He had everything to live for—but most of all, he lived for Jesus Christ. He believed it was not enough to serve his Lord through preaching and writing alone; he knew he had to live out his faith in costly obedience to God.

In one of his letters from prison, Bonhoeffer frankly confessed his fears, saying, "When I think of the worst that could happen to me, I find myself trembling." Bonhoeffer was afraid, but he subordinated his fear to his love for Jesus Christ.

Forty years later, the world came to know another man of bold Christian courage. The year was 1983. Benigno Aquino was returning home to the Philippines from the safety of exile in the United States. His friends, his wife, and his two daughters had tried to persuade him not to go, fearing he would be harmed or arrested, but he could not be dissuaded.

Aquino was an outspoken political opponent of Philippines' dictator Ferdinand Marcos, and had been a member of the Philippines Senate until he was jailed without trial in 1972. A moderate statesman caught in the vicious power struggle between left and right, Aquino was a lone voice pleading for the needs of the forgotten common people.

Aquino's plane, laden with reporters and concerned observers, landed at Manila International Airport and taxied to a stop. Philippine soldiers immediately boarded the plane and separated Aquino from the rest of his entourage, shoving him toward the door of the plane. Moments after he disappeared through the doorway, a volley of shots exploded outside the plane. Conflicting stories were later told about the next few agonizing seconds, but one fact was certain: Benigno Aquino was dead. His murder aroused outrage throughout the world— and it raised questions: "Why did he go back? Wasn't he afraid?"

Despite the intensive coverage this tragedy received from television, newspapers, and newsmagazines, the most compelling aspect of Aquino's story—his motive for going—was never

disclosed by the news media. The truth is that Aquino returned
to the Philippines for the same reason Bonhoeffer returned
to Germany: his love for Jesus Christ.

In 1976, while still in a Philippines prison, Aquino had
been given a copy of *Born Again* by Charles Colson,[1] and
later saw a television interview in which the former Watergate
defendant described his new life in Christ. For weeks before,
Aquino had been so bitter and despondent that he was seriously
contemplating suicide. But now, alone in his cell, Aquino suddenly felt the relentless love of God tugging at his heart—
and he yielded himself to that love, committing himself to
Christ.

Aquino was released from prison in 1980 so he could have
emergency surgery in the United States—a stay which turned
into a three-year exile in America. One day he was surprised
to find himself on the same flight with Charles Colson. He
introduced himself and shared how much Colson's testimony
had meant to him while he was confined in prison. A friendship
was immediately forged between them.

While in America, Aquino made a searching study of Dietrich Bonhoeffer's life—and it was the example of Bonhoeffer's
courage that moved Aquino to begin his final trek home. "I
consider Benigno Aquino a Christian martyr," Colson later
told an interviewer, "because he had the courage to act on
his beliefs. . . . The media glossed over his religious faith,
and it explains everything about the man." [2]

What a glorious epitaph for any Christian, to have it said
that our Christian faith explained *everything* about us. Ultimately it is only our love relationship with Jesus that enables
us to make the healing choice for the hurt of fear.

The three opposites of fear

We have so many things to be afraid of these days. The
things we read in the newspaper or see on television frighten
us; surveys show that people who watch a great deal of television are generally more fearful than those who watch little
or none at all. The threat of nuclear annihilation troubles our
sleep. We fear crime, economic crisis, war, accident, illness,
old age, natural disaster, and death—especially death. All of
us have known the anxiety of wondering, "How will I endure

the suffering of my death?" Many of us even dread what lies beyond the grave, and there is a paralysis in the fear of death that prevents us from being able to truly live.

"My heart is in anguish within me; the terrors of death assail me. Fear and trembling have beset me; horror has overwhelmed me." Those lines may sound like something out of Edgar Allan Poe, but they actually come from the heart of David, from Psalm 55. But Jesus never intended His own followers to be defeated by the hurt of fear. "Do not let your hearts be troubled," He told His disciples in John 14:1. "Trust in God; trust also in me."

That master psychologist of the first century, the apostle Paul, tells us that fear has not one but *three* opposites: (1) power, (2) love, and (3) inner wholeness ("a sound mind"). In 2 Timothy 1:7 (NKJV) he writes, "God has not given us a spirit of fear, but of power and of love and of a sound mind." Notice, first, that the person who is burdened with fear lacks *power;* he is powerless to dare great things for God. But the spirit we have received from God is one of boldness, courage, and power through the Holy Spirit.

Secondly, the person burdened by fear is not fully able to receive and give *love.* The fearful person is a guarded, wary person who seeks to be invulnerable and safe in his relationships. But the person who loves unconditionally is willing to take risks in relationships. He can't be afraid to be hurt; he must be prepared to be hurt again and again for the sake of loving others. God has not given us a spirit of fear, but of Christlike, unconditional love.

Finally, the person burdened with fear cannot experience *inner wholeness,* or soundness of mind and heart. He is unable to experience life fully because he is haunted by dangers, both real and imaginary. Like the security-obsessed fanatic who lives behind iron-barred windows and triple-bolted doors, surrounded by alarm systems and weapons and attack dogs, the fearful person one day awakes to find himself in a prison of his own making. God didn't give us a spirit of fear, but of a sound mind and a whole personality.

God seeks to turn our fears inside out and transform them into healing for others who are afraid. "Strengthen the feeble hands, steady the knees that give way; Say to those with fearful hearts, 'Be strong, do not fear; your God will come . . . to save you,' " says Isaiah 35:3–4. And in 1 Thessalonians 5:14 we're urged to "encourage the timid" and "help the weak." God calls us to make the healing choice to encourage those around us who are fearful.

Life without a net

"Living in the lap of luxury isn't bad," the late Orson Welles once said, "except that you never know when luxury is going to stand up." This is an apt restatement of Proverbs 23:5— "Cast but a glance to riches, and they are gone, for they will surely sprout wings and fly off to the sky like an eagle." Through the accumulation of wealth—investments, real estate, Individual Retirement Accounts, pensions, and Social Security—we seek to insulate ourselves from all risk by the time we reach retirement age. We want to be safe and secure, free from all worry and uncertainty. And thus we put our trust in the goods of this world, which could "take flight" at any moment.

And just as there is no security in wealth, neither is there security in health. I'm something of a fitness fanatic. I run two or three miles every day. I do aerobics with my children at the YMCA once a week. I enjoy anything physical—swimming, basketball, tennis, soccer, touch-football. I take a handful of vitamins every day, and carefully watch the food I eat. But no matter how well we take care of ourselves and try to minimize stress and risk in our lives, our health can disappear in a instant through accident or disease.

Our lives are balanced on a tightrope. We're living life without a net. The sooner we acknowledge this truth, the sooner we can begin investing in the real health and wealth that lasts eternally. That is why Jesus tells us in Matthew 6:31–33, "Do not worry, saying, 'What shall we eat?' or 'What shall we drink?' or 'What shall we wear?' For the pagans run after all these things, and your heavenly Father knows that you need them. But seek first his kingdom and his righteousness, and all these things will be given to you as well."

If you're a follower of Christ, then the only choice you can make is to seek your security in God's kingdom and His righteousness. But if you're not committed to Jesus Christ right now, then you've got to play it safe. You've got to base your life on the false security of the things of this world—even though striving to save your life will ultimately cost you everything, *including* your life. As Jesus said, "Whoever wants to save his life will lose it, but whoever loses his life for me and for the gospel will save it. What good is it for a man to gain the whole world, yet forfeit his soul?" (Mark 8:35).

Following Christ means counting the cost and accepting the risks of being His disciple. God calls Christians out of the temporal security of the things of this world to the ultimate security of those things that will last for eternity. When that is our security, we're free to wager all we are and have on the promises of God.

Risky obedience

It is said that one of the chief functions of fairy tales is to illuminate our darkest fears. This is certainly true of J. R. R. Tolkien's *The Hobbit*. Tolkien, a close friend of C. S. Lewis, wove stories that are rich in the truths of the Christian life.

Tolkien's hobbits are easy-going folk about three or four feet tall. The average hobbit lives a well-ordered, sheltered life in a quiet, comfortable hole in the ground. One day, a fellow named Gandalf comes calling on a hobbit named Bilbo, inviting him along on an adventure he is arranging. Bilbo is aghast. "We hobbits are plain quiet folk and have no use for adventures!" he replies. "Adventures are nasty disturbing uncomfortable things! Make you late for dinner! I can't think what anybody sees in them." [3]

Isn't this a lot like the reply we make to God as He calls us to the adventure of the Christian life? Tolkien has something to teach us about fear in this story. He allows his hobbits—symbolic of plain, ordinary people like you and me—to be drawn into a harrowing, thrilling adventure. Ultimately, the obedient courage of a few lonely, fearful hobbits enables a kingdom to be saved from a terrible evil.

The adventure of the Christian life is like that: a journey of risky obedience as we trust God to accomplish His victory through our weakness, despite our fears and our trembling. God uses the weak and fearful things of this world—hobbit-hearted Christians like you and me—to tear down the strongholds of evil and declare salvation to a dying world.

Helen Keller was right when she said, "Life is either a grand adventure, or it's nothing." How it must break our Savior's heart to see so many of His people going to church every Sunday, singing bold hymns like "Onward Christian Soldiers" and "A Mighty Fortress Is Our God," claiming to trust in God—yet basing their lives on the false security of this world.

The freedom of risk

St. John Chrysostom (A.D. 347–407), the Archbishop of Constantinople during the reign of the Empress Eudoxia, understood the meaning of Christian courage. One day, he was commanded to appear before the Empress. "I hear you preach most ardently," she said, "that this man Jesus is Lord."

"I do," said Chrysostom.

"This teaching cannot be tolerated," Eudoxia replied, "for the only lordship recognized in Constantinople is that of this Throne. If you continue to preach these myths, then you will be banished from your home."

"Banish me? Why, the whole world is my home," said Chrysostom. "My Lord has said, 'Blessed are the meek, for they shall inherit the earth.' "

"I tell you that I am your ruler, not this crucified Jew!" said the Empress, her eyes flashing. "I will order all your treasures confiscated if you persist in calling this Jesus your 'Lord.' "

"You cannot take my treasures from me," he replied, "for I have hidden all my treasures in Heaven, where the Lord has promised that no one may break in and steal."

"You will cease calling this dead man your 'Lord'!" retorted Eudoxia, rising to her feet and shaking with rage, "or I shall confine you alone and friendless in the blackest pit in my dungeon!"

"That is impossible," Chrysostom gently replied, "for Jesus, my risen Lord, has promised, 'I will never leave you nor forsake you.' "

"Still you defy me!" shrilled the Empress. "Don't you know I have the power to order your *life* taken from you?"

"You have no power to take my life," he softly replied, "My life is hidden with Christ in eternity. If you slay me, I shall live again."

And the witness of history is that the Empress Eudoxia was frustrated in her attempt to force Chrysostom to deny the Lordship of Jesus. Ultimately, she deposed him and exiled him from Constantinople—but she was never able to silence him or intimidate him. What do you do with a man like John Chrysostom? He is *free!*

True freedom lies in *risk.* Your safety is your prison. If you knew what the future held, it wouldn't take any faith to live it. Our prayer before God should not be, "Lord, give us safety," but, "Lord, *increase our risks!* Give us boldness! Help us to dare great things for you!"

A few years ago, Bruce Larson was talking with the noted Christian counselor and physician, Paul Tournier. Larson asked Dr. Tournier how he was able to help his patients get rid of their fears. "Oh, I don't," Tournier quickly replied. "That which does not frighten does not have meaning. All the best things in life have an element of fear in them." I've seen this truth proved again and again: A life that is insulated from risk and fear is a life without meaning.

If we don't risk, we won't change. And if we don't change we won't grow, and we won't become conformed into the image of Christ. But it's our nature to resist change, isn't it? Even though our past has been unproductive and unfulfilling, most of us would rather return to the dreary security of the past than face the adventure of tomorrow. We're like the Israelites in the time of Moses, who wanted to return to the slavery of Egypt rather than trust God to lead them toward the Promised Land. We long for the bygone days when things were easier, when there was less pressure, when things were more familiar. We dig in our heels and say, "Let's camp here. Let this be my Mecca, my comfort zone."

I've heard that soon after a baby elephant is born, the animal trainer will chain him to a sturdy tree. The baby elephant will do all he can to get free, pulling and pulling on the chain until he is worn out. Finally he will begin to walk in a slow circle around that tree.

Over time, the elephant will continue testing his chain—but with decreasing persistence: just a tug on the chain, and then he gives up and begins walking around and around the tree. Eventually the elephant becomes so conditioned to his chain that the trainer no longer attaches it to the tree. He simply drops the chain on the ground—and the elephant will circle hour upon hour around that chain. The elephant is free to go anywhere—and he doesn't even know it. He's enslaved by the chains of the past.

We're so much like that elephant: we're completely free in Christ, yet we're enslaved by the chains of the past. There's an adventure waiting for us—but we prefer the same old familiar path, even though it only leads us around and around in safe, secure, unproductive circles.

Counting the cost and paying the price

One of the great old anthems of the faith is a hymn to the freedom of adventure: "Like a mighty army moves the church of God!/Brothers, we are treading where the saints have trod!" The church is not camped out for security, but moving forward against the gates of hell. We are in a war against spiritual darkness, and no war was ever won without paying a price.

My friend Jack knows what it means to live the adventure of faith. He also knows what it means to be afraid, and to pay a price. Jack is a missionary in one of the largest and most neglected mission fields in Christian history: the Muslim world. He is making Christian disciples in countries where evangelism is illegal, and where conversion to Christianity is punishable by imprisonment or death.

A few years ago, Jack and several of his associates were in a militant, fanatical Muslim country, preparing to begin a daring new penetration of that land with the gospel. Shortly after his arrival, Jack wrote a letter to his mother which concluded with these words: "I have peace, but also much fear." The day after he mailed that letter, Jack and his friends were arrested. They spent almost a year in prison for the crime of telling Muslim people about the love of Jesus Christ.

Jack was obedient to the call of God in his life, and he paid a price for that obedience. Undeterred, he is still reaching the Muslim world with the gospel. He continues to have peace in the knowledge he is doing God's will—and he continues to know fear.

Sometimes God delivers us from the furnace of our afflictions—and sometimes He gives us grace to stand the heat of that furnace. In Acts 7, the deacon Stephen didn't look for deliverance, but endured a martyr's death by stoning for the sake of Jesus Christ. Paul, in Philippians 3:10, didn't look for safety and security as he wrote, "I want to know Christ and the power of his resurrection and the fellowship of sharing in his sufferings, becoming like him in his death." Dietrich Bonhoeffer and Benigno Aquino did not look for deliverance or safety, but chose instead to follow their Lord and pay the heavy price of commitment.

Heaven is crowded with witnesses who can testify that while God does not promise to spare us from the trials of life, He is always *with* us in our trials, leading us through the fire. The healing choice for the hurt of fear is the decision to completely trust God with our lives, to risk everything for Him, and to truly live the adventure of the Christian life.

Not afraid to die

"In the real dark night of the soul," writes F. Scott Fitzgerald, "it is always three o'clock in the morning." The 3:00 A.M. fear that haunts the dark night of most human souls is the fear of death. This fear is common to mankind—though some of us try desperately to deny the reality of death. One poet has said, "Nothing can happen more beautiful than death." Another wrote, "Why fear death? It is the most beautiful adventure in life." There is something pitiable in these words—a poignant denial of the terrible truth of the grave.

There is nothing "beautiful" about death. First Corinthians 15:26 calls death an enemy to be destroyed, and Romans 5:12 says that death entered the world through sin, and now overshadows us all. So let's speak the truth: death is our enemy, a powerful destroyer. Many of the things we fear in life are so trivial or unlikely to occur that our worry is truly wasted—but death is truly worthy of our fears.

Fortunately, that's not all there is to know about this enemy called death. God has given us victory over the grave through the death and resurrection of Jesus Christ. Paul concludes 1 Corinthians 15 with these words of triumph: "Where, O Death, is your victory? Where, O Death, is your sting? . . . Thanks be to God! He gives us the victory through our Lord Jesus Christ." Though fully God, Jesus became a man in order to

endure death, disarm it, and conquer its fear. Hebrews 2:14–
15 tells us that Jesus took part in our humanity "so that by
his death he might . . . free those who all their lives were
held in slavery by their fear of death."

I am not afraid to die. I fear the physical suffering that
may accompany my death. I have moments of anxiety when
I contemplate the separation death will cause between myself
and those I love. But I'm at peace with the reality of death
because I'm convinced of the greater reality Christ has given
us: "Because I live, you shall live also." I know I will live
forever, not because of any good works I have done, but because
by faith I have committed myself to Jesus Christ as my Savior
and Lord. The healing choice for the fear of death is to commit
ourselves to the resurrected Christ, to receive by faith the gift
of eternal life He bought for us on the cross.

Several years ago, I and several others in my previous church
in Minneapolis received a letter from a friend who was dying
of leukemia. Only twenty-eight years old and approaching the
close of her life, she wrote,

> Many people have asked me if I feel any bitterness about
> my long illness and imminent death at a young age. No,
> I feel no bitterness or anger. Many people would demand
> to know, "Why me?" But I can't help but ask, "Why
> *not* me?"
>
> I have felt so much pity for the millions of people
> starving to death all over the world, for those who are
> so poor they can barely subsist, for those who are physi-
> cally handicapped. I can't expect that God owes me any-
> thing more than these people have—but God has given
> me more! My life has been filled with every blessing a
> person could want.
>
> I was raised by loving parents, and I had a happy child-
> hood. I've had eight years of marriage to a wonderful
> man. Our love has grown so much over the years that
> our marriage is much more beautiful now than when it
> began. I've been blessed by more precious friends than
> one could ever hope for.
>
> My life has been permeated by a faith in the resurrected
> Christ. He has been my purpose in life. He has been my
> peace in death. So mourn for those that I leave behind,
> but don't mourn for me.

I'm not afraid to die because the resurrection of Jesus Christ is not just some doctrine to me; it's my *reality*. I've settled the matter of my own death, and that sets me free to truly live. The same can be true for you. I can think of no finer benediction to offer you than this: May you live your life courageously, victorious over your fears—and may you die gloriously in a great cause for Jesus Christ!

Epilogue

Joy—Even When It Hurts

We should be watchful lest we lose any blessing which suffering might bring.

—A. W. Tozer

In this you greatly rejoice, though now for a little while you may have had to suffer grief in all kinds of trials. These have come so that your faith—of greater worth than gold, which perishes even though refined by fire—may be proved genuine and may result in praise, glory and honor when Jesus Christ is revealed.

—1 Peter 1:6–7

The early years of Carolyn Koons's life were spent in a series of rough, dirty logging towns. Violence and mistreatment were just part of growing up for her. Her mother and father repeatedly abused her, and finally abandoned her on the streets.

As a teenager, Carolyn was befriended by some Christian young people who cared enough to patiently, persistently win this hardened young woman to Christ. Carolyn went on to college and seminary, eventually becoming a professor of Christian Education at Azusa Pacific University. In 1975, she founded Mexicali Outreach, an evangelistic ministry which takes hundreds of Christian students into northern Mexico for short-term missionary work. The first year she led a team to Mexicali, they toured a youth prison housing three hundred boys, some as young as five years old. There she met nine-year-old Tony.[1]

Tony was raised in the streets of Tijuana, surrounded by crime, narcotics, and prostitution. Tony's childhood, like Carolyn's, had been filled with violence and mistreatment. One day when five-year-old Tony was playing in the street, he heard his baby brother screaming. Tony went to the door of his house, heard a loud thud, and froze. The screaming had

175

stopped. Looking inside, Tony saw his mother and father bending over his brother's body, a bloody club nearby.

Tony fled and his parents reported him to the police, accusing him of the murder. So five-year-old Tony was thrown into prison—and he stayed there for four years before being discovered by Carolyn Koons. There had never been any investigation of the charges against him.

After a long and expensive battle against bureaucratic red tape, Carolyn Koons won Tony's freedom and brought him to the United States, whereupon she found herself a single parent to a twelve-year-old boy. In the hardness and resentment of this terribly wounded boy, Carolyn confronted the scars of her own childhood. Her own long-buried hurts surfaced again as she sought to help Tony overcome his painful memories—and she *used* those hurts to bring healing into Tony's life. She saw the love of Christ begin to change his heart.

Today, Tony is a Christian college student at Azusa Pacific. Carolyn and Tony are living proof of the power of God not only to heal our hurts, but to *transform* our hurts into healing for others. Theirs is a story of the power of God to penetrate the darkness of human suffering with the light of *joy.*

Joy in our trials

The Bible promises that we can actually have *joy* no matter how hard our circumstances are. "Consider it all joy, my brethren, when you encounter various trials," says James 1:2 (NASB). Yet joy is usually the *last* thing we think of as we face our trials—and understandably so. The first thing that occurs to us in the hard places of life is not joy, but, "Why me? And why this? And why now?" When we're hurting, we have some questions to ask God—and God accepts our questions. He understands our hurt.

But there comes a time when we need to make the healing choice to move beyond our questions. We have to get on with our lives, even when it becomes clear that our hurts are not going to immediately go away. And the promise of God is that we can go on with *joy.*

How, then, do we find joy when we encounter various trials?

There is joy, first of all, in knowing that our trials have a purpose. James 1:3 says, "The testing of your faith develops perseverance." God is building endurance in us.

The Greek word for "testing" in this passage is *dokimos,* which means "approved." Many of the jugs and pots which have been unearthed in ancient ruins of Greece and the Middle East are marked on the bottom with this same word, *dokimos,* "approved." In this way, the valuable pieces of pottery were set apart. They had gone through the refiner's fire without cracking.

Similarly, when we go through the furnace of affliction and withstand the heat without cracking, then we build endurance, and we receive God's *dokimos,* His seal of approval. As Jesus described it in Matthew 25:23, this is the joy of hearing God say to us, "Well done, good and faithful servant! . . . Come and share your master's happiness!"

This is the kind of joy a man named Ignatius was learning to experience through a terrible trial of persecution. Ignatius was one of the early church fathers, the bishop of the church of Antioch in Syria. He was arrested by the Roman government for the crime of being a Christian, and sentenced to be executed for the Emperor's amusement in Rome. He was chained to a detachment of cruel, hardened Roman soldiers who led him on a forced march to Rome, a trek of over 1500 miles. Along the way, Ignatius wrote a letter to some Christian friends which included these words:

> The soldiers who guard me behave like animals, treating me with bewildering cruelty. They are like a pack of leopards, enjoying their sport, with myself as their prey. Still, this trial has its advantages. I'm growing accustomed to the ravages of leopards, which is just as well, since it will be real lions I face at Rome. As bitter as my present sufferings are, I am gaining spiritual endurance and mental fortitude for the trial that lies ahead.
>
> No power must hinder my going to Jesus Christ. Whether the path be fire or crucifixion or wild animals in the arena, I can bear it if it leads the way to Him, for He is my joy.

Ignatius willingly, courageously faced some of the cruelest trials imaginable—and he faced them with *joy,* knowing that he was building endurance, and that his trials led the way to Jesus.

A journey of discovery

I've sometimes observed two Christians suffering under similar trials, but making very dissimilar choices in their trials. One will choose to respond to his trial by giving up on life and wrapping himself in self-pity. The other will look for God's perspective on his hurts, and he will cooperate with God in *growing* through his trial. He prays for endurance, not mere escape—for joy, not mere comfort—and he always emerges from his trials a stronger and more joyful Christian.

Throughout our lives we are faced with tremendous opportunities. The problem is that these opportunities come disguised as unsolvable trials. Joy in the Christian life comes as we respond to our trials by allowing them to bring forth our character and wisdom and courage. These qualities reside in every human spirit; they are part of the image of God in which we are all molded. Whether these qualities are *displayed* in us in a time of crisis, however, depends primarily on the conscious choices we make: the choice to accept responsibility for our problems; the choice to take up the challenge of our trial rather than to moan about it; the choice to keep our gaze on God while glancing at our problems.

Life is a journey of discovery, and there is great *joy* in the adventure of spiritual and emotional growth. Sadly, most people just drift through life, evading its challenges, afraid of its risks. Unwilling to learn and to change, such people miss the deep joy of living. True joy is reserved for those who are willing to make the effort to *master* this thing called Life, to become *experts* in the art of growing with God and enjoying His grace.

If we are attentive, we can learn something new about the reality of God every day of our lives. Just think of all the ways, great and small, in which you've experienced God's goodness: a narrowly averted accident in your car or home; a letter or call from a distant friend; a new and unexpected insight into a passage of Scripture; a recovery from a painful illness; a sunny, fragrant, perfect day; a good friend or a good book that happened to come into your life at just the right time; that rare and inexpressible sense of well-being that sometimes comes upon us for no apparent reason.

The grace of God comes to us in many small ways that

we tend to overlook—or if we notice them at all, we ascribe them to "luck" or "chance" or "coincidence." But as we open our eyes widely to all the different ways God's grace is demonstrated in our lives, our day-to-day existence is dramatically transformed into a thrilling *adventure* of spiritual discovery. We gain a sense of direction and progress in our journey. No detail of life can be considered insignificant anymore, for now we see God's intimate involvement in every aspect of our lives. He is even involved with us in our hurts—and that heightened awareness of the presence of God brings us *joy*.

We all need some help along this journey to wholeness and joy. We need a few trusted Christian friends to whom we can disclose ourselves. God intended for us to be a *family* in the body of Christ—brothers and sisters who transparently share our hurts with one another. I really believe that only what we hide is going to hurt us.

Many of us have been brought up to believe it's a sign of weakness to confess our hurts and ask for help. Yet I'm convinced it's a sign of courage to admit we need help. Part of the job of mastering the art of living is *unlearning* what we have been taught about what it means to be mature. True maturity is proved not by stolid self-reliance, but by a willingness to be vulnerable and a desire to be known. The journey of spiritual discovery requires that we allow a few trusted people to see into the depths of our lives, so that we can mutually encourage each other toward maturity in Christ.

And some of us need to go a step further.

I've counseled many people over the years, and people often assume that a person who counsels others would have a handle on all his own problems. But the truth is that there have been times in my life when I have needed someone outside myself, listening to me and mirroring my feelings back to me, giving me a word of counsel to point me in the direction of wholeness.

There have been two occasions in my life when my hurts were so great that I knew I needed the help of a professional counselor. These two Christian psychologists were able to help me reassemble my broken self-image and to guide me further along the journey of spiritual discovery. As a result of the time I spent in counseling, I am today more whole and more effective as a Christian, as a husband, and as a father.

How about you? If you really want to be healed, then I

urge you to join me in doing whatever it takes to achieve that healing. Let go of your excuses and your pride, and open up your life to a few other Christian friends. If you are struggling with truly deep hurts, then begin now to seek the counseling you need.

You can begin by talking with your pastor, who can either help you or refer you to someone who is trained to help you with your particular problem. A friend who has been helped by counseling can also give you a reference. If finances are a problem for you, many churches have a counseling fund to assist people in getting help. Remember to seek a Christian counselor; many secular therapists see "religion" as the enemy of mental health and would not be understanding of your spiritual needs. Recognize, too, that people often become afraid of the effort and self-disclosure that's involved in becoming whole, and they drop out before any real progress has been made. When you begin counseling, make a commitment to persevere until you achieve genuine healing.

I invite you to join me in this quest for inner wholeness and maturity, and I wish you courage and endurance for your journey. But most of all, I wish you a deep and genuine sense of *joy,* even in your time of trial.

A glimpse of spring

Joe Bayly tells of an experience he had of joy in a time of trial, shortly after his five-year-old son died of leukemia. It was a windy, below-zero Saturday morning in January, and there was more than a foot of snow on the ground. Looking out the window of his home, Bayly saw the postal truck pull up to his mailbox. Without pausing to put on a coat, he ran out of the house, took the mail out of the box, and was about to rush back into the house when something among the letters caught his attention: a colorfully printed seed catalog.

On the front of the catalog were brilliant zinnias; on the back, luscious red tomatoes. Standing in his shirtsleeves, Bayly seemed not to even notice the cold as he leafed through the pages of roses, daffodils, dahlias, marigolds, corn, peas, and cucumbers. The fragrances of springtime seemed to rise from the pages, and for a brief moment the winter was past and he felt warmed and cheered.

Then the cold wind whipped up around him, and he rushed back inside and closed the door behind himself. Bayly later reflected on how our experiences as Christians are like that moment at the mailbox. "We feel the cold," he wrote, "just as those who do not share our hope, the biting wind that penetrates us as it penetrates them. But in our cold times, we have a seed catalog called The Bible. We open it, and we smell the promised spring, the eternal spring, and the first fruit that settles our hope is Jesus Christ, who was raised from death and cold earth to glory eternal." [2]

That is what our Christian joy is like—a fragrance of Christ and the coming spring amid the wintry trials of life. It's easy to give God praise when the sun is shining; it's another and much deeper thing to experience real joy when the bitter December wind is blowing hard in our faces and the light around us is failing.

Our lives are just a gleam of Time between two Eternities—but God is at work in our lives to fan that gleam into a shining glory, the glory of His own reflected image. The choice is ours: we can surrender to the cold and darkness of our trials—or we can allow God's light and warmth to shine through our lives in spite of our trials. In all the hurts you face in life, may you make the truly healing choice—the choice that leads to Christlike maturity, wholeness, and *joy.*

Notes

Chapter 1

1. John Gunther, *Death Be Not Proud* (New York: Modern Library, 1953).
2. Marie Rothenberg, *David* (Old Tappan, N.J.: Fleming H. Revell Co., 1985).
3. Ibid, 91.

Chapter 2

1. Paul Brand, "A Surgeon's View of Divine Healing," *Christianity Today,* 25 November 1983, pp. 15–16.
2. Kathryn Lindskoog, "What Do You Say to Job?" *Leadership* (Spring 1985):93–94.
3. M. Scott Peck, *The Road Less Traveled* (New York: Simon and Schuster, 1978), 239–40.
4. Charles Farr, *Leadership* (Spring 1985):16.
5. David Ireland, *Letters to an Unborn Child* (New York: Harper and Row, 1974), 117–18.
6. Kenneth L. Bakken, *The Call to Wholeness: Health As a Spiritual Journey* (New York: Crossroad Publishing, 1985), 11–12.
7. Norman Cousins, *The Healing Heart* (New York: Avon Books, 1984), 185–86.
8. Ron Lee Davis, *Gold in the Making* (Nashville: Thomas Nelson Publishers, 1983).
9. Lindskoog, "What Do You Say to Job?" 91.
10. Brand, "A Surgeon's View of Divine Healing," 20.

Chapter 3

1. John White, *The Golden Cow* (Downers Grove, Ill.: InterVarsity Press, 1979), 92–93.
2. C. S. Lewis, *A Grief Observed* (New York: Seabury Press, 1963), 11.
3. Ibid, 4.

4. Don Baker, *Pain's Hidden Purpose* (Portland: Multnomah Press, 1984), 63–64.

Chapter 4

1. Erich Fromm, *The Art of Loving* (New York: Harper and Row, 1956), 8–9.
2. Lloyd Ogilvie, *The Bush Is Still Burning* (Waco, Tex.: Word Books, 1980), 159.
3. *Newsweek,* 30 November 1981, p. 106.
4. Bruce Larson, *There's a Lot More to Health Than Not Being Sick* (Waco, Tex.: Word Books, 1981), 59.

Chapter 5

1. Peck, *The Road Less Traveled,* 32–33.
2. Lorraine Hansberry, *A Raisin in the Sun,* quoted in Tony Campolo, *It's Friday, but Sunday's Comin'* (Waco, Tex.: Word Books, 1984), 64–66.
3. Richard Selzer, *Mortal Lessons: Notes in the Art of Surgery* (New York: Simon and Schuster, 1976), 45–46.
4. Stephen D. Shores, *Discipleship Journal* 28 (1 July 1985):20.

Chapter 6

1. James Dobson, *Hide or Seek* (Old Tappan, N.J.: Fleming H. Revell Co., 1974).
2. *TV Guide,* 16 March 1985, pp. 5–10.

Chapter 7

1. A. W. Tozer, *The Root of the Righteous* (Harrisburg, Pa.: Christian Publications, 1955), 119.
2. T. M. Kitwood, *What Is Human?* (London: InterVarsity Press, 1970), 128.
3. Baker, *Pain's Hidden Purpose,* 34.
4. C. S. Lewis, *The Screwtape Letters.*
5. J. I. Packer, *God Has Spoken* (Downers Grove, Ill.: InterVarsity Press, 1979), 29.
6. C. S. Lewis, *Prince Caspian,* vol. 2 of *The Chronicles of Narnia* (New York: Macmillan, 1951), 135–36.

Chapter 8

1. David Augsburger, *Caring Enough to Confront* (Glendale, Calif.: Regal Books, 1980), 77–78.
2. A. W. Tozer, *Of God and Men* (Harrisburg, Pa.: Christian Publications, 1960), 75.

3. Josh McDowell, *Evidence That Demands a Verdict* (Arrowhead Springs, Calif.: Campus Crusade for Christ, 1972), 374.
4. Augsburger, *Caring Enough to Confront,* 53–54.

Chapter 9

1. Bob Considine, "Could You Have Loved This Much?" *Guideposts,* January 1966, pp. 4–7. Copyright 1966, 1985, by Guideposts Associates, Inc., Carmel, N.Y. 10512. Used by permission.

Chapter 10

1. Charles W. Colson, *Born Again* (New York: Bantam Books, 1976).
2. *Christianity Today,* 7 October 1983, pp. 53–54.
3. J. R. R. Tolkien, *The Hobbit.*

Epilogue

1. Carolyn Koons, *Tony: Our Journey Together* (New York: Harper and Row, 1984).
2. Joe Bayly, *The View from a Hearse* (Elgin, Ill.: David C. Cook Publisher, 1969), 120–21.

Acknowledgments

Robert Browning, in *Pauline* (1833), wrote to his dear friend Shelley, "Live forever, and be to *all* what you have been to *me.*" I would like to offer these words as a gift to all the special friends who have so significantly contributed to the development of this book.

My friend and brother in Christ, Jim Denney, has tirelessly edited, developed, and refined this book. His efforts are obvious on every page and every line, and there would have been no book without him.

Dr. Tom Granata, an outstanding Christian psychologist, has carefully critiqued each chapter of this book. His insights have contributed to both the biblical and psychological integrity of these pages. Tom has been my own personal friend and counselor for several years and has helped me gain greater understanding of my own trials. Many of the insights I share in this book were discovered through my relationship with Tom, and I will always be deeply grateful for his impact on my life.

For the past five years I have served as pastor of the First Presbyterian Church in Fresno, California, and many within our family of faith have contributed to the shaping of this book. My associate pastoral staff team of Dr. Ernest Bradley, Rev. Joe Pettit, Lydia Pugh, and Dr. Dwight Trowbridge have all added their loving suggestions and counsel to this book. I feel deeply privileged to be able to minister with such an outstanding staff.

Other friends from my church and my community who have offered suggestions, insights, and prayers during the writing of this book include Debbie Denney, Steven and Gayle Jaurena, Russ and Jan Koch, Jim and Carol Gartung, Hilary Chittick, Mike Flavin, Tess Mott, Meredith Hicks, Dr. Tom Griffin, Janet Nichols, Nancy Jen, Mary Lawrence Allen, Patricia Stivers, Bud Richter, Jim Helzer, Dr. Harold Haak, Lou Herwaldt, Bob Duncan, and Jeff Baggett. Many others in our congregation have also contributed to this work, and I am grateful for the friendship and insight of each one.

Dr. Bill Richardson, my life-long friend, offered his wise counsel to this material from the perspective of a Christian physician.

My new friend, Ernie Owen, Vice President and Editorial Director of Word Books, believed in the message of this book before it was ever committed to paper. I am very thankful for his suggestions, support, and encouragement.

I must acknowledge loving appreciation for my family. My wife, Shirley, and our children, Rachael and Nathan, have been a special support and encouragement to me throughout the months of study and preparation of the message in this book.

Finally, I am thankful to the scores of friends who have courageously permitted me to share the stories of their trials with you. Their transparency and vulnerability for the sake of others have given this book a dimension of realism and practicality that would otherwise have been impossible to achieve.

A NOTE TO THE READER

This book was selected by the same editors who prepare *Guideposts*, a monthly magazine filled with true stories of people's adventures in faith.

If you have found inspiration in this book, we think you'll find monthly help and inspiration in the exciting stories that appear in our magazine.

Guideposts is not sold on the newsstand. It's available by subscription only. And subscribing is easy. All you have to do is write Guideposts Associates, Inc., Carmel, New York 10512. A year's subscription costs only $7.95 in the United States, $9.95 in Canada and overseas.

When you subscribe, each month you can count on receiving exciting new evidence of God's presence and His abiding love for His people.